coolcamping
britain
FIRST EDITION

Jonathan Knight

with

Alf Alderson, Jules Brown, Dan Davies, Sophie Dawson, Keith Didcock, Martin Dunford, Richard Happer, Norm Longley, Scott Manson, Paul Marsden, Robin McKelvie, Mirio Mella, Andrea Oates, Sam Pow, Hayley Spurway, Andy Stothert, Paul Sullivan, Alexandra Tilley-Loughrey, Mandy Tomlin, Richard Waters, and Dixe Wills

The publishers assert their right to use *Cool Camping* as a trademark of Punk Publishing Ltd.

Cool Camping: Britain (1st edition)
This edition published in the UK in 2013 by
Punk Publishing Ltd, 3 The Yard, Pegasus Place, London SE11 5SD
www.punkpublishing.co.uk
www.coolcamping.co.uk

A catalogue record of this book is available from the British Library.

ISBN 978-1-906889-61-6

10   8   6   4   2   1   3   5   7   9

KEY
CDP – chemical disposal point
1W, 1M – one women's, one men's (for loos and showers)
Vanners – collective term for campervans and caravans
SSSI – Site of Special Scientific Interest
AONB – Area of Outstanding Natural Beauty
Public transport options are only included where viable

introduction

Welcome to the very first edition of *Cool Camping Britain*.

Although we've previously published individual editions for England, Scotland and Wales, we've never produced one volume with all the camping highlights of mainland Britain. So here it is!

Compiling a new book is always great fun. Revisiting lovely sites we've been to before – and meeting fellow campers who have discovered these places in a *Cool Camping* book – is immensely rewarding. But finding new places to share with our readers is perhaps the most exciting part of the process, and for this book, we've found some real winners.

One of my personal favourites is The Secret Campsite in Sussex, (p104). With just 15 pitches, it's exclusive enough, but it's the unusual entrance to the camping meadow that sets the tone for a special, chilled-out stay – a disused railway bridge, over which you must pull all your kit in a trolley. Owner Tim spends his spare time planting edible plants for campers to use in their campfire concoctions – that's the sort of attention to detail that we at *Cool Camping* like to see from a campsite owner!

Fellow author Richard loves Cleadale campsite (p294), on the Isle of Eigg in Scotland. It's as close to wild camping as a campsite can get, perched beneath an eagle-haunted cliff with views out to the Middle-Earth mountains of Rum.

Mountain-biking author Alf loves Beudy Banc campsite (p249) near Machynlleth – surely the only campsite in the world with its own private single track? It's also within easy reach of all of North Wales world-class trail centres.

Of course, there are many more new finds in the book – and no doubt you will have your own favourite in time. And if you do, why not let us know? You can write campsite reviews on our website – you can also add your own photos and create a handy pinboard of your favourite places, or easily invite several friends on a camping trip at once. Go to www.coolcamping.co.uk to get involved.

Whether it's this book or the *Cool Camping* website that inspires you to get out there and discover beautiful new places to camp, I hope you have a great time. Maybe you'll be one of the happy campers I meet on my next trip.

See you out there,

Jonathan Knight
Chief Camper, Cool Camping

england

campsite locator

continued overleaf

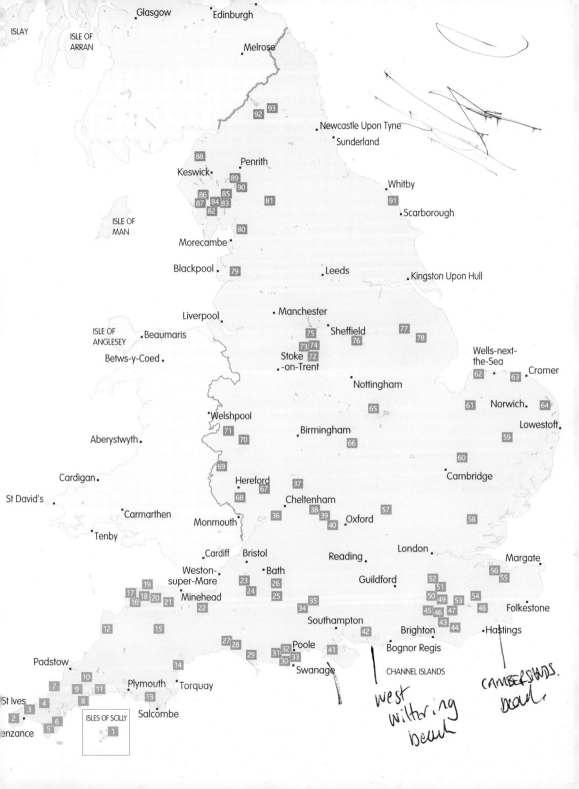

ISLAY

ISLE OF ARRAN

Glasgow

Edinburgh

Melrose

ISLE OF MAN

92 93

Newcastle Upon Tyne

Sunderland

88

Keswick

Penrith

89
90

86 85
87 84 83
82

80

Morecambe

Blackpool

79

Leeds

Whitby

91

Scarborough

Kingston Upon Hull

Liverpool

Manchester

ISLE OF ANGLESEY

Beaumaris

75

Sheffield

77

Betws-y-Coed

73 74

76

Stoke
-on-Trent

72

Welshpool

71
70

Birmingham

Nottingham

65

78

Wells-next-the-Sea

62

63

Cromer

61

Norwich

64

Aberystwyth

66

Lowestoft

59

Cardigan

69

60

St David's

Hereford

67

37

Cambridge

68

Cheltenham

57

Carmarthen

36

38 39

Oxford

58

Monmouth

40

Tenby

Cardiff

Bristol

Reading

London

Margate

Weston-
super-Mare

Bath

23

26

Guildford

56

52

55

Minehead

24

25

51

Folkestone

17 19
18 20
16 21

22

34

35

Southampton

50

49 53

54

48

45 46 47

43 44

Hastings

12

15

27 28

Poole

42

Brighton

Padstow

29

31 32
30 33

41

Bognor Regis

14

Swanage

CHANNEL ISLANDS

7
10

St Ives

9 11

Plymouth

Torquay

13

3
4

8

Salcombe

2

6

5

ISLES OF SCILLY

1

enzance

West
wittering
beach

CAMBERSANDS.
beach.

campsite locator (continued)

campsites at a glance

For more options, including dog-friendly and campervan-friendly campsites, please visit **www.coolcamping.co.uk**

troytown farm

Troytown Farm Campsite, St Agnes, Scilly Isles, Cornwall TR22 0PL   01720 422360   www.troytown.co.uk

If camping on the tiny island of St Agnes isn't exciting enough, it's certainly an adventure getting there. Take your pick from a boat or plane for the journey to the Isles of Scilly's main islands, Tresco or St Mary's.

Then it's on to a catamaran for the trip to St Agnes. If it's a bright day, you'll be greeted by the almost Mediterranean sight of boats moored on the turquoise waters of Porth Conger as you arrive. Next is a tractor ride – for your luggage at least – although most people choose to walk the 20 minutes to the campsite, a scenic stroll that provides a stunning introduction to the island.

At just one mile in diameter, St Agnes is one of the smallest inhabited islands of the Scilly archipelago. There are only a handful of B&Bs on the island, but most people come to stay at Troytown Farm, England's westernmost campsite.

This site is all about the panoramic backdrop... Atlantic waves undulating on to puzzling rock formations, heather-covered coastal landscapes, a sweeping curve of sand at nearby Pereglis Beach, and that night sky – an awe-striking bedazzlement of stars illuminating the blanket of sky above you. The downside is that you're exposed to the elements, though a couple of low walls and the odd wild-fern hedge provide some respite. When the sun shines, though, this place is perfect.

It's a simple site with no more than a few grassy fieldlets, but there aren't many other places in England where you can pitch as close to the sea and watch the burning crimson sunsets from your doorstep.

COOL FACTOR Extreme Atlantic isolation, one of England's most naturally beautiful campsites.

WHO'S IN? Tents, dogs (arrange in advance), groups – yes. Campervans, caravans – no.

ON SITE Campfires allowed. The site comprises a few fieldlets. Clean facilities: toilets, showers (tokens required), coin-operated washing machines and tumble-dryers, shaver points, and baby-changing facilities. The onsite shop sells dairy basics, homemade ice cream, meat and seasonal veg, and camping fuels.

OFF SITE The whole of Scilly is an Area of Outstanding Natural Beauty and there are plenty of walking opportunities around the isle with Island Wildlife Tours (01720 422212). Seals can be seen around the island, but if you want a closer look then arrange a snorkelling experience (Scilly Diving – 01720 422848). And with St Agnes and her views all around, you won't struggle for entertainment.

FOOD AND DRINK The Turks Head (01720 422434) in Porth Conger is the only pub on St Agnes, but it does serve great food and has a gorgeous beer garden. If it's seafood you're after, High Tide (01720 423869; www.hightide-seafood.com) is one of the most regarded restaurants in Scilly (advance bookings essential).

GETTING THERE Cars and other vehicles must be left on the mainland. Contact Scilly Travel (08457 105555; www.ios-travel.co.uk) for plane and boat travel. Contact Troytown Farm for details of transportation to the campsite, including luggage transfer.

PUBLIC TRANSPORT From Penzance train station take a skybus, boat or ferry to St Agnes.

OPEN March–October. Advance bookings essential during July and August.

THE DAMAGE £7.50–£9 per person, per night.

secret garden

Secret Garden, Bosavern House, St Just, Penzance, Cornwall TR19 7RD   01736 788301   www.secretbosavern.com

The greatest difficulty this small campsite could ever encounter is living up to its name. After all, those two simple words, 'secret' and 'garden', when put together, promise so much: your very own slice of Eden-like paradise full of natural pleasure.

The fact that this tiny campsite is situated on the mystical far-western edge of Cornwall, where travellers only find what they earnestly seek and don't just drop in by chance, only adds to the anticipation and allure of the Utopian vision. And the way to the Secret Garden is indeed enchanting, along the rugged coast westwards, fleeing the crowds of St Ives, or across the empty granite-strewn hills, escaping any Pirates of Penzance.

The sign outside Bosavern House, where the Secret Garden hides away, stating there are cream teas available, is yet another promising prospect for keen gastro-campers. But this doesn't look like a place where there is, or can be, a campsite. Instead it's a rather grand-looking granite mansion. 'Where's the campsite?', you ask the distinguished-looking chap who comes to the door. 'It's in the garden round the back', says he, and your heart dares to wonder if all those wild imaginings of a secret garden can really be true.

You push past the hens and brush off the embrace of the palm trees and other exotic plants, and there it is – the Secret Garden. But what's this – other campers taking up residence here too? So you aren't the only person to make it here after all. Seems unbelievable after such an epic journey, but it's true. In fact, there are 12 spacious pitches (each with a hook-up), within this private oasis, and quite often in high season they are all occupied.

However, though it may not be solely yours, after a day or three has passed and the outside world is just a distant memory, the realisation dawns that this garden campsite, with all its hidden-away intimacy, really feels like a secret – and a perfect one at that. The onsite facilities are spotlessly maintained, and there are pleasingly homely touches, with the lounge in the main house open for campers' use, alongside the library and bar.

The feeling that you've happened upon a secret location endures once you step outside, where little-trod footpaths lead off towards the coast. One such magical trail leads to Porth Nanven, through a mile of scenery that you never want to end, to yet another seemingly undisclosed place, despite being just a few miles from the tourist throng at Land's End. Another footpath strikes out across farmland, before burrowing its way through dark, damp, overgrown tree-tunnels to the cliffs, and to Cape Cornwall: one more well-kept secret. It's fortunate the Cape doesn't poke out into the Atlantic just a little further, or it would have been Land's End, and this beautiful, empty place might have ended up being smothered by visitor footfall. As it is, you can stroll here from your Secret Garden, enjoy a swim in the cove or tidal pool, climb to a lookout to see if you can spot a basking shark, watch the fishermen winch their boats out of the sea, then wander back to the campsite for a cream tea in the garden… And all without encountering more than a handful of other retiring and secretive folk. So, does the Secret Garden live up to its name? As Churchill (the dog, that is) would say, 'Oh yes!'

COOL FACTOR A secret campsite, hidden away in secret Cornwall.

WHO'S IN? Tents, campervans, caravans – yes. Dogs, groups – no.

ON SITE This place is genuinely the garden of Bosavern House B&B, and the washing facilities are fairly minimal, providing toilets, free showers (1W, 1M), laundry and a washing-up sink. It's a homely place, and the proprietors will cook you breakfast if you possess the personal organisational skills to have ordered it the night before. No campfires.

OFF SITE There are many remnants of Cornwall's mining heritage scattered about on both the moors and cliffs hereabouts (see also Beacon Cottage, p28). The Levant Engine House (01736 786156; see www. nationaltrust.org.uk) is a very beautiful 4-mile walk along the coast path and contains a functioning Cornish Beam engine. There's also the Geevor Tin Mine (01736 788662; www.geevor.com), just inland a couple of miles north of St Just, which was the area's last mine to be shut. It has been restored as a museum that gives you the chance to view at close-hand just how hellish the life of a tin miner was. About 4 miles in the opposite direction, at the far end of the stunning stretch of sand that is Whitesand Beach, is Sennen Cove, where there is often some serious surf action, while a bit closer to the site (a mile away) is Porth Nanven, where a bracing dip awaits the adventurous. Between St Just and Penzance are the exotic (and slightly secretive) gardens at Trengwainton (01736 363148; see www.nationaltrust. org.uk), where plants that grow nowhere else in Britain thrive in the shelter of the walled garden. Less than a mile from the Secret Garden is Land's End Airport, where there are pleasure flights and regular flights to the Scilly Isles (08457 105555; www.ios-travel.co.uk); you can also reach the Scillies on the *Scillonian*, which sails from Penzance. Plus, of course, there's Land's End itself, just beyond, where you can have your photo taken (along with crowds of other visitors) next to the sign for John O' Groats (874 miles away, since you ask), and invest in the pure hokum of the Land's End Experience, all lasers, lights and amazing facts (0871 720 0044; www. landsend-landmark.co.uk).

FOOD AND DRINK For gargantuan classic Cornish cream teas look no further than the front garden where, from 2.30pm to 6pm, the fat factor is put aside – the Cornish hevva cake, with clotted cream and strawberries, is sublime. For an alternative twist on this Cornish classic, seek out The Cook Book in nearby St Just, a café-cum-secondhand-bookshop serving Cheese Teas – savoury scones, Cornish cheeses and red-onion marmalade (01736 787266; www.thecookbookstjust. co.uk). Local pubs in St Just include the Commercial Hotel (01736 788455; www.commercial-hotel.co.uk), where the food is unquestionably good, and the Star Inn (01736 788767; www.thestarinn-stjust.co.uk) – an ancient, atmospheric inn, though with no food. For a slap-up meal bang on the beach, it's a short hop down the road to The Beach at Sennen Cove, where the menu is crammed with Cornish ingredients (01736 871191; www.thebeachrestaurant.com). Nearby, there's also the Old Success Inn (01736 871232; www.oldsuccess.com), a large pub with rooms that serves food either in the bar or its attached restaurant.

GETTING THERE Follow the A30 towards Land's End and turn right a few miles short of it, on to the B3306 after passing Crows An Wra. Bosavern House, and its Secret Garden, is on the right after 2 miles.

PUBLIC TRANSPORT Trains run to Penzance, where the summer-only Coast Bus (no. 300, operated by First from April–October) can be boarded and passes the site. It's also a useful means of reaching walking expeditions on the coastal path.

OPEN 1 March–31 October.

THE DAMAGE Tent plus 2 people £16.20 per night; additional person (over 2 yrs) £3.80; hook-up £4.50.

ayr holiday park

Ayr Holiday Park, Ayr Lane, St Ives, Cornwall TR26 1EJ   01736 795855   www.ayrholidaypark.co.uk

Many an artist has gravitated towards St Ives for its quality of light and inspiring coastal scenery since big names like Barbara Hepworth first settled here after the Second World War. In 1993, Tate opened an impressive gallery in St Ives in recognition of resident artists and sculptors' contributions to the British art scene. The building has a view over the sandy stretches of Porthmeor – St Ives' main beach – with its consistent surf and spectacular sunsets. Also overlooking the pretty reaches of this bay is Ayr Holiday Park – best of the campsite crop here.

Away from the rows of caravans, the camping fields are very much their own domain on the brink of the wave-lashed Atlantic scenery, yet along with this wild and beautiful location comes a far tamer camping experience. Everything about Ayr Holiday Park is organised and professional – from the spotless facilities block and soft-landing of the children's play area, to its well-placed picnic benches and outside showers for salty wetsuits.

Unfortunately, the tariffs reflect all the care and attention that goes into maintaining the site, so all this luxury does come at a price. But when you consider Ayr's location, and peer down over that incredible vista, the cost seems justifiable.

You can also make the most of Ayr's proximity to St Ives and stroll down the hill to find wide-open beaches, trendy bars and cafés, any number of restaurants – from chip-cheap fish shops to contemporary fusion affairs – and, of course, the galleries. So it's fitting that Ayr, enjoying its position in the midst of a town steeped in creativity, has got the art of camping just right.

COOL FACTOR Ocean vista and prime spot in arty St Ives.

WHO'S IN? Tents, campervans, caravans, small-to medium-sized dogs (not in July–August) – yes. Large dogs, huge tents, single-sex groups – no. Other groups – by arrangement.

ON SITE 80 pitches in total, 40 with electric hook-ups, 30 of which are hardstanding. There's a main shower and loo block with magnificent showers with hot water aplenty (6W, 6M) as well as disabled and family rooms, hairdryers and shaving points. Laundry; kids' playground; games room; wi-fi; direct access to the coastal path. No campfires or disposable BBQs.

OFF SITE Head to the beach and try your balance at surfing; go for walks along the coastal path; or don your art-critic persona and explore the Tate St Ives (01736 796226; www.tate.org.uk/stives).

FOOD AND DRINK Blas Burgerworks (01736 797272; www.blasburgerworks.co.uk) is a treat for meat-eaters and veggies alike. Book ahead for beachside Porthminster Café (01736 795352; www.porthminstercafe.co.uk), a friendly place serving beautifully presented, scrummy food. Stock up on provisions at the Cornish Deli (01736 795100; www.cornishdeli.com).

GETTING THERE Follow signs for St Ives from the A30, the take the B3311 then B3306 to town; then follow the brown campsite signs to Ayr and Porthmeor Beach. The entrance to the campsite lies at a sharp S-bend.

PUBLIC TRANSPORT Train or bus to St Ives and then taxi/bus/walk to the site.

OPEN All year.

THE DAMAGE Caravan/campervan/tent £7.50–£20 (seasonal) per night; adult £4.75–£7.50; child £2.25–£3.75; dog £2–£3.50; serviced pitch £5.

sandy acres

Sandy Acres, 22 Sandyacres Road, Hayle, Cornwall TR27 5BA   07768 320505   www.sandy-acres.co.uk

This campsite is made for thos campers who want to fall asleep to the sound of the waves and wake up metres from the sand – three miles of sand in this case, stretched between Hayle rivermouth and Godrevy Lighthouse. It's perfect for kitesurfers, surfers, coastal-path walkers, beach-lovers, and, well, anyone really, though it's probably best suited to those who seek a lifestyle with sand between their toes. There are no airs and graces – and relatively sparse facilities – at this simple campsite tucked behind and among the coastal dunes.

The dunes themselves are lovely, and a natural playground for children; they're also part of a designated SSSI and a haven for wildlife. When the sun shines you can kick off your shoes and do away with the car keys; in fact, the only world you'll be interested in is the one in view over the jungle of marram grass knitting the dunes together. As for the beach, it's made for every type of sea-and-sand-based activity, from paddle-boarding to simply, er, paddling. Once you've tired of what the beach has to offer, you could pull on some footwear for a stroll along the coastal path or, for a 'big' day out, hop on the coastal train to St Ives, whose relative urban vibe, with great restaurants and galleries, makes a pleasant change. However you decide to spend your time, though, come prepared: the scene may look like the Caribbean on a balmy day, but it can get breezy here, so howling onshore winds aren't unusual. And don't forget your wetsuit and your waterproofs – this is Cornwall, after all.

COOL FACTOR Beach bliss: roll out of your tent, down the dunes and on to 3 miles of sand.

WHO'S IN? Tents, campervans, dogs – yes. Groups – no.

ON SITE 32 pitches, 2 loos and showers (unisex) and a couple of outdoor sinks. There's also a bell tent for hire (sleeping 4–5). BBQs must be kept off the grass. No campfires.

OFF SITE There's a beach café footsteps away at the top of the sand dune (summer holidays only), where you can hire wetsuits (£5 per day) and boogie boards. If you're serious about learning to surf, head to the Gwithian Academy of Surfing (01736 757579; www.surfacademy. co.uk). You're also bang on the South West Coast Path, with St Ives to the west and the shipwreck coast around Hell's Mouth to the east.

FOOD AND DRINK Grab a bacon bap from the kiosk just metres away from the site or, if you fancy doorstep sandwiches and homemade cakes, you can wait in line at the Godrevy Beach Café (01736 757999; www.godrevycafe. co.uk). For a decent pint, delicious pub food and a friendly welcome (for dogs too) you can't beat the Red River Inn (01736 753223; www.red-river-inn.com), a 5-minute drive away in Gwithian village.

GETTING THERE Come off the A30 at Hayle, turn right at the double mini-roundabout (towards Gwithian) and take the first left, signposted 'beach car park'.

PUBLIC TRANSPORT It's a 45-minute schlep from Hayle station, or take a bus from Penzance or Truro to Hayle (get off at the stop nearest Lidl supermarket), from where it's a 25-minute walk.

OPEN June–September. Phone for availability for groups out of season.

THE DAMAGE £12–£15 per pitch (includes 1 tent, 1 car, 2 people).

teneriffe farm

Teneriffe Farm, Predannack, Mullion, Helston, Cornwall TR12 7EZ   01326 240293   www.nationaltrust.org.uk/teneriffecampsite

Don't expect the wow-factor to hit you as soon as you arrive at Teneriffe Farm. On first impressions it's just a very pleasant place to pitch up, hemmed by farmland, and with a blaze of Atlantic blue peeking above the hedges. Beyond this there are no obvious frills, save for the swings and slide of the children's play area. But that's just the point: camping should be a simple pursuit, and it's always best if your focus is on nature, starry nights and the Great Outdoors. And Teneriffe Farm is a place for all three.

Close to the Lizard National Nature Reserve, 10 minutes on foot from the South West Coast Path and a 40-minute stroll from the pretty harbour of Mullion Cove, the location is a gem. The recent acquisition of this cliff-fringed site by the National Trust is part of a project to breathe life into the landscape by re-joining the land with its neighbour and making a viable farm where there hasn't been one for years. So, starry skies and the simple life aside, the knowledge that the campsite is helping to enhance the landscape and boost the local economy makes you feel pretty good about staying here.

COOL FACTOR Embrace the simple life on this National Trust site that aims to boost the local farming landscape.

WHO'S IN? Tents, campervans, caravans, dogs – yes. Groups – no.

ON SITE No campfires. 24 generous pitches (14 hook-ups) and an overflow field. Shower/loo block being renovated, but will include a laundry, ice pack and phone-charging facilities.

OFF SITE Mullion Cove is a short drive or 40-minute walk; from here you can go on a kayaking trip with Lizard Adventure (07845 204040; www.lizardadventure.co.uk) or walk over the cliffs to Poldhu via the Marconi Centre, where the first transatlantic message was sent in 1901. Turn the walk into a 4-mile loop via Mullion village (www.southwestcoastpath.com/walksdb/133).

FOOD AND DRINK For the best fish and chips in the area it's worth the 10-minute drive to The Smugglers in Lizard village (01326 290763).

GETTING THERE From the A3083 (Helston–Lizard) head right on the B2296 through Mullion. Before Mullion Cove turn left to Predannack.

PUBLIC TRANSPORT The bus between Helston and Lizard stops at Mullion, just over a mile away.

OPEN Easter–November.

THE DAMAGE £13–£15 per pitch including 2 people.

buzzards bridge

Buzzards Bridge, Cury Cross Lanes, nr Mullion, Cornwall TR12 7AY   07973 488526   buzzardsbridge@hotmail.co.uk

Squirrelled away down a country lane, on the banks of a stream burbling through a secret valley, there are no camping signs beckoning you to stop at Buzzards Bridge. But with just six pitches, this place isn't designed to attract passing crowds.

The style of Buzzards Bridge is strictly rustic, but it takes the business of cool camping quite seriously. There are two covered decking areas raised above the babbling brook, with barbecues and outdoor furniture. Then there are bell tents to hire – not luxury ones, just big, beautiful bell tents that you can fill with your own camping paraphernalia. Taking being green to extremes, there's a tree bog (a compost loo in a tree house) and an off-grid den – a giant Wendy house run off solar power and rainwater, with a double bed, kitchen and wood-burner.

Being a no-car zone (there are wheelbarrows on which to trundle your kit between car and canvas) the only vehicle in the field is the Big Blue Tractor, a favourite plaything for kids. There's also a rope-buoy and swingball for little campers, plus plenty of opportunities to spot dragonflies and water voles in the stream.

COOL FACTOR Small and rustic – buzzards and water voles probably outnumber campers.

WHO'S IN? Tents, campervans – yes. Dogs, groups – by arrangement. Caravans – no.

ON SITE Campfires allowed. Communal firepit, 3 covered decking areas and 6 pitches, 3 of which have bell tents for hire. Basic facilities, with a tree bog, portaloo and washing-up area. No electricity/phone signal but there is wi-fi.

OFF SITE It's about an hour's walk to the beach at Poldhu Cove, 2 miles away, where you can try surfing (07974 941575; danjoelsurf.com). Other beaches a short drive away include Dollar Cove, Polurrian and Church Cove (Gunwalloe).

FOOD AND DRINK It's a mile-long trot up the hill to Mullion, where the family-friendly Mounts Bay Inn serves real ales and decent pub grub (01326 240221; www.mountsbaymullion.co.uk). Roskilly's, 20 minutes away, sells ice cream made from the herd's Jersey milk (01326 280479; www.roskillys.co.uk).

GETTING THERE Strictly secret. Please contact the owner for directions.

PUBLIC TRANSPORT Buses between Helston and Lizard stop at Mullion.

OPEN July and August only.

THE DAMAGE £20 per pitch or £35 per bell tent per night.

beacon cottage

Beacon Cottage Farm, Beacon Drive, St Agnes, Cornwall TR5 0NU   01872 552347   www.beaconcottagefarmholidays.co.uk

Cornwall is not simply one place; its north and west fringes are very different from those on the south and east, which are sheltered, lush and very lovely, in a mild-mannered sort of way.

Beacon Cottage, however, is on the other side of Cornwall, on a hillside directly facing the wrath of the Atlantic, amid some of the wildest, roughest and most dramatic seaside scenery in Europe. It's not a 'nice' place, perhaps, but it is an awesome one.

That Beacon Cottage is knocked about by the wind on this rocky, wave-lashed and very beautiful section of Cornish coast just makes it even more amazing. The campsite itself is superbly sited, with a choice of pitches either facing whatever the weather can throw at them or sheltered from the elements in the more intimate orchard.

For the surf dudes and dudettes, sandcastle builders and ice-cream fanciers there's an eminently suitable beach for every one of their preferred activities, and although it is about 150 (very vertical) metres below the site, it's less than a mile away along the coastal path. The ice cream is provided from a stone hut in the small car park, but nothing else is allowed to spoil Chapel Porth's immaculately wild looks.

This part of Cornwall is also littered with haunting ruins from its mining history; walk a couple of miles along the coast to the former mining village of St Agnes and you'll pass engine houses and mine shafts perched precariously on the cliffs, before the path drops down into the rocky cleft of Trevaunance Cove.

COOL FACTOR Slap bang in the middle of some very intriguing coastal scenery.

WHO'S IN? Tents, campervans, caravans, dogs – yes. Groups – no.

ON SITE 43 of the total 70 pitches are equipped with hook-ups. Facilities are modern and well maintained with toilets, CDP, showers (4W, 4M) and 2 family bathrooms. There's a laundry and washing-up sinks, and ice packs, milk, eggs, gas and newspapers are sold at the farmhouse. No campfires.

OFF SITE A 3-mile walk away along the cliffs, at Blue Hills Tin Streams (01872 553341; www.bluehillstin.com) you can see the process of tin extraction and smelting. For a break from the wild coast, wander the cobbled streets of Truro, just a 20-minute drive away.

FOOD AND DRINK Within walking distance (between 2 and 3 miles), and both in St Agnes, the St Agnes Hotel (01872 552307; www.st-agnes-hotel.co.uk) offers a decent selection of food and drink in a traditional-looking dining room, and Sally's Bistro (01872 552194; www.sallysrestaurant. co.uk) serves well-presented meals with a slightly exotic Mediterranean theme. Closer to Trevaunance Cove, 1½ miles from the site, is the Driftwood Spars Hotel (01872 552428; www.driftwoodspars.com) with its cosy bar, sea-view dining room and microbrewery.

GETTING THERE Take the B3277 to St Agnes and, at the first mini-roundabout, head left into Goonvrea Road. After a mile, turn right into Beacon Drive, and Beacon Cottage is on the right.

PUBLIC TRANSPORT From Truro there are regular bus services (nos. 85 and 85A) to St Agnes.

OPEN Easter/1 April–end September.

THE DAMAGE Tent plus 2 adults £16–£23; backpacker £8; child £3.20; dog £3.

THE STRAWBERRY MAN THURSDAY. MORNING

treveague farm

Treveague Farm Campsite, Gorran, St Austell, Cornwall PL26 6NY   01726 842295   www.treveaguefarm.co.uk

A family farm perched in divine clifftop countryside, within easy reach of three sandy coves, Treveague Farm has everything a really good seaside campsite needs. So when you consider its extras – a café serving organic food, farm animals, a badger hide and an aviary with bantams, lovebirds and more – it really does notch up a few credits as a superb place to stay.

Spread across three meadows, with glorious sea views in two directions, even with 80 pitches it's impossible to feel hemmed in here. However, it can be an exposed location, so you might want to opt for a space by the hedgerows rather than a front-row view. While kids gravitate to the farm animals, playground and storytelling sessions in the Secret Garden (great distractions when you want to chill out), make sure you tear them away from all this for a trip to the beach, because that's what this location is really all about. It's an easy stroll down to Hemmick Beach (though it's advisable to avoid the short-cut through a field of bulls if you have a dog in tow), and the calf-grinding walk back up is always a great excuse for a generous scoop of the Cornish ice cream they serve back at camp.

COOL FACTOR There are 3 beaches within reach, farm animals, and an organic farm café.

WHO'S IN? Tents, campervans, caravans, dogs – yes. Groups – no.

ON SITE No campfires. 80 pitches (40 hook-ups) with facilities including indoor/outdoor sinks, fridges/freezers, laundry and baby changing. Showers are 50p and you have to pay for wi-fi. There are pigs, cows and sheep, a wildlife hide for badger watching, a resident barn owl and other creatures.

OFF SITE Of the beaches, Hemmick is the closest (10–15 minutes' walk), but Gorran Haven has more facilities. There's also the stunning Vault Beach, though this is a longer walk.

FOOD AND DRINK There's little need to stray beyond the onsite café and restaurant, open from breakfast to 9pm. You can also buy meat for the barbie, or catch your own dinner on a 2-hour mackerel fishing trip (£13pp, 07973 957550).

GETTING THERE From St Austell take the B3273 to Mevagissey; past Pentewan, turn right at the crossroads at the top of the hill. Follow the signs to Heligan, then to Seaview campsite, and you'll see the signs to Treveague.

PUBLIC TRANSPORT Bus 526 from St Austell station stops a 500m walk from the site.

OPEN Easter–end September.

THE DAMAGE £7–£22 per pitch (including 2 people).

pleasant streams farm

Pleasant Streams Farm Camping, Lower Sticker, St Austell, Cornwall PL26 7JL   01726 74837   www.cornwallfarmcamping.co.uk

'There's very little to do here, no bells and whistles', says Tony Hedges, proprietor of Pleasant Streams Farm with his wife Lesley. Yet this is indeed a pleasant field in which to pitch a tent. Campfires are encouraged, and often the crackle-pop of wood on the fire is the only noise of the evenings here. There is, though, quite a lot to do on and around the site. There's a lake in the centre of the field, which not only attracts wildlife, but also beckons you to hop in the rowing boat for an afternoon afloat; a summerhouse has books and games for rainy days; and, of course, there are the animals: Matilda, Snowflake, Billy and Gruff the goats, Rodney and Del Boy the pigs, and the chickens and ducks that lay fresh eggs for your breakfast. And that's not even counting the field mice, owls, herons and badgers. You can always break the tranquillity with a ten-minute stroll to the local pub in Sticker, just don't expect wild nights and karaoke. Most people that stray from the site do so by day, by biking along the nearby Pentewan Valley Trail or hiring the campsite's kayak and exploring the beautiful coast around Gorran Haven and Charlestown.

COOL FACTOR It's all about simple pleasures when you pitch up by a lake in rural Cornwall.

WHO'S IN? Tents, campervans, caravans, groups – yes. Dogs – no.

ON SITE Campfires allowed. 50 pitches with basic showers/toilets and a water-tap for washing up. 2 vintage caravans.

OFF SITE The Eden Project (01726 811911; www.edenproject.com) is the biggest nearby attraction. Explore the coast by kayak (on hire from the campsite for £25 per day), or freewheel along the Pentewan Valley Trail with Pentewan Valley Cycle Hire (01726 844242; www.pentewanvalleycyclehire.co.uk).

FOOD AND DRINK It's a 15-minute stroll to the Hewas Inn (01726 73497; hewasinn.co.uk), which serves a traditional pub menu. The Polgooth Inn (01726 74089; www.polgoothinn.co.uk) – a 5-minute drive – offers a more contemporary choice, and an impressive range of cask ales.

GETTING THERE From the A390 between St Austell and Truro take the Hewas Water exit and turn right towards Lower Sticker. Go straight over a crossroads and it's on the right.

PUBLIC TRANSPORT A bus service runs from St Austell and stops at Sticker, 10–15 minutes' walk from the site.

OPEN Easter–September.

THE DAMAGE £10–£16 (2–8-person tent), £2 per child.

south penquite

South Penquite Farm, Blisland, Bodmin, Cornwall PL30 4LH   01208 850491   www.southpenquite.co.uk

Occasionally at South Penquite Farm, on the edge of Bodmin Moor, when it's long gone midnight and there's the sound of rustling in the undergrowth, you might find yourself wondering whatever happened to the elusive Beast of Bodmin Moor?

Supposedly a large wildcat that had either escaped from a sci-fi lab or was a throwback to some kind of sabre-toothed ancestor, it was reputed to prowl the moor scaring the wits out of anyone unlucky enough to cross its path. The story was at its height some years ago, and the hoo-ha has long since died down. But when you're creeping to the loo in the middle of the night and hear a twig snap behind you, you'd better pray that the big cat hasn't come back looking for a midnight snack.

Actually, within the boundaries of South Penquite Farm, any scuffling in the undergrowth is more likely to be one of the free-range chickens pecking around in your wake or, at worst, it might be the footfall of one of the horses grazing by the gate; but in the pitch blackness of a moorland night, you can never be quite sure.

Come daylight you can forget all about it and just enjoy the site: a fully certified organic 200-acre farm that takes sustainability very seriously, from using solar energy and rainwater to recycling absolutely everything – check out the roomy showers that are lined with psychedelic panels made from recycled yogurt pots and plastic bottles.

The farm education centre is a fantastic resource for learning all about organic farming and the local environment, while the bushcraft courses they run will introduce the whole family to field skills such as den building and cooking on an open fire.

Numbers are limited in the camping fields, so you shouldn't ever feel penned in. Campfires set the tone of the evenings here, and there's a whopping amount of space to run around in. As well as fellow campers you'll also be sharing the fields with wandering turkeys, ducks and chickens – an endless source of entertainment for children, who also have a games barn, swings and a climbing frame to keep them occupied. Plus, there's walking galore to be done even before you break out on to the moors, with a farm trail that brings you face-to-face with sheep, cows and horses, while taking in disused quarries, prehistoric hut circles and the banks of the De Lank River.

Since its beginnings as a farm site with just a basic loo and shower installed for the campers that flocked to Cornwall for the 1999 solar eclipse, South Penquite has adapted to the camping scene with style. Owner Dominic reckoned that once he had a family farm with a campsite on the side, whereas now he has a campsite with a farm on the side. And now, even here in the wilds of Bodmin Moor, you can opt for the luxury of one of Goldilocks and the Three Bears – four Mongolian yurts that occupy their own field. Daddy Bear and Goldilocks are the biggest, sleeping six; then there's Mummy Bear, who sleeps four; and Baby Bear, a snug little place for two. And when you do lace up your hiking boots and strike out on to the rolling moors, it's not the three bears you've got to watch out for. Er, is it?

COOL FACTOR Location, location, location.

WHO'S IN? Tents, campervans, groups – yes. Dogs – no.

ON SITE Campfires allowed and wood can be purchased from the farm. New facilities include a shower block with roomy showers, a loo block (watch out for the psychedelic panels made from recycled yogurt pots), with a disabled toilet and shower, and covered washing-up areas. There's a children's play area, board games and books in a basic lounge area and a games room in the barn. As well as geocaching, there is a farm education centre, and family bushcraft courses are on offer (£20pp for the latter), along with art courses and photography workshops. You can also fish for brown trout on the farm's own stretch of river between April and September, and walk the 2-mile-long South Penquite Farm trail, spotting sheep, cows and horses, and taking in standing stones, stone circles, a canyon and a quarry.

OFF SITE There's no end to glorious footfall territory on Bodmin Moor so, if you dare face the wrath of the Beast, don your boots and strike out to the ancient standing stones of The Hurlers and The Cheesewring or the peaks of Rough Tor and Brown Willy (Cornwall's highest points). Being on the Sustrans Route 3 between Bristol and Land's End, the moorland tracks are very popular with cyclists, and you can explore various trails on horseback from Hallagenna Farm (01208 851500; www.hallagenna.co.uk). There are pony treks, which are ideal for kids (over 5), or hacking and trail rides for the more experienced. However, if the endless shades of green make you feel a little land-locked, you're only a short drive from the town of Bodmin, and 25 minutes' drive from the dramatic seascapes of Trebarwith and Boscastle, and the legendary, stupendously sited castle of King Arthur at Tintagel. Consider, also, a trip to Jamaica Inn, a few miles east, the eponymous inn of Daphne du Maurier's novel and home to a great Smuggler's Museum (which also has a room devoted to the writer). Jamaica Inn is also a good place from which to head out on hikes across the moor, and you can leave your car in the car park if you ask nicely. They even offer advice on circular walks you can do from the pub, one to the peak of Brown Willy, at 420m the highest point on the moor, and another an easy stroll to Dozmary Pool, a mysterious place where, according to Arthurian myth, Excalibur was returned to the watery depths.

FOOD AND DRINK Sausages, burgers and fabulously fresh seafood are available from the pop-up catering van that shows up at the farm every week. If you fancy something else there's the Blisland Inn (01208 850739), which serves an extensive selection of cask ales alongside great bar snacks in the village of Blisland, about a mile away. The Old Inn, St Breward (01208 850711; www.theoldinnandrestaurant.co.uk), is another cosy local serving decent home-cooked food, sourced locally, including a popular all-day carvery on Sundays; plus, if you don't fancy hopping in the car you can walk here in 45 minutes or so. For a slightly more sophisticated menu but all the character of a 15th-century inn, it's worth the 20-minute drive to the award-winning St Kew Inn (01208 841259; www.stkewinn.co.uk); it's pub grub, but a cut above most other offerings.

GETTING THERE As you head west into Cornwall on the A30 just short of Bodmin the dual carriageway narrows to a single lane. There's a right turn signposted St Breward. Follow this road over the moor for 2½ miles until you see the large South Penquite sign by a rough track on the right.

PUBLIC TRANSPORT The closest you can get by public transport is Bodmin Parkway railway station, but it's nearly 10 miles away.

OPEN May–October.

THE DAMAGE Adult £8, child (5 to16) £4. Yurts £125 (3 nights in the smallest) to £390 (per week in the biggest).

botelet farm

Botelet Farm, Herodsfoot, Liskeard, Cornwall PL14 4RD   01503 220225   www.botelet.com

Fancy this. A farm that's like its own little village, with its own phone box and genuine Victorian red postbox, a couple of yurts and room for a couple of tents. Actually there's room for hundreds of tents in Botelet's 300 acres, but it's a working farm and the owners want to keep the camping small and special. The two tent pitches change with the seasons, based on where the cows are grazing, how high the grass is, and a number of other mostly random factors, like what's in the tea leaves that morning.

This, of course, means that if you were to come here every year for the rest of your camping days the chances are you'd still never pitch in the same place twice. You may be in one of the fields close to the little village of farm buildings, with views across the valley, or you may be banished to the wilderness somewhere. As for the two yurts, there's one in the field out the front and another in a field above the farm. Both have views across the rolling valley, and wood-burning stoves to you on warm those chilly nights and to boil the kettle for your morning cuppa. Just remember to hide the tea leaves afterwards, or the folk in the tents might be asked to move.

COOL FACTOR Remote farm with freedom to roam.
WHO'S IN? Adults only. Room for 2 tents – maximum of 2 people per tent. Motorhomes, caravans, dogs, groups – no.
ON SITE There's a single hot shower (with piped Radio 3 so you can hum along in the morning) and 1 loo. Cold taps are dotted around and there's a trough for washing dishes. No campfires, but the yurts have wood-burning stoves.
OFF SITE The nearby Polmartin Riding School (01503 220428; www.polmartinfarm.com) offers lessons for all ages and abilities. The coast is just 6 miles from the site.
FOOD AND DRINK They serve a veggie breakfast in the farmhouse at £10 per person (book the night before). A nearby pub making a name for itself for the quality of its food is the Plough Inn at Duloe (01503 262556; www. ploughduloe.co.uk), where it's fish night on Thursdays.
GETTING THERE Come off the A390 between Liskeard and St Austell at East Taphouse and take the B3359 south towards Pelynt. After about 1½ miles, turn right at the sign for Botelet; the site is on the right.
PUBLIC TRANSPORT Train to Liskeard, then bus to East Taphouse, 2 miles away. They will collect you from there.
OPEN Easter–mid September (yurts)/end September (tents).
THE DAMAGE £7.50 per person for tents. Yurts (sleeping 2), from £230 for 3 nights, £350 for a week.

bakesdown farm

Lower Bakesdown Farm, Marhamchurch, Bude, Cornwall EX23 0HJ   01288 341105   www.bakesdownfarm.co.uk

'So, where's the Showman's Wagon?' I ask one happy camper at this camping field in the back of beyond. There are just four pitches at the top of a farm-side meadow petering out into waist-high grass. No bells and whistles; just children racing around on bikes and jumping in puddles. The campsite is perfect as it is, but I still want to find the 1930s wagon I've heard about. 'I've seen no sign of it,' comes the reply.

So I ask an even happier camper, who is changing her muddy boots by the farm entrance. 'I'm staying in it', she beams. 'You'll never find it, come with me.' And she leads me further into the back of beyond, along a path and through another field, and there it is: a traditional showman's wagon in a private meadow. Inside it's like a Granny's living room with mahogany furniture, floral prints and a wood burner; outside there's a wind turbine, firepit and compost loo. Even if I'd missed my guided tour to this classic abode I'd be very happy with the rustic camping field that makes up most of Bakesdown Farm. But the knowledge that this campsite hides something else behind its simple façade makes it even more special.

COOL FACTOR Just 4 simple pitches in a farmside meadow, plus a quirky 1930s showman's wagon with eco-facilities.

WHO'S IN? Tents, campervans – yes. Dogs, caravans – no. Groups by arrangement.

ON SITE Campfires allowed by all 4 pitches in the car-free field. The shower room and loo are a few footsteps up the lane at the farm. The Showman's Wagon sleeps up to 3. There is also a yurt for hire.

OFF SITE There are plenty of beaches around Bude, but for something a little different try zorbing (08458 725634; www.zorbude.co.uk). There's horse riding at Broomhill Manor Stables (07796 470625; www.broomhillmanor.co.uk/riding).

FOOD AND DRINK Bude has plenty of eating options, including the River Life Café (01288 355994). The Bay View Inn in Widemouth (01288 361273; www.bayviewinn.co.uk) is a family-friendly bar and restaurant with great views.

GETTING THERE Turn left from the A39 to Marhamchurch, heading into the village before turning left at the T-junction. Keep going for 3 miles, then turn left to Titson, where you take the first right by a little chapel. Bakesdown Farm is about ½ mile further on the right.

OPEN April–October.

THE DAMAGE Camping £7 per person, Showman's Wagon from £60 a night.

karrageen

Karrageen Caravan and Camping Park, Bolberry, Malborough, Kingsbridge, Devon TQ7 3EN   01548 561230   www.karrageen.co.uk

Karrageen. In a region long steeped in folklore, the name of this South Hams hideaway conjures up mythical times; a Devon of misty moorlands and pagan priests; of elusive mermaids and spectral ships, enchanted forests and cavernous underwater kingdoms. Indeed, the South West is the original home of the pixie. In nearby Challacombe, the mischievious creatures are said to dwell beneath the fabled 'Pixie Rocks', keeping a watchful eye on the comings and goings around these parts.

The relationship between the wee folk and humans has not always been a harmonious one, though. Further to the east of the county, in the town of Ottery St Mary, legend has it that the once peaceful coexistence was shattered by the arrival of Christianity. The pixies and their impish ilk took umbrage to this new human belief that denied their very existence. What's more, they loathed the sound of church bells. On Midsummer's Eve in 1454, the newly installed church bells rang out from the belfry of Ottery St Mary, thus sounding the death knell of the ruling pixie kingdom. With the pixies forced to leave their homeland on the banks of the River Otter and beat a hasty retreat for a cave (now known locally as 'Pixie's Parlour'), the fiendish little sprites hatched a plot to exact revenge. Once again, the hapless hobs were foiled… but that's not to say they won't recapture their ancestral home one day. So, just to be on the safe side, Devonians commemorate their forefathers' battle with the little creatures every July at the annual 'Pixie Day' celebrations.

Happily, at this wonderfully laidback campsite, the only wrath of the little folk you need fear is from your own little pixies should you not indulge their yearnings for the Devonshire ice cream the area is so famous for. Karrageen is all about giving its lucky occupants plenty of room to breathe, think, play and relax. There's no tangle of guy ropes here, and there's even room for those multi-bedroom monstrosities that can take up a good few pitches on their own.

This unadorned site harks back to traditonal camping from days of yore. You'll find nothing fancy, nothing flash, and nothing gimmicky (with the exception of the brand-spanking new and immaculately clean toilet block); just a simple, very well-maintained and nicely landscaped site in an ever-so-lovely location – with space to spare.

The immediate locality of Karrageen is peaceful and only accessed along a tortuous narrow lane leading down (eventually) to the sea at the lost world of Hope Cove and its little village. After wandering through the sleepy rows of fishermen's cottages you'll think it eminently possible that this is still a place for clandestine meetings of pirates and smugglers – such is the sense of detachment and timelessness in the air. There are a couple of pubs in the village that serve food, should lethargy – or the desire not to leave this lovely site – rob the legs of movement. Karrageen's amiable cooking proprietor also does a mean line in freshly baked croissants, baguettes and *pain au chocolat* every morning. With the smell of warm bread lingering gently in the morning air and the breathtaking vista of the Celtic Sea, Karrageen truly feels like a place plucked straight from Devonian myth.

COOL FACTOR Space for families to spread out and relax in.

WHO'S IN? Tents, vanners, dogs – yes. Groups – no.

ON SITE A terraced hillside split into small, intimate cul-de-sacs. Excellent facilities: loos and 9 showers (20p; 4W, 4M; wash basins; shaver/hairdryer points, 1 family/disabled room equipped for baby changing). There's a utility room with 3 sinks for dishwashing; 3 washing machines; and a tumble-dryer. There are 50 hook-ups and freezer access. A well-stocked and fully licensed onsite shop sells all the basic provisions plus chilled lagers, beers, ciders and wines. Fresh pastries, baguettes and loaves of bread are baked every morning. They also stock some camping equipment including calor gas and camping gas for your stove. Downsides: some static caravans lurking about; it's not easily reached by public transport. No campfires but BBQs off the ground are okay.

OFF SITE There are beaches aplenty within walking distance or a short drive from Karrageen; South Milton Sands, Thurlestone and Bantham (the prime surfing beach) are some of the best. Consider also a trip to the stretch of sand between Bigbury-on-Sea and Burgh Island, which lies just offshore and is reachable via the stretch of sand in between at low tide; you can also ride across on its customised tractor, perhaps stopping for tea at the Art Deco Burgh Island Hotel (01548 810514; www.burghisland.com). There's lots of other great ways to explore this magnificent region. You could hop on the South West Coast Path (www.southwestcoastpath.com) and check out this majestic stretch of the so-called English Riviera on foot. Or book a boat trip, either sailing from Kingsbridge to Salcombe and back (01548 853607) or from Totnes to Dartmouth on a River Dart trip (01803 555872; www.dartmouthrailriver.co.uk), or from Dartmouth up to Dittisham or combine the best of both worlds with the Dartmouth Steam Railway & River Boat Company (01803 555872; www.dartmouthrailriver.co.uk). The

600-year-old Dartmouth Castle (01803 833588) is well worth a visit, as is Totnes Castle (01803 864406) for the stunning views it commands over the River Dart; it also hosts open-air theatre events in the summer months. For the oenophiles (that's the wine connoisseurs, for the uninitiated), Sharpham Vineyard (01803 732122; www.sharpham.com) is an essential day out. Sample some of the region's internationally renowned plonk in a refreshingly snobbery-free environment. For the kids, Paignton Zoo Environmental Park (01803 697500) is both educational and entertaining.

FOOD AND DRINK Beachhouse (01548 561144; www.beachhousedevon.com) is a shabby-chic hangout overlooking the always-popular family beach at South Milton Sands. Sophisticated lunches such as herby crab cakes are served alongside doughnuts, Chelsea buns, pasties and the assorted stodge-tastic foodstuffs trips to the seaside are all about. They also do a great fish-and-chip supper on high-season weekend evenings; be sure to book in advance. The Oyster Shack (01548 810875; www.oystershack.co.uk) in Bidbury is a local institution. There's posh nosh with a view at the South Sands Hotel (01548 859000) in Salcombe, while the Sun Bay Hotel (01548 561371) does very good food too. The Hope & Anchor (01548 561294; www.hopeandanchor.co.uk) in Hope Cove specialises in locally caught fish. For a real taste of South West bohemia, the Pig's Nose Inn (01548 511209) in the tiny village of East Prawle is always lively.

GETTING THERE From the A38 at Wrangaton take the A3121 south, then turn left on to the B3196 to Kingsbridge then the A381 towards Salcombe. After 3 miles take the second turn, signposted Hope Cove; the site is 2 miles further on.

OPEN Easter/early April–late September.

THE DAMAGE Tent, car, plus 2 adults and 2 children £13–£27 (depending on season and tent size) per night. Hook-up £3; dog £1.

manor farm

Manor Farm, Daccombe, Newton Abbot, Devon TQ12 4ST   01803 328294   www.manorfarmcows.com

Manor Farm is a charming, isolated Devon campsite, located so near the M5 that campers can fall into step with the West Country's calming, unhurried way of life quickly and easily. Signposts to the farm line the main Torquay Road, and just five miles from the motorway a steep detour promptly descends into rural calm. As you pootle along between high hedgerows the site jumps into view. Nestled at the foot of a lush green valley is a sprawling farmhouse with a few dozen grazing cows, and not a mobile home in sight. Better still, far from overflowing with tourists, the nearby dinky (okay, minuscule), thatched-cottage villages of Daccombe and Coffinswell are crowd-free.

The resident owner, Thea, is a chatty lady who raises calves, keeps chickens and has all manner of friends and family mucking in to keep the farm in tip-top condition. Simplicity is key to her success and she's never advertised the campsite and never needed to. The field is spacious and airy and there's a half-hour walking trail through the neighbouring woods of Orestone Plantation, overlooking fields.

Nearby kiss-me-quick Torquay is a typically British seaside resort; its numerous restaurants and bars vie for custom, and the main beach is heaving in high summer. Prettier, quieter sandy coves in the area include Watcombe and Hollicombe: reached by either a steep decline or a long walk, they tend to put off a lot of visitors and are all the better for it. We say, be a proud tourist – Manor Farm's chilled aura and surroundings can be as relaxing or as energetic as you need them to be.

COOL FACTOR An easily accessible, simple and calming Devonshire idyll.

WHO'S IN? Tents, campervans (with tents), dogs, groups – yes. Caravans, radios – no.

ON SITE There's room for 75 pitches, plus an overflow field that can fit a further 75. A clean, functional shower block has 15 loos and 8 electric showers; 3 sinks for washing dishes and clothes, plus a lower-level sink for kids, and washing machine. A mini playground at the bottom has rope swings and a slide. A small shop sells drinks, ice creams and bacon butties. BBQ blocks are free or there are 3 BBQ areas behind the washroom. No campfires.

OFF SITE P-p-pick up a ticket to see a penguin at Living Coasts (www.livingcoasts.org.uk), Torquay's coastal zoo and conservation charity.

FOOD AND DRINK Torquay's inaugural Michelin-starred restaurant, The Elephant (01803 200044; www.elephantrestaurant.co.uk), is stylish and serves up posh grub and sea views. The Linney (01803 873192; www.thelinney.co.uk) is a local and lovely pub in Coffinswell offering more traditional cooking.

GETTING THERE Simple: take the M5 and A38 south then A380 (Torquay Road). Turn left at the traffic lights, following the brown camping signs, then turn right at the top of the hill and you'll see Manor Farm as you descend.

PUBLIC TRANSPORT Take a train to Newton Abbot, then it's £10 by taxi, or take a bus to Torquay and catch bus 31, alight at Barchington Avenue, and walk down Daccombe Hill (10 minutes).

OPEN May–September.

THE DAMAGE £10–£20 (depending on tent size) per pitch, per night; gazebo £1; dog £1.

west middlewick farm

West Middlewick Farm, Nomansland, Tiverton, Devon EX16 8NP   01884 861235   www.westmiddlewick.co.uk

Ellie and her family are on their third visit to West Middlewick Farm. She's given her dad strict instructions to wake her up each morning in time to feed the lambs and help out with anything else they might need doinghere. In fact, Ellie has become such an able farmhand that she's even been given her own set of overalls. Because at this working dairy farm, just outside the sleepy (and wonderfully named) hamlet of Nomansland near Tiverton, campers and their kids are encouraged to take an interest in – and help out with – the daily activities.

The farm itself sits between the camping fields and the facilities block, so you'll inevitably wander past and find popping your head into one of the barn doors, with their welcoming labels and friendly residents, irresistible. Indeed getting to know the animals and helping with their care comes hoof in hoof with a stay at West Middlewick, and has done since 1933. As Ellie's parents find out, this refreshing ethos is a huge hit with kids, with some actually begging their parents to leave the beach early so that they're back in time to watch the cows being milked and to help distribute the pig feed. Rabbits in hutches sit on the driveway, guinea pigs snuffle around, chickens roam freely by the barns, and companionable cats prowl around on the hunt for attention. The atmosphere is one of community and conviviality; grown-ups chat cheerfully while their children race around together. And it's not just the kids who get caught up in the West Middlewick way; people of all ages return year after year to fuss over the animals and relax at this no-frills site.

COOL FACTOR Lend a hand on a friendly farm.

WHO'S IN? Tents, campervans, caravans, dogs (on leads), groups (in lower field) – yes.

ON SITE The upper field has a large space in the centre for playing and a track for cycling, as well as hook-ups and water taps. The more informal lower field has taps and hook-ups at the top. Facilities are a walk away from the site, near the farmhouse. There's one ladies' block – loos, basins, 2 (metered) hot showers plus a disabled loo/shower room with baby changing. Around the corner are 2 washing-up sinks and a washing machine. The men's block has loos and a shower (also metered). There are 3 cabins sleeping 6 in another field. No campfires, but BBQs off the ground are okay. Firepits are planned for 2013.

OFF SITE Tiverton Castle (01884 253200; www.tivertoncastle.com) is a compact castle that is educational as well as fun. Or find out how honey is made at Quince Honey Farm (01769 572401; www.quincehoney.co.uk).

FOOD AND DRINK The farm has a small shop selling locally-made sausages, burgers, cheese, jams and chutneys and Devon ice cream. The ivy-covered Thelbridge Cross Inn (01884 860316; www.thelbridgecrossinn.co.uk) does cream teas and mouthwatering fish and fowl mains. Slightly further afield, in Bickleigh, check out the Fisherman's Cot pub (01884 855237; www.fishermanscotpub.co.uk), on the banks of the Exe, which offers fabulous views from its garden.

GETTING THERE Take the A361 towards Tiverton. After 7 miles take the B3137 from the roundabout towards Witheridge. A mile after Nomansland you'll see the farm on the right.

PUBLIC TRANSPORT Train to Tiverton, then bus 155 right to the farm.

OPEN All year.

THE DAMAGE Pitch plus 2 people £8–£10 (extra £2 if it's 1 night only); extra adult £4, child £2, dog £1. Hook-ups £2.

mitchum's

Mitchum's Campsites, Moor Lane, Croyde, Devon EX33 1NN   07891 892897 (9am–6pm only)   www.croydebay.co.uk

Thinking of Devon often evokes sepia-toned scenes of cream teas, chocolate-box cottages and rambling on wild Exmoor. Yet this genteel image of the county is only as true as you make it around here. Sure, there's the traditional Devonian charm of sleepy village Georgeham; not to mention the typical seaside 'candy-floss 'n' kiss me quick' chic of the family resorts at Woolacombe. But if you've descended on the North Devon coast with tent on back, board under arm and adventure on the mind, you've come to the right place – for Croyde Bay is undoubtedly England's surf capital.

Acres of sand, pounding surf, and bronzed lifeguards…welcome to the Gold Coast. It may be a tad cooler than the Aussie version but, more importantly, it is much nearer for us Poms. Okay, so our cousins down under might enjoy near perma-sunny skies, but on an early summer morning, with the breeze just right, we'd take Croyde over Byron Bay any day of the week. With its lush green hills ravining down to blustery expanses of open beach, there's no disputing the beauty of Croyde Bay. This wide sweep of dune-backed sand flanked by the finest field-green North Devon hills is the closest thing you'll find to an Aussie surf beach in this part of the world, gifting awesome waves to pros and beginners alike.

As Guy, the owner of Mitchum's Beach, is all too aware, surfers are an enthusiastic bunch (to put it mildly). Hours can pass as they scan the endless blue horizon for that elusive perfect wave.

Happily, with its enviable elevated vantage point, Mitchum's is one of the few campsites in the area with direct beach views, meaning you can keep an eye on the surf from your tent and race down with your board when the waves are good. And if you're not here for the surf, it's just as great being able to wake up and see the ocean each morning while you cook your breakfast sausages. This stunning bay provides a perfect canvas for this unparalleled campsite masterpiece, and the site is on the coastal path, so it's easy to reach the neighbouring beaches on foot.

As all Cool Campers know, some of the best camping experiences are made infinitely better when the people running the show are attentive to your camping needs. Guy certainly knows how to make you feel welcome, but he also appreciates that his site is rather popular, to say the least. So during the busy summer period, Guy opens up his other campsite in Croyde. This one's called Mitchum's Village campsite, and has the same ambience as its neighbour, just without the ocean outlook. As the albatross flies, it's less than a jiffy to Croyde's quirky collective of pubs and restaurants. Those who've stayed find the village name of this adjacent site is echoed in the jovial friendliness and all-round bonhomie that pitching up by the sea brings out in people.

Regardless of which Mitchum's site you end up in, you're still just a flip-flop away from the beach and guaranteed to fall asleep every night in one incredible location, to the sounds of the crashing Croyde Bay waves.

COOL FACTOR Devon-like chilling with awesome Aussie-like surf.

WHO'S IN? Small tents, small VW campervans without awnings – yes. Motorhomes, large campervans, caravans, dogs, under-17s (unless accompanied by an adult) – no.

ON SITE Approximately 36 pitches; no hook-ups; 2 clean facilities blocks with free hot showers, immaculately clean toilets and 'ladies powder room'. There are also hairdrying, shaving, and phone-charging points. Campers are provided with an alfresco washing-up area with hot water (for dishes) and an outside cold shower (for wetsuits). Freezer packs available (£1 deposit, 50p for freezing). Friendly staff are on site 24 hours a day. There's onsite surf-board, body-board and wetsuit hire. No campfires are allowed but BBQs off the ground are permitted.

OFF SITE Book some lessons with Surfing South West (01271 890400; info@surfsouthwest.com) or take advantage of the stunning heritage coastline path with a walk to Baggy Point. Croyde Bay also hosts the annual Oceanfest (01271 817000; www.goldcoastoceanfest.co.uk) – a beach, sports and music festival in June. To see how it all began, visit the Museum of British Surfing (01271 815155; www.museumofbritishsurfing.org.uk) in Braunton. Here you'll find a detailed history of the long board in our native waters, including sketches of Hawaiian surfers by Captain Cook's crew, airbrushed surf art on early boards and photos of the locals riding the waves on wooden planks in the 1920s. You may also be surprised to learn that Devon's most famous daughter, none other than Agatha Christie, was an early surf pioneer who mastered the art of stand-up surfing in Waikiki. Horse riding on Croyde beach is a must-do experience, whether a leisurely beach trot or epic country trek, exploring Croyde on horseback is a great way to soak up the atmosphere. The family-run, pretention-free Roylands Riding Holidays (01271 890898; www.roylands-stables.co.uk) is based in central Croyde and welcome experienced riders and first-timers all year round. Discover the area on 2 wheels by hopping on the Tarka Trail and exploring the beautiful coast and countryside. Bikes can be hired from Otter Cycle Hire (01271 813339) in Braunton.

FOOD AND DRINK Scoff a Devon cream tea at Centery Farm (01271 879603; www.centeryfarm.co.uk). The Thatch (01271 890349; www.thethatchcroyde.com) pub is a lively surfers' hangout with decent food. The Blue Groove (01271 890111; www.blue-groove.co.uk) combines laid-back beach-bum vibe with trippy artwork and an internationally eclectic menu that includes Thai curries, Mexican pancakes and Japanese noodles. In the village of Georgeham, just inland, try the food and real ales at the Rock (01271 890322; www.therockgeorgeham.co.uk), where they do a great Sunday lunch and serve lunch and dinner daily in a light, bright conservatory. For some of the best fish and chips you're likely to have on the North Devon coast, go to Squires (01271 815533; www.squiresfishrestaurant.co.uk) in neighbouring Braunton. They've been frying the freshest Devon-caught fish here since 1969 and the stylish 2-floor restaurant attracts many celebrity admirers, not least Rick Stein. For a quick bite, grab one of the delicious pasties from the village shop (just don't call them Cornish!).

GETTING THERE Follow the A361 to Braunton, then take the B3231 into Croyde. Turn left in the centre of the village, then left again on to Moor Lane. The Village site is on the left, the Beach site further down on the right.

PUBLIC TRANSPORT From Barnstaple train station walk the 10 minutes to the bus station and take bus 308 to Moor Lane.

OPEN Mitchum's Beach: late July–early September; Mitchum's Village: late May–end August.

THE DAMAGE Book well in advance. Prices vary; contact Mitchum's at www.croydebay.co.uk. for details.

secret spot

Secret Spot Camping, Moor Lane Nursery, Saunton Road, Devon EX33 1HG   07818 423498   croydebay@aol.com

Never has there been a campsite more aptly named. It took this reviewer 20 minutes and two phone calls to find the place, despite the satnav indicating that I was around 200 metres away. Persevere, though, and the determined camper is rewarded with a brilliant little piece of England to call their own. Our tip is to look out for the sign for Moor Lane Nursery as, rather sweetly, the day-to-day business here is growing and selling gorgeous plants.

What this means is that the whole place is beautifully designed, with stunning plants at every turn. A stroll through the site is a revelation, revealing nooks and crannies peppered with comfy chairs, a barbecue, picnic tables and a wishing well along with essential amenities such as a fridge-freezer, microwave, kettle and so on. Its proximity to Croyde Beach means that it's a favoured hangout of the surf crowd but, thanks to its tranquil, private vibe, it attracts the more chilled variety of surfer. There's unspoilt countryside in every direction and you'll share your stay with butterflies, owls, egrets, bats and dragonflies. Back to nature, then, but with the bonus of the lively village of Croyde just down the road.

COOL FACTOR Finding the place is like making it on to the best VIP guest list in town.

WHO'S IN? Tents, small campervans – yes. Caravans, big groups, dogs – no.

ON SITE Fires must be on stone and off the ground. 10 pitches, clean washrooms with 2 toilets and 2 showers (price included), free wi-fi. Microwave, tea/coffee-making facilities. Picnic tables and BBQ, no electric hook-ups.

OFF SITE Look no further than the beach at Saunton Sands and the wonderful dunescape of Braunton Burrows.

FOOD AND DRINK For an excellent sandwich and good ice cream, check out CJ's (01271 812007); for fish and chips, Squires (01271 815533; www.squiresfishrestaurant. co.uk) brings folk from miles around, both for its chippy and sit-down restaurant; surf dudes and dudettes make a beeline for the White Lion (01271 813085; www.whitelionbraunton. co.uk) for its rib-sticking burgers; or, if you want to venture further and fancy more of a party vibe, try the Thatch in Croyde (01271 890349; www.thethatchcroyde.com).

GETTING THERE Look for signs for Moor Lane Nursery, tucked away just off the main Braunton–Croyde road, just 2 miles from Saunton Sands.

OPEN Opening dates change – best to contact them direct.

THE DAMAGE From £12.50 per person per night.

brightlycott barton

Brightlycott Barton, Shirwell, Barnstaple, Devon EX31 4JJ   01271 850330   brightlycott.wordpress.com

Travel writing is littered with clichés. Mountains are almost always majestic, villages usually nestle and great views are invariably jaw-dropping. But, at Brightlycott Barton, for once the clichés ring true: a four-acre campsite and working farm, it has a stunning south-facing view of the North Devon hills as its backdrop, and a cute 400-year-old farmhouse at its heart. It's run by the husband and wife team of Charles and Julia, who have crafted a fine campsite out of fallow fields, even moving 300 tons of topsoil to create a more even pitch. It's not big on facilities, but that's the point. There are chickens to provide the morning eggs for hungry campers and, in a revamped, rough-and-ready barn, one of the biggest games rooms you'll ever see, with table tennis, table football and assorted toys. In truth, though, with a site that commands such dramatic views, the canny camper will simply crack out the folding chair, fill their glass and raise a toast to mother nature in all her glory. And once the novelty has worn off, there are some of Britain's best sandy beaches to enjoy, from the surf dude's paradise of Croyde to the more tranquil charms of nearby Putsborough, one of Britain's cleanest and prettiest stretches of sand.

COOL FACTOR Fab views, peaceful site, and a great jumping-off point for coast and country activities.

WHO'S IN? Tents, campervans, caravans, well-behaved dogs, big groups, families – yes. Groups of teenagers – no.

ON SITE 20 level pitches for tents or caravans, hook-ups available. Clean washrooms with 6 showers, parent and baby washroom, disabled facilities, washing machine, fridge-freezer. Kids' play area with swings. No campfires, but ready-made BBQs allowed, providing they are raised off the grass.

OFF SITE Apart from the beaches, there's Exmoor Zoo (01598 763352; www.exmoorzoo.co.uk), and the excellent Combe Martin Wildlife and Dinosaur Park (01271 882486; www.wildlifedinosaurpark.co.uk).

FOOD AND DRINK Bratton Fleming Farmers' Market gets the thumbs-up from campsite owner Charles. At nearby Blakewell Fisheries (01271 344533; www.blakewell.co.uk) you can catch fresh trout for the barbecue. The Muddiford Inn (01271 850243; www.muddifordinn.com) serves fabulous seasonal cuisine at keen prices.

GETTING THERE From Barnstaple follow the A39 towards Lynton, take the Lynton turn-off and a right to Brightlycott.

OPEN Mid March–mid November.

THE DAMAGE From £8 per tent (sleeping 2 people); extra adults £4 each. Campervans/caravans from £10.

little meadow

Little Meadow Campsite, Watermouth, Ilfracombe, Devon EX34 9SJ   01271 866862   www.littlemeadow.co.uk

The ancient South American tribes of Inca and Maya might have invented terracing to help with their crop cultivation, but seldom can they have done it so well as the folk have here at Little Meadow. By levelling off the land in a series of flat lawns they've ensured that campers benefit from being plumb-line level with the well-tended soft grass for easy tent pegging, while still enjoying views of the stunning North Devon coast. This Area of Outstanding Natural Beauty has everything: dramatic cliffs, wide sandy beaches and quaint little coves and harbours.

The terracing also helps create privacy – you'd never guess there are 50 pitches on this unassuming, environmentally friendly campsite, all set in a beautifully kept 100-acre organic farm. Part of this is down to their sensible policy on dwelling size, with the campsite owners actively discouraging mega-size tents or massive motorhomes. Everywhere you walk brings another unexpected delight, whether it's a rabbit hip-hopping across a nearby meadow, or a set of swings for kids tucked away in a corner. There's also an outdoor table tennis-table set up for use by all guests, and you can buy bats and balls at reception. While here, why not pick up some of the store's lovely regional products – from bacon, eggs and local meats to truly moreish homemade cakes. Bright splashes of flowers border the pitching areas, providing colourful framing to the views over Watermouth Bay, the Bristol Channel and the cliffs of Hangman Point. Its proximity to all things nautical is also in evidence, with huge old anchors, carved driftwood and colourful

floats and buoys scattered around the reception area. It's a magnificent spot in which to settle comfortably into a deckchair, or one of the giant hammocks, and survey the scenery – you might even spy a seal or a basking shark if you're lucky (and in possession of a good pair of binoculars).

If you can drag yourself away, though, there are several must-dos in the area. A day trip to Lundy Island, by ferry from nearby Ilfracombe, offers outstanding views of England, Wales and the Atlantic. It might be just 11 miles from the mainland, but the sense of remoteness is incredible. There's no ferry between November and March, but well-heeled folk can always opt for the daily helicopter service (Mon–Fri). You should also consider taking a fishing trip from Ilfracombe to catch bass, pollack, whiting, cod and mackerel, which are all plentiful here. Gut them on the boat – under the tutelage of the skipper, of course – and you could have your breakfast, lunch and dinner sorted for the day. Alternatively, spend a day learning to ride the waves at one of the many surf schools in the area, at Woolacombe, Croyde or Saunton Sands; or take a beach horse-riding lesson courtesy of Woolacombe Riding Stables (woolacombe-ridingstables.co.uk). There's also Exmoor on your doorstep, of course, which is fabulous for walking. Plus it's not far from the site to the Hunter's Inn pub, from where there are any number of glorious treks you could do, including an easy stroll to the sea at Heddon's Mouth, after which you'll definitely have earned yourself a pint at the pub.

COOL FACTOR Well-tended terraces providing magnificent ocean views.

WHO'S IN? Tents, campervans, caravans, dogs (on leads) – yes. Groups, mega-size tents and huge motorhomes – no.

ON SITE Approximately 50 pitches (draughty in high winds), plus an octagonal camping pod is being built. The washblock has toilets (disabled access), hot showers, a washing machine and hairdryers. There's also ice-pack freezing and a basic shop selling essentials, fresh organic milk, homemade cakes and local farm meats. Hook-ups available. There's a small, wooded play area for kids, as well as table tennis, wi-fi and a dog-exercising area. No campfires.

OFF SITE The closest attraction to the site is Watermouth Castle (01271 867474), a large stately home with old-fashioned exhibitions inside and a theme park behind – good fun for children. Just the other side of nearby Combe Martin, the Combe Martin Wildlife and Dinosaur Park (01271 882486; www.wildlifedinosaurpark.co.uk) is a zoo-cum-theme park with a dinosaur slant – including some fantastic roaring animatronic creatures, alongside seals, monkeys, a spot of falconry and whatever else they have been able to squeeze in. In the opposite direction you can explore the rockpools at the unique Victorian Tunnels Beaches in Ilfracombe (01271 879882; www.tunnelsbeaches.co.uk), and enjoy the landscaped seafront nearby, with its Landmark Theatre, which doubles as the local information centre. Ilfracombe also has a couple of museums that are worth visiting on rainy days – the Ilfracombe Town Museum, on the seafront, (01271 863541; www.ilfracombemuseum.co.uk) and a small aquarium in the harbour (01271 864533; www.ilfracombeaquarium.co.uk), not to mention the long-standing Walker's Chocolate Emporium (01271 867193; www.chocolate-emporium.co.uk), which makes and sells its own chocolates and sweets. For a beautiful, tucked-away coastal spot, check out Barricane Beach at nearby Woolacombe, a lovely inlet that is the final destination for millions of small shells that are whisked here from the Caribbean. Woolacombe Beach itself is a beautiful spot, whether you are surfing or just beach-lounging – the latter is best done at its far end, known as Putsborough Beach, where a lovely café overlooks the sea. Further around the headland there are the glorious expanses of Croyde and Saunton Sands – and the dunescape of Braunton Burrows just behind, which is a fabulous natural soft-play environment for kids.

FOOD AND DRINK Gazpacho (01271 862545; theboathouseilfracombe.co.uk) offers fabulously authentic paella cooked by a Spanish chef; Espresso (01271 855485; www.seafoodrestaurantilfracombe.co.uk) is a seafood restaurant famous for its crab and lobster dishes – all caught locally. La Gendarmerie (01271 865984) and Brit-art wonderboy Damien Hirst's Number 11 The Quay (01271 868090; www.11thequay.co.uk), both fly the flag for modern British cuisine, and the latter has great sea views from its main dining room, as well as a convivial downstairs bar with outside tables. Try also the renowned Sri Lankan curry shack pitched on the edge of the sand at Barricane Beach during the summer months. There's not much in Combe Martin itself, although the large Pack o' Cards pub (01271 882300; www.packocards.co.uk), halfway up the long high street (Britain's longest in fact), does pub grub and has a nice beer garden with lots of activities for kids.

GETTING THERE Take the A361 to Barnstaple. Just past the South Molton exit, turn right at Allercross roundabout (signposted Combe Martin). Go through Combe Martin; the campsite is just past Watermouth Castle on the left.

PUBLIC TRANSPORT Train to Barnstaple then catch a taxi or the infrequent 301 bus to Watermouth Castle.

OPEN Easter–late September.

THE DAMAGE Tent, 2 people and a car £14.50–£20 per night.

westland farm

Westland Farm, Bratton Fleming, Devon EX31 4SH   01598 763301   www.westlandfarm.co.uk

For city dwelling campers especially, there are few things that bring the reality of camping home as much as taking a stroll through a dewy early morning field to use a shower block. Pausing to inhale the clear air – still scented with the smoky fragrance of last night's campfire – while watching the mist rising off the rolling fields, even the most jaded urbanite can't fail to be stirred.

Westland Farm is the perfect place for such epiphanies: a beautifully tranquil site that looks out over a small lake, rolling hills and sheep. There's a variety of accommodation, too, ranging from pitches in a lush, grassy field to a brilliant Shepherd's Hut, set in a quiet corner at the top of the farm, close to the loos and showers and next to a babbling brook, that comes complete with a 5-ft double bed and small child bunk-bed and airbed if you want it – perfect for a family of four – plus a giant yurt that comfortably sleeps six. You can even snag a B&B room in the farmhouse if the outdoor life is not for you and, in case you're feeling lazy, they'll even cook you breakfast. A beautiful spot, and perfect for both a romantic getaway and an escape from the urban jungle.

COOL FACTOR Feeling like you're part of a working farm.

WHO'S IN? Everyone, really. Tents, campervans, caravans, dogs (although not in the yurt), all kinds of groups – yes.

ON SITE Campfires allowed (in pits), 5 pitches, clean washrooms with 2 toilets and 2 (free) showers, fridge-freezer, mobile-charging point and fresh eggs available from the farm's hens. Kids can also help feed the horses or lambs.

OFF SITE Exmoor Zoo (01598 76335; www.exmoorzoo. co.uk) is close by, as is Combe Martin Wildlife and Dinosaur Park (01271 882486; www.wildlifedinosaurpark.co.uk).

FOOD AND DRINK The Black Venus Inn in Challacombe, a 5-minute drive away (01598 763251; www.blackvenusinn. co.uk), has superb home-cooked food in nice surroundings. The New Inn at Goodleigh (01271 342488; www. thenewinnatgoodleigh.co.uk) offers locally sourced produce and excellent views from its garden.

GETTING THERE Take the A39 and then turn off left on to the A399. The farm is about 5 minutes down on the left.

OPEN All year.

THE DAMAGE Camping £6–£7 per person, children half-price, under-4s free; shepherd's hut from £60 per night; yurt from £65–£70 per night for up to 4 people – extra people, camping or staying in the yurt £6–£7, children half-price, under-4s free.

westermill farm

Westermill Farm House, Exford, Exmoor, nr Minehead, Somerset TA24 7NJ   01643 831238   www.westermill.com

In 1938, fed up with army life, Great Grandpa Edwards paid a visit to an unkempt farm hiding in a Somerset valley. On stepping inside, he said simply, 'This'll do'. Within a few years he'd planted thousands of trees, made a home for his cattle and sheep, and transformed the boggy land into something nearing the subtle splendour of today's farm. Split into four adjoining fields at the base of the valley, Westermill enjoys the clear, trout-inhabited waters of the River Exe as it swishes past, and the sturdy protection of mottled hills on either side. Furthest from the farmhouse, the fourth field is perfect for those fancying a late night by the campfire. Awaken neglected hunter-gatherer instincts by foraging for wood and then building a crackle-tastic fire. By the time you settle down to sleep beneath a star-spattered sky, the neighbouring cattle may have morphed into woolly mammoths.

Exmoor provides a backdrop of scenic eye-candy. And if you're lucky enough to be here at the right time, there's an annual skittles tournament held in the lambing barn, with lots of beer, homemade grub and all proceeds going to local charities. In Great Grandpa Edwards' words, 'This'll do'.

COOL FACTOR A secluded, riverside valley in Exmoor.

WHO'S IN? Tents, campervans, caravans, groups, well-behaved dogs – yes.

ON SITE Campfires in the fourth field. BBQs off the ground. Roughly 60 unmarked pitches. Each field has a spring-water tap. Two separate washblocks with toilets, hot showers and washing-up sinks. Washing machine and tumble-dryer.

OFF SITE The pretty village of Dunster with its castle is nearby, and it's not far to the resort of Lynton and Lynmouth, with its cliff-top funicular.

FOOD AND DRINK Onsite shop sells bread, eggs and meat reared on the farm. The Crown (01643 831554; www.crownhotelexmoor.co.uk) in Exford and the Rest and Be Thankful (01643 841222; www.restandbethankful.co.uk) at Wheddon Cross both do good food.

GETTING THERE From Exford take the road to Porlock. After ¼ mile, fork left. Continue along this road and look out for the Westermill sign on a tree.

PUBLIC TRANSPORT Train to Tiverton, then bus 398 towards Minehead. This stops at Exford – the site is a 20–30-minute walk away. In summer the Exmoor Explorer open-top bus (no. 400) travels from Minehead to Exford.

OPEN All year.

THE DAMAGE Adults £6.50, child £3.50.

huntstile organic

Huntstile Organic Farm, Goathurst, nr Bridgwater, Somerset TA5 2DQ   01278 662358   www.huntstileorganicfarm.co.uk

Huntstile is foodie heaven. Owners Lizzie and John radiate a passion for good food, which the whole place lives and breathes. The farm covers over 650 acres of organic land, nursing vegetables, soft fruit, wheat, oats and barley, as well as medicinal crops and sheep and chickens galore. This isn't a dedicated campsite but a farm-cum-campsite/glamping-sort-of-a-place – and it's amazing...You can even get married here.

There are technically 25 pitches, located in a separate field just down from the farmhouse, but you're more or less welcome to hunker down anywhere. If that seems like too much hard work, then cosy up in the beautiful bowtop gypsy caravan, complete with dinky little log burner and double bed – also with an outdoor firepit and cauldron for cooking – or the gorgeous, sky-blue painted shepherd's hut trailer which, believe it or not, sleeps four, albeit at a squeeze.

You're in Quantock country, so the farm lies in an enviable position circled by stunning rural Somerset and all its outdoor possibilities, not to mention a lovely stretch of coastline within striking distance. There are also onsite walks that seek out ancient woodland or stone circles – hard to believe you're only ten minutes from the M5 as all you can hear around here is wildlife. Just a short stroll across the farmyard is a gorgeous little café, where you can tuck into a cream tea or a Full English, happy in the knowledge it's all fair trade without a GM ingredient in sight. Lizzie also runs sausage-making courses, so you can have a ball creating, then sampling, your very own British banger.

COOL FACTOR Bijou camping and glamping by a 14th-century farmhouse with valley views and organic food.

WHO'S IN? Tents, campervans, caravans, children, dogs – yes. Groups – by arrangement.

ON SITE Campfires allowed. 25 pitches. No hook-ups or CDP. There's an eco-shower for a quick rinse (eco-friendly soap only), and 2 electric showers next to the main loo and washing-up area. Private shower cubicle and compost loo for the gypsy caravan and Shepherd's hut. Onsite organic café, shop, restaurant and veg garden. Breakfast available every day; supper by request.

OFF SITE The Quantock Hills (www.quantockonline.co.uk) are close by. The fossils and freshwater ponds of Kilve Beach, on the north Somerset coast, are only a 20-minute drive away.

FOOD AND DRINK All yummy basics can be bought on site. Chomp on juicy burgers at the Pines Restaurant & Diner (01823 451245; www.pinescafe.com) in Broomfield, 3 miles south, or homemade venison and Stilton pies at the Lamb Inn (01278 671350; www.lambinnspaxton.co.uk), 4 miles north in Spaxton.

GETTING THERE From junction 24 of the M5 take the second exit to North Petherton; turn right just before the village into Old Road (signposted Goathurst and Broomfield); after about 1½ miles, take the second right marked Huntstile and Goathurst, and the farm is a further mile up the road.

PUBLIC TRANSPORT Bridgwater train station is 6 miles away, from where you can take a taxi (01278 455565). Buses from Bridgwater go to North Petherton, from where it's a 1½ mile walk.

OPEN April–October.

THE DAMAGE Tent plus 2 people £15 per night. Family tent/campervan/caravan £20. Gypsy caravan £60, shepherd's hut £75 (both 2-night minimum stay; breakfast included).

greenacres

Greenacres, Barrow Lane, North Wootton, Shepton Mallet, Somerset BA4 4HL   01749 890497   www.greenacres-camping.co.uk

Once upon a time, an enchanting couple created a peaceful outdoor living area that was both safe and comfortable for young families and lots of fun for children. They called this place Greenacres – a gigantic four-and-a-half-acre field with just 40 pitches spread around the perimeter. The entire central swathe, meanwhile, is reserved for various dragon-slaying and spell-casting playtime activities, which are run by the Lazy Dayzee Crew, who pitch up here at weekends and during the week during school holidays – thereby giving mums and dads an opportunity to kick back without the little ones for an hour or so. When that's not happening, there's the occasional 30-a-side football match taking place in the field, and perhaps a spot of ping-pong (aka wiff-waff), too. There's no visual electronic entertainment here, just a host of classic old-fashioned toys and activities, such as Wendy houses, see-saws, swings and bikes.

If all this has left you imagining a site full of noisy spellbound kids chaotically running through the place among all the cars and tents, then relax. All the magic takes place in car- and tent-free zones. Except, that is, at sundown on summer evenings, when the lanes around the campsite come alive with magic beetles, and they host their ever-popular Glow Worm Safaris. There's plenty of fun to be had in the environs of this fairy-tale campsite, as well. The moody Somerset Levels provide excellent walking opportunities or, if you fancy something that doesn't require wearing boots, then hippy-central Glastonbury is only three miles away – and just the spot for picking up a magic wand…

COOL FACTOR Spellbinding family campsite.

WHO'S IN? Tents, small campervans, groups – yes. Caravans, motorhomes, dogs – no.

ON SITE Campfires allowed off the ground. BBQs allowed off the ground. 40 good-sized pitches; electric hook-ups. Washblock with WCs, clean showers, washbasins, fridge-freezers, microwave (for sterilizing only) and washing-up sinks. Hut with local info and books to borrow. Bike hire from £7.50 per day.

OFF SITE Explore the famous caves at Wookey Hole (01749 672243; www.wookey.co.uk), 5 miles away, or partake in some thrills and spills at nearby Cheddar Gorge and Caves (01934 742343; www.cheddargorge.co.uk). Check out the myths and legends of the Glastonbury Tor – and the town – in nearby Glastonbury (www.glastonburytor.org.uk).

FOOD AND DRINK Drinks, milk and eggs are available from reception, while two fantastic local producers sell their wares here in high season, including meat treats for the BBQ. The family-friendly Lion (01749 890252; www.thelionatpennard.co.uk), a 20-minute walk away at West Pennard, offers hearty pub fare and some terrific ales but, for a special dining treat, you can't beat Goodfellows Seafood Restaurant (01749 673866; www.goodfellowswells.co.uk) 4 miles away in Wells, which does lovely set menus based on what's good that day – £23 for 3 courses at lunch, £39 at dinner – as well as à la carte fare.

GETTING THERE Take the A361 towards Glastonbury; after Pilton, turn right at the brown campsite sign to North Wootton; turn left and the site is 1 mile further, on the left.

PUBLIC TRANSPORT Train to Castle Cary, then a taxi; or regular buses from Bristol/Bath to Wells, then a taxi..

OPEN April–September.

THE DAMAGE Adult £8.50 per night; child (2–14) £4.

batcombe vale

Batcombe Vale, Shepton Mallet, Somerset BA4 6BW   01749 831207   www.batcombevale.co.uk

The first time you enter this secretive place is a memorable moment. As the lane reaches the hill's crest it drops suddenly to reveal a breathtaking view of a veritable Shangri-La – the slice of heaven, dropped into the midst of rural Somerset, that is Batcombe Vale, where the camping is not so much 'cool', as 'chilled-out-to-the-point-of-being-horizontal'. Around here, rabbits scoot across the grass, buzzards soar on thermals above, and herons pose majestically on the lakesides. Listening to the plops of fish in the water, you half expect the cast of *The Wind in the Willows* to come marching out of the hedges.

The 30 variously sized pitches are positioned on different levels, with caravans and campervans allocated spots on higher ground and the tent brigade safely tucked away among lush tropical-looking vegetation lower down – though the views are glorious from wherever you are. There are four small lakes – one of which has four colourful rowing boats for Batcombe's campers to mess about in – from where hidden paths snake off through the valley's rampant undergrowth. The central patch, meanwhile, is a small oasis of green, with wonky wooden posts positioned at either end for those all important football matches.

There are numerous activities to undertake beyond this sheltered enclave: walkers have a choice of paths radiating outwards from Batcombe Vale. Alternatively, within half-an-hour's drive, there are the magnificent Stourhead Gardens, and Longleat Safari Park. But many visitors just stay put once they've bashed the last peg into the ground of Somerset's answer to paradise.

COOL FACTOR A beautiful and tranquil valley haven.

WHO'S IN? Tents, campervans, caravans, dogs (except certain breeds), small groups (up to 4 units, and only if there's room) – yes. Big group celebrations, noisy types – no.

ON SITE There are 30 pitches, 17 with electric hook-ups; 4 lakes, 2 of which are stocked, though you must hold a licence to fish. You'll find excellent if eccentric washing facilities in a log cabin under a huge climbing plant – toilets, free hot showers, basins, laundry (£3), and freezer. Free rowing boats. Gas or charcoal BBQs only – no campfires.

OFF SITE Stourhead Gardens (01747 841152; www.nationaltrust.org.uk/stourhead), near Mere, makes for a terrific family day out, as does Longleat Safari Park (01985 844400; www.longleat.co.uk) near Warminster. Check out, too, the Royal Bath & West Showground just up the road, where there's something going on most weekends during the summer (www.bathandwest.com).

FOOD AND DRINK In Bruton, Gilcombe Organic Farm Shop (01749 813710; www.somersetorganics.co.uk) is noted for its meat and can supply organic packs for the BBQ, while At the Chapel (01749 814070; www.atthechapel.co.uk) is a restyled coaching inn and chapel offering pizzas and superb wine. As for pubs, try the 17th-century Three Horseshoes Inn (01749 850359; www.thethreehorseshoesinn.co.uk), a mile's stroll away, in Batcombe.

GETTING THERE The easiest approach is via Bruton or Evercreech on the B3081, then follow the brown campsite signs to Batcombe Vale.

PUBLIC TRANSPORT The campsite is 3 miles from Bruton train station, from which the only transport is taxi – call one on 01963 351168.

OPEN Easter–end September.

THE DAMAGE Pitch plus 2 adults £17.50 per night; child (3 –15 yrs) £3.30; under-3s free.

bush farm

Bush Farm Bison Centre, West Knoyle, Wiltshire BA12 6AE   01747 830263   www.bisonfarm.co.uk

As if a coterie of cool animals – bison, elk, raccoons, chipmunks and more – wasn't enough, how does 30 acres of gorgeous oak woodland sound? While the Bison Farm and shop is well known in these parts, the campsite is a bit of a secret. The small, sheltered paddock is reserved exclusively for caravans and campervans and also holds a fabulous wooden pod sleeping four, while the main field is primarily for groups. But Bush Farm's real draw is its vast woodland area, throughout which are half a dozen super-sized clearings, each easily big enough to accommodate several tents. You'll also find a picnic bench and brick firepit for use in each clearing and, if you need wood, there's a designated area where you can chop your own. With so much frolicking about to be done among the woods – including a small brook for the kids to splash around in – a neat play area (including zip wire), and what basically amounts to a mini-zoo, there should be little temptation to leave the site. But, if you fancy a wee excursion, Stonehenge is just up the road, and there are a handful of gentle walks nearby.

COOL FACTOR A magical woodland setting.

WHO'S IN? Tents, campervans, caravans, children, groups – yes. Dogs – no.

ON SITE Campfires allowed in the woodland area. Paddock for around 6 caravans and campervans, plus 1 field and extensive woodland for tents. Amenity block with male and female showers, washbasins and loos. Play area. Shop selling naturally reared meat, eggs, milk and other refreshments.

OFF SITE 25 minutes' drive away, Stonehenge (0870 333 1181, www.stonehenge.co.uk), is a must-visit attraction. Look out, too, for local farmers' markets taking place in the area, notably at Warminster, Wincanton, Frome and Salisbury.

FOOD AND DRINK 2 very agreeable pubs in Mere, 4 miles away, are the Walnut Tree Inn (01747 861220; www.walnut-tree-inn.co.uk), with a fabulous Sunday carvery, and the convivial George Inn (01747 860427; www.thegeorgeinnmere.com) – good for both food or just a pint.

GETTING THERE From the A303, follow the signs to West Knoyle, some 4 miles distant. The site is just beyond the village, well signposted down a narrow track.

OPEN April–September.

THE DAMAGE Adults (and children over 4) £7 per night; caravan/campervan £11 per night per person; pod £40 per night. Half-price entrance to the Bison Centre for guests.

stowford manor farm

Stowford Manor Farm, Wingfield, Trowbridge, Wiltshire BA14 9LH   01225 752253   www.stowfordmanorfarm.co.uk

We can't all be to the manor born, but camping in the grounds of Stowford Manor – a delightfully relaxed campsite on the verdant Wiltshire/Somerset border – gets you close. A stunning 13th-century farmhouse, with accompanying mill and assorted workshops, provide the backdrop to two camping fields bisected by a stream, itself a great little spot for boating and paddling. If this seems like too much effort, afternoons at Stowford Manor can instead be whiled away in the garden, where sumptuous cream teas are served. From here you can watch hens peck around the millpond as the gurgling River Frome flows by. Bliss…

Camping here isn't about being completely indolent, though. The local River Swimming Club is a half-mile downstream; many wild-swimmers stay here, and campers are allowed to use the club for £1 a day. Alternatively, you can cycle along the canal to Bath, less than an hour away. Knowing what makes their campers tick, the Bryants have also printed a map of three pubs within walking distance, all of which have views and serve good ales and terrific food. What more could you want? Another cream tea? Oh, go on then…

COOL FACTOR Rural England at its finest.

WHO'S IN? Tents, campervans, caravans, dogs, groups – yes.

ON SITE Campfires allowed off the ground. 30 pitches with hook-ups spread across 2 fields. Washroom with 2 showers (50p coins), washbasins and washing-up area; plus 3 loos. Tea and scones £4.50, served 3–6pm.

OFF SITE Farleigh Hungerford Castle (01225 754026) is just up the road in Norton St Phillip, but if you fancy a spot of water-bound activity, head to the Kennet and Avon Canal (0800 1214679; www.kennetandavontrust.co.uk) in lovely Bradford-on-Avon, itself a sort of Bath in miniature.

FOOD AND DRINK There are 3 super pubs (all with good food) in close proximity: the New Inn (01225 863123; www.thenewinnwestwood.co.uk), less than a steep mile's walk away in Westwood; Poplars (01225 752426; www.poplarsinn.co.uk), in Wingfield; and the Hungerford Arms (01225 754949; www.hungerford-arms.co.uk) in Farleigh Hungerford.

GETTING THERE From Bath take the A36 south, then turn east on to the A366; the site is 3 miles before you reach Trowbridge.

OPEN Easter–October.

THE DAMAGE Tent and 2 people £14 per night; family tent £17; campervan £15; hook-ups £2.

hook farm

Hook Farm, Gore Lane, Uplyme, Lyme Regis, Dorset DT7 3UU   01297 442801   www.hookfarm-uplyme.co.uk

Picturesque and peaceful, but within a stone's throw of the lively harbour town of Lyme Regis, Hook Farm offers the best of both rural and urban worlds. Tucked away in the small village of Uplyme, with views up the pretty Lym Valley, it's a lovely, leafy site that feels quite remote: being in a designated Dark Valley there's no light pollution at night – just lie back and watch the stars emerge on a clear evening.

The site itself is well-kept and welcoming, with pitches on several different levels, some spacious and open, others secluded and sheltered behind trees and bushes. Friendly, quiet and gently undulating, it's a perfect spot for families: children will enjoy the playground, complete with an old boat to clamber around, while their parents will appreciate the well-stocked shop selling fresh bread and croissants in the mornings and a village pub within easy strolling distance that serves local real ales and wholesome pub grub. And if the peace and quiet of the countryside isn't enough, there's a great 45-minute walk down the valley which runs alongside the River Lym and into the cobbled backstreets and alleyways of Lyme Regis, with its bustling harbour, arty gift shops, sandy beach and array of restaurants and cafés. You can either make it a round walk and return via the coastal path and the cliff-top (the camp shop can provide details of the walking route and maps) or, if you can't face the steep walk back uphill, call the resident tuktaxi, which will come and pick you up and take you back to the campsite for about a fiver.

COOL FACTOR A lovely countryside site made easy.

WHO'S IN? Tents, campervans, caravans, dogs (only certain breeds), families, groups by appointment only – yes. Single-sex groups – no.

ON SITE 100 spacious tent pitches (58 with hook-ups), and 17 static caravans. Large, clean toilet blocks with solar-powered showers, freezers, a washing machine and dryer. Childrens' playground and a well-stocked shop selling local meat and eggs. No campfires, but off-ground BBQs okay.

OFF SITE Great walks down the valley to Lyme Regis and along the coastal path; fossil hunting beneath the local cliffs; and exploring the shops, cafés and restaurants of Lyme Regis. Oh, and if the weather's good, you can just go to the beach.

FOOD AND DRINK Hugh Fearnley-Whittingstall's River Cottage (01297 630302; www.rivercottage.net) is less than 2 miles away – book the tuktaxi to take you there and back. Or take your pick of the many places in Lyme Regis, from Thai on the seafront at Largigi (01297 442432; www.largigi.com) to high-end cuisine at Hix Oyster and Fish House (01297 446910; www.hixoysterandfishhouse.co.uk) and the fantastically elaborate and delicious ice cream sundaes at Rinky Tinks (www.rinky-tinks.co.uk) on the prom.

GETTING THERE Head south on the A35 beyond the Lyme Regis turn-off, then left on to the B3165 and carry on through Yawl to Uplyme. Turn right opposite the Talbot Arms into Gore Lane. The campsite is on the right.

PUBLIC TRANSPORT The nearest train station is Axminster, from where the 31 bus runs to Uplyme, stopping at the Talbot Arms, a 5-minute walk from the campsite.

OPEN March–October half-term.

THE DAMAGE Small tent plus car or campervan and 2 adults £13–£23; medium tent, motorhome or caravan £16–£27; large tent £18–£29. Extra adult £3; child (5–16) £1.75; electric hook-ups £3.

brig's farm

Brig's Farm Camping, Wootton Fitzpaine, Bridport, Dorset DT6 6DF   01297 561267/07967 794038   www.brigsfarmcamping.co.uk

Tucked away along winding, hidden country lanes, Brig's Farm offers real back-to-nature wild camping at its simplest. Little more than a beautifully located field dotted with apple trees and surrounded by woodland, the campsite has stunning views over rolling countryside to the Jurassic coast, just a few miles away.

There are no marked pitches or electrical hook-ups – just pick your favourite spot and set up camp. Most people head up to the top of the sloping field, where they can tuck in beside the woodland and enjoy the best of the views. It's a relaxed and informal place, run by the laid-back Mew, who farms the 12-acre smallholding according to organic principles and is building his own eco-friendly house in one corner of the site. The campsite's eco-footprint is low, with compost toilets and its own running spring water. Campfires and families are welcome, and on Friday nights, the brick-built wood-fired pizza oven is fired-up for Mew's pizza and salad nights. Plus there's a wooden swing and a trampoline for the kids. The real joy of this site, however, is its location, with fantastic footpaths, winding through bucolic landscapes, and quiet country lanes for cyclists to explore. It's also just a short drive down to the beach at Charmouth, where fossil hunting and swimming in the sea are popular activities, while the arty and foodie town of Lyme Regis is also nearby. Seasoned campers and children will particularly enjoy the get-away-from-it-all atmosphere, ; here you can escape from the tyranny of technology, and kids can climb trees, build campfires and roam free.

COOL FACTOR Back-to-nature, environmentally friendly camping with great views over countryside to the sea.

WHO'S IN? Tents, campervans, dogs – yes. Caravans, motorhomes, parties – no.

ON SITE Campfires allowed. The free portable showers are clean and high-pressure and there are 2 compost toilets (with 2 more planned). No marked pitches or electrical hook-ups. No shop or café, but you can buy firewood for campfires, and home-grown veg and eggs when available. The site can get muddy when it rains – bring your wellies.

OFF SITE Fossil hunting in nearby Charmouth is a great activity for children and adults alike. Book onto one of the fascinating 2-hour tours at the Charmouth Heritage Centre on the beach and you'll be amazed by what you can find (01297 560772; www.charmouth.org/chcc).

FOOD AND DRINK A traditional 16th-century village pub, the Bottle Inn in nearby Marshwood (01297 678484; www.bottle-inn.net) serves food and, er, hosts the annual World Nettle Eating Championships in July. Alternatively check out the 14th-century Shave Cross Inn in Shave Cross (01308 868358; www.theshavecrossinn.co.uk): it's got a pretty garden, Britain's oldest thatched skittle alley and a highly rated restaurant serving Caribbean-style food.

GETTING THERE Turn off the A35 at Charmouth then head back under the road towards Wootton Fitzpaine, where you turn left and follow Meerhay Lane into Champernhayes Lane. Look out for the campsite sign on your left.

PUBLIC TRANSPORT The nearest train station is Axminster, which is on the main line to Waterloo; for a small fee, the campsite owner will pick you up.

OPEN Open August and some weekends in July only.

THE DAMAGE Adult £7.50; child aged 5–14 yrs £5; under-5s are free.

sea barn farm

Sea Barn Farm Camping Park, Fleet, Weymouth, Dorset DT3 4ED   01305 782218   www.seabarnfarm.co.uk

Tucked down single-track country roads, shaded with tall trees on either side, this little tenters' campsite is perfectly pitched atop Fleet Lagoon, Lyme Bay and the Jurassic Coast. Many of the pitches have countryside or sea views, and a low-key ambience thrives. This is a traditional campsite with a well-stocked shop and cubicle facilities which include the two most impressive-looking and well-sized family bathrooms we've seen at any UK campsite, with self-contained WC, shower, sink and even a bath). The site is part of a larger operation that includes an adjacent site, and guests can use their facilities, which include an outdoor heated swimming pool and a bar. So, it's the best of both worlds – quiet and peaceful camping, with extra entertainment just next door. Regulars to the site tend to be visitors who travel from afar on their long holiday break. Parents like to pitch near the small children's playground. Older families enjoy all the grassy space for ball games. Climbers come to be near Portland's cliffs and quarries. And walkers just love the Fleet Lagoon – a unique and protected nature reserve that attracts migrating waterfowl in spring and autumn – which is just a 500m stroll down the South West Coast Path. The tidal lagoon is home to Moonfleet Manor Hotel, formerly called Fleet House by its well-to-do owner who, so legend has it, was heavily involved in smuggling. During the summer months you can book a guided tour with a costumed re-enactment group that will talk you through the history of the once-booming local smuggling community, making a fun day out for the kids.

COOL FACTOR Sea views and farm landscapes.

WHO'S IN? Tents, campervans, motorhomes, dogs (on leads) – yes. Groups – by arrangement. Caravans – no.

ON SITE Up to 250 pitches in peak summer, including 50 with hook-ups. 2 blocks with free hot showers and toilets, 2 beautiful, large family shower rooms and disabled facilities. There's a laundry, bar and swimming pool at adjacent West Fleet Farm during peak season, a 15-minute walk along flat roads. No campfires.

OFF SITE You can walk from the site down to the Fleet Lagoon – a protected nature reserve. A re-enactment group offers guided tours along the South West Coast Path covering its smuggling history and influence on the book *Moonfleet*. Tickets are available from the camp shop.

FOOD AND DRINK Some of Dorset's best seafood can be enjoyed at the famous Hive (01308 897070; www.hivebeachcafe.co.uk) while, slightly closer, the Elm Tree Inn at Langton Herring specialises in game (01305 871257; www.theelmtreeinn.co). Nearer still, the pedigree cattle grazing the working farmland produce amazing steaks, which are on the menu at the all-new Bar in the Barn, which opens daily at West Fleet Campsite (www.westfleetholidays.co.uk).

GETTING THERE Take the A354 and follow the signs for Abbotsbury and the B3157. After Chickerell, turn left at the mini-roundabout towards Fleet. At the top of the hill, after the church, turn left at the crossroads and you're pretty much there.

PUBLIC TRANSPORT Take bus 8 from Weymouth to Chickerell, then it's a short walk.

OPEN March–October.

THE DAMAGE Pitch plus 2 adults £12–£22; child £1–£2.50, hook-ups £15–£25 per night.

tom's field

Tom's Field, Tom's Field Road, Langton Matravers, Swanage, Dorset BH19 3HN   01929 427110   www.tomsfieldcamping.co.uk

A piece of manicured heaven exists in the rural Isle of Purbeck called Tom's Field; a quiet site encased within an old stone wall, with just a neighbouring field of cows for company. We've always loved this site. It's been in the same hands for two decades now, but no one could ever accuse the owners of resting on their laurels. The shop just keeps expanding (they've recently added hot drinks, local jams and hand-drawn artist cards to their shelves); there's a new tourist information booth, and the new Breakfast Bar behind the washrooms sends delicious wafting wake-up calls around the site. The Nissen Field is opposite this; a dinky, good-looking, tucked-away corner with space for seven tents, which can be booked out in the school holidays. There's also an upper field that has long views seaward across Swanage Bay or, on a clear day, to the Isle of Wight, and a lower or 'family' field that allows a little more freedom to scatter around, with a stone wall running along the length of one side, keeping out the cows and sheep. Pitches in the lower field can be booked, but again only during school holidays.

With so many attractions in the area, what you do depends on your mood and, of course, dear old Mother Nature. But really you're here for the stretch of coast – aka the fossil-rich Jurassic Coast – now a UNESCO World Heritage Site (along with the Great Barrier Reef and the Grand Canyon). Getting here by public transport is easy, then you can hire bicycles and embrace the many coastal walks to see why.

COOL FACTOR Peace, tranquility and a UNESCO world wonder on its doorstep.

WHO'S IN? Tents, motorhomes, dogs (on leads) – yes. Groups – by arrangement. Tents with a diameter of over 8 metres, caravans – no.

ON SITE Approximately 100 pitches; shower block with solar hot-water system, traditional (refundable) token-operated showers, 2 family shower rooms, disabled facilities, laundry room, baby-changing area, washing-up areas and hook-ups. Onsite shop for daily essentials, camping goods, food plus ice packs to rent (daily 8am–11am/4pm–6pm). Breakfast Bar (8am–10.30am weekends, and every day in school hols). No campfires. BBQs off the ground okay.

OFF SITE The National Trust's Corfe Castle (01929 481294; see www.nationaltrust.org.uk) is so near it would be criminal not to visit or to dig into one of their cream teas.

FOOD AND DRINK The best-loved pub in the area – the Square & Compass in Worth Matravers (01929 439229; www.squareandcompasspub.co.uk) – is an all-weather hit: on sunny days, sit on the hill outside sipping ciders; in cooler weather, tuck into tasty ales and pasties. For supplies, stock up on local, organic and fair-trade produce at the onsite shop, or for greater variety seek out the fortnightly (Weds) local produce farmers' markets in Wareham, and monthly (Sat) Purbeck Products stalls at Swanage Middle School.

GETTING THERE Take the A351 to Harman's Cross and turn right on to Haycrafts Lane; after a mile turn left on to the B3069 and then take a right, on to Tom's Field Road.

PUBLIC TRANSPORT Train to Wareham and then one of numerous local buses towards Swanage that stop at the site.

OPEN March–October.

THE DAMAGE Tent plus 2 people and a car £14 per night.

downshay farm

Downshay Farm, Haycrafts Lane, Swanage, Dorset BH19 3EB   01929 480316   www.downshayfarm.co.uk

Campsites with sprawling views, wide-open spaces and big skies don't come much better than Downshay Farm. The hospitable owners – who live in the large Victorian farmhouse – have struck gold with their location, near to the historically rich Jurassic coastline in one direction and stunning Corfe Castle in the other. This is a campsite with stately views, in fact; the castle perches on the Purbeck Hills in sight of campers and looks eerily spectacular shrouded in early morning mist.

The facilities are fantastically clean (guests must mop up after their own shower and it works, the cubicles are spotless) and the pitches are sheltered and un-numbered, bordered by tall trees. Kids love the steam train, of course, that stops at the bottom of the hill at Harman's Cross station every hour during high summer. Non-petrolheads can travel conscientiously to the farm's doorstep, therefore, and later hit the family-friendly Swanage beach two stops away within minutes. Yup, Downshay is an amazing spot.

Sadly the site is only open for camping during the school holidays, and you have to be quick or lucky or both to find a flat pitch on the lower ground, but those of us who don't mind sleeping on a slope will scale the peak to enjoy a wide-angle view of sprawling countryside every morning (it's also a good place to be if it rains). Walks across the Vale of Purbeck also run right by the campsite, including an unmissable – if energetic – day-trek to Studland Bay and Lulworth Cove.

COOL FACTOR Fantastic, spacious countryside spot accessible by a steam train running to the coast.
WHO'S IN? Tents, small campervans, caravans (in a separate field), well-behaved groups, dogs (on leads) – yes. Transit vans, motorbikes – no.
ON SITE Room for about 90 tents. There is no specific limit – the owner just brings out the 'full' sign when he thinks it's time. The caravan field has 12 pitches (all with hook-ups) and separate facilities block. Each block contains hot showers (5W, 4M, 2 unisex), and toilets. Hairdrying point; freezers for ice packs; washing-up areas. BBQs off the ground are okay, and barrels are available for fires. A football and frisbee play area.
OFF SITE On sunny days head to Swanage, Studland or Shell Bay beaches or take the ferry to Sandbanks. Plus there is the evocative ruin of Corfe Castle (01929 481294; www.nationaltrust.org.uk).
FOOD AND DRINK Corfe Castle's ice-cream shop – Box of Delights – sells Purbeck specialities (01929 481060).
GETTING THERE Take the A351 past Corfe Castle to the crossroads at Harman's Cross. Turn right into Haycrafts Lane and continue for half a mile past the steam railway station and up the hill. The campsite signs are on the right.
PUBLIC TRANSPORT Train to Wareham/Swanage, Purbeck Breezer bus 40/44 to Harman's Cross, then a short walk up the hill. Or take the steam train from Norden or Corfe Castle (01929 425800; www.swanagerailway.co.uk).
OPEN For 10 days around Whitsun weekend, then mid July–early September. Caravan field April–October.
THE DAMAGE Adults £5 per night; children (over-11) £2, (under 11) £1. Plus £2/£3/£4 for small/medium/large tent; car £1. Minimum fee per night £10.

harman's cross

Harman's Cross, Haycrafts Lane, Swanage, Dorset BH19 3EB   07970 804928   book@harmanscrosscamping.co.uk

A new campsite on the Purbeck block on the southern tip of Dorset, this wide, spacious eight-acre pasture adjacent to the Swanage Railway line is open for a brief period in high summer, and the rest of the time is home to grazing cattle. Pitch around the top edges for sheltered, level ground and views of the neighbouring campsite Downshay Farm (see p74); there are also a few hideaway corners for those seeking privacy.

A few roly-polys downhill is all it takes to reach the station where steam trains tootle by on their hourly missives to and from the coast. Swanage is the closest town to explore, and the steam train will whizz you there in minutes. Its Victorian pier and fabulous views across to the Needles on the Isle of Wight are popular with families. Studland features a beautiful, natural, sweeping sandy five-mile bay where Old Harry Rocks lives; an impressive chalk headland that has seen many shipwrecks in its time. The water is shallow and the beach is clean: another hit among parents. Behind the beach lots of rare birds flit in and out of the Nature Reserve. Back at the ranch, cleaning off the sand takes place in new facilities, a basic cabin with hot, free showers.

COOL FACTOR Verdant, lush pasture with steam trains chuffing by.

WHO'S IN? Tents, campervans, groups, dogs on a lead – yes. Caravans, young groups – no.

ON SITE Campfires allowed off the ground. 50 unmarked pitches. Brand new block with sinks and shower cubicles. Kids' playground with rope swings and wooden bridges.

OFF SITE The Jurassic Coast is probably the main draw to these parts and is just a few miles away – take bikes and feel the English Channel wind in your hair. If it's not beach weather you can head up towards Corfe village for some old-fashioned trinket shopping and a stroll around the castle.

FOOD AND DRINK The Isle of Purbeck microbrewery churns out delicious ales with names such as Studland Bay Wrecked and Fossil Fuel, available at many pubs in the area.

GETTING THERE Take the A351 towards Swanage, turn right at Harman's Cross, into Haycrafts lane; take the second right into Faryls Way, and the site is at the end of the lane.

PUBLIC TRANSPORT Train to Wareham/Swanage, then Purbeck Breezer bus 40/44 to Harman's Cross station; turn left and into the field and you're there.

OPEN End of July–end of August.

THE DAMAGE Tents £4, adults £3, children £2.50, cars £3, gazebo £3, child's tent £3.

burnbake

Burnbake Campsite, Rempstone, Corfe Castle, Dorset BH20 5JH   01929 480570   www.burnbake.com

There are those rare occasions when you arrive at a site and within minutes know that you'd like to stay all season. Burnbake is one of these instantaneous hits. Its many plus points quickly add up to create a vibe so agreeable that, before you know it, you're down at the office negotiating a second week's stay. Children in particular will love being able to run free through the woods, swing on the rope tyre, climb in wooden boats or build dams in the stream.

There are no designated pitches among Burnbake's woodland site – 12 acres of secluded, level ground, complete with burbling stream – so have a nose around to find a suitable nook or cranny. During high summer it can be busy, and as a result it's not the quietest site, but there are some more peaceful places to pitch away from the main circuit.

In low season it's quieter and at any time of year it's a prime location for the National Trust Studland beaches and for exploring the Isle of Purbeck, particularly on bike or foot. You can also cycle to Swanage or Wareham avoiding the main roads, or indeed to Corfe Castle itself, which is an iconic and uplifting old ruin.

COOL FACTOR Woodland campsite that kids love.

WHO'S IN? Tents, campervans, groups, hikers, cyclists, dogs – yes. Caravans – no.

ON SITE Campfires allowed in containers off the ground. 130 pitches. 2 large wooden huts house showers (free), plus a baby changing room, 2 washing machines and outside washing-up sinks. A shop opens for 2 hours each morning and evening, selling sweets, breakfast buns, camping food and equipment. Woodland play area with slide and swings.

OFF SITE Studland Bay is an hour's walk or a 20-minute cycle. Hire bikes from cyclexperience in Wareham (01929 556601; www.cyclexperience.co.uk).

FOOD AND DRINK Onsite café open mornings and evenings for cream teas, burgers, etc. The Greyhound Inn at Corfe Castle (01929 480205; www.greyhoundcorfe.co.uk) is a good spot, with sharing plates and Purbeck ice cream.

GETTING THERE From Wareham take the A351 to Corfe Castle, turn left on to Studland Road, then take the third left turn, signposted Rempstone. Then follow the campsite signs for a mile; Burnbake is on the right.

PUBLIC TRANSPORT Train to Wareham, then a taxi.

OPEN Easter–September.

THE DAMAGE Tent and 2 adults £11–£15 per night. Extra adult £3–£5, child (3–16yrs) £1.50–£2.50.

riversidelakes

Riversidelakes, Slough Lane, Horton, Wimborne Minster, Dorset BH21 7JL   01202 821212   www.riversidelakes.co.uk

We've always believed this is one of the top campsites in the UK, but this utter gem has just been getting better and better since our last visit. The owners Maggie and Nigel are as affable as they are creative, and they don't do anything by halves. At the beginning of summer 2010, the couple and their two sons took on this 15-acre site, along with the resident Chinese geese, duck, swan, cat, chickens – and an entire season's bookings. Since then, both their business and their animal farm have been booming. The wild flowers and rope-tyre swings have been swaying, new little piglets grunting and, most importantly of all, the punters are smiling.

The low-key signposting (if you hit Drusilla's Inn you've gone too far) does little to hint at the magic that lies ahead, where the pitches are spacious and the atmosphere is almost other-worldly, despite its convenient location not far from the M27. Once you're in, park up and head for reception, where you'll probably meet Maggie. The camping area comprises 12 acres of dreamy natural meadow and woodland, with three lakes enclosed by circumferential paths and thick shrubbery. All the pitches are accessible by car so you can drive and unload before parking in the car parks. Mown pathways separate the clusters of pitches and the long, wild grasses create walls in between, so that all that sedentary campers can see of their neighbours is the smoke rising from their braziers. At dusk the overall vista resembles the basecamp of an intrepid expedition into the wild unknown. There's a stillness in the air.
This is total enchantment.

Groups (quiet ones) really do love it here, booking out entire pitch clusters. Each cluster bears its own helpful name. So you can choose your spot according to your needs – great lake views, proximity to the facilities, sheltered woodland, treelined and ridgeway pitches, and isolated individual hideaways – you choose.

The facilities are top-notch: a new shower room has been upgraded so the water is always hot and there's a sheltered area for recycling with plug points. The area beyond is full of great pubs and restaurants, though you'll need a car or a taxi to sample the fish and chips or the Chinese and Italian establishments at Verwood; failing that you can just dial for a takeaway – many leaflets can be found on site. The narrow country lane outside of the campsite isn't ideal for young children to walk or cycle along, but just a few miles up the road is the fabulous Moors Country Valley Park, which has cycle paths, tree-top walkways and scavenger hunt trails. A sandpit play area for the very young and a larger adventure park for older kids are the cherries on top. It's expensive to park there but a lot of the areas are free – which is always a bonus. Take a packed lunch to enjoy in the picnic area before jumping on a steam train for a ride through the woods.

Alternatively you can just stay put on the site: many families bring bicycles so their charges can tear along the kale and woodland paths. If they're not doing that they're climbing trees, playing on swings or watching their dads fish. As for everyone else, well, they're just kicking back and enjoying the magic of the place.

COOL FACTOR Spacious, relaxing and comfortable – just lovely.

WHO'S IN? Tents, campervans, caravans, dogs, groups (not young or noisy ones) – yes.

ON SITE Campfires in firepits or borrowed braziers. Logs are £5 a bag, which includes matches, firelighters and kindling (delivered to your tent). There are 55 pitches, no minimum stay, in different areas, and room for 5 campervans or caravans with hook-ups. Areas include: Viewpoint, which allows parents to keep an eye on toddlers as they run up and down the meadow; Isolation spots suit single bookings and are nearest to the showers; Chill Out is in the furthest corner. Three woodland pitches offer protection from the elements among the trees: Overview looks out across the middle lake and suits small tents; and at the top the Treeline and Ridgeway clusters have views of the site and also share an eco-loo. The new shower block has 8 showers supplied with renewable energy, loos, hairdryers, a family bath and baby-changing facilities. There are 3 washing-up sinks, a freezer and microwave. New Soul Pad bell tents come with camp kitchens, mattresses, wooden decking outside and a bench table. A communal area, 2 washing-up sinks, and an electric powerpoint faces a huge firepit that groups can use. Recycling bins include a swap shop, where you leave/pick up anything that campers might use. Experienced anglers can acquire an Environment Agency rod licence to fish in the lakes (from the post office, 1 day £3.75; 8 day £10). Two tyre swings; ice packs are available.

OFF SITE If you want to do more than just kick back by the lakes, the historic market town of Wimborne Minster has a farmers' market on Fridays and flea market on Saturdays. The town also boasts a remarkable, originally Norman minster church of St Cuthberga, with a rare chained library. The Moors Valley Country Park (01425 470721; www. moors-valley.co.uk) is down the road, and has picnic areas, cycling tracks, forest walks with wooden climbing structures, golf, croquet and high-wire tree-climbing. One of England's most magnificent country mansions, Kingston Lacy, is just outside Wimborne Minster to the north-west (01202 883402; www.nationaltrust.org.uk/kingston-lacy), plus there's the Iron Age fort of Badbury Rings, in what feels like a very wild and remote spot a mile or so further north. In the opposite direction, the relatively urban vibe of Bournemouth and its lovely beaches are just a 20-minute drive away.

FOOD AND DRINK Pretty Drusilla's Inn (01258 840297; www.drusillasinn.co.uk) is a right turn out of the campsite and serves a whole range of pub grub including Sunday roasts, cider-roasted hams and kids' meals. Friday morning is market day at Wimborne Minster – great for campfire supplies. Wimborne pubs are much of a muchness, but you could try the White Hart (01202 886050), right in the heart of town, which does decent pub grub and has a small beer garden. The Long Crichel Bakery Café (01258 830852; www.longcrichelbakery. co.uk) is perhaps the best place for lunch, with lots of choice based on its own beautiful bread and delicious savoury pastries.

GETTING THERE Take the M27 west and then the A31. After Ringwood, take the exit for Bournemouth, keep right on the slip road and take 3rd exit for Moors Valley Country Park/Three Legged Cross, and the site is 3½ miles after the Country Park on the right, after 2 mini-roundabouts.

PUBLIC TRANSPORT Bournemouth train station is a 20-minute taxi ride away (£30). National Express run coaches to Ringwood, from where a taxi costs about £16.

OPEN April–September.

THE DAMAGE Adult £10 high season/£8 low season; child £7/£6, under-5s free. Soul Pad bell tent £40–£90 per night. Riversidelakes is a Camping and Caravanning Club Certified site so annual membership is required if you stay outside August – join on arrival.

hillside campsite

Hillside Campsite, Gotham, Verwood, Dorset BH21 5QY   01202 824460   www.hillsidecampsite.co.uk

Life seems to stand still at Hillside Campsite, a rustic, natural coppice in the heart of the east Dorset countryside. This undiscovered gem not far from Ringwood is reached by narrow lanes through picturesque villages has been here for ever. While guests are greeted by a scene straight out of the film *Babe*, with chickens, geese and dogs sharing the garden, the dishevelled house looks like it's been transported from Australia's bohemian Byron Bay. The facilities, however, are another thing altogether, featuring a fancy, modern sea-green tiling reminiscent of the Mediterranean.

Once the domain of hippy travellers, Hillside now attracts anyone looking to jump off the treadmill of daily routine, feet first into a green, enclosed wilderness. Health and emergency services workers are offered discounts, the owners are keen to welcome special-needs adults and kids, and they work with a charity to help re-socialise homeless people. Pitches are often arranged in a circle with the BBQ in the centre, to 'aid peaceful socialising', but if you're travelling solo or with partners/family and wish to be private, you can do that, too. There really isn't anything to do on site except sit in a chair, cook, gently imbibe, bat a ball and gaze at the leaves rustling in the trees. But when that gets too much, there are 30 miles of forest walking trails on the doorstep. Bring a good book or three, and when you feel more adventurous, take the kids down the road to the Heavy Horse Farm Park to enjoy wagon rides, go-karting, a straw barn play area and some serious heavy horse swooning.

COOL FACTOR A true, back-to-basics, peaceful camping hideaway next to a forest.

WHO'S IN? Tents, campervans, dogs, caravans, family groups, young groups – yes. Noisy groups – no.

ON SITE There are 15 marked pitches with electric hook-ups and around 7 additional pitches in 2 overflow fields. Hot, modern shower cubicles (50p), one for disabled. Washing-up sinks. Ice pack hire (15p). Free wi-fi. Chish & Fips [sic] van passes by Saturday lunchtimes. Large play area with badminton net, hens, ducks, horses and geese to pet. The nearest shop is 1 mile away. Local butcher sausages are given to guests. BBQs okay. No campfires.

OFF SITE Head to Burley to browse the shop that sells witch cauldrons and enjoy a cream tea in the village before burning it off on a lovely walk around the New Forest. More adventurous travellers with wheels can hit the south coast, go to Mudeford Quay for crabbing, or to Kimmeridge, which offers great views, snorkelling and fishing, but fewer tourists than Lulworth.

FOOD AND DRINK Verwood has enough to satisfy anyone staying here for a while, so having barbecued your delicious sausages, dial in a superb Indian takeaway from the village's Spice of India (01202 813017).

GETTING THERE From Verwood follow the Ringwood Road/B308 onto Champtoceaux Ave, then Edmondsham Road, turn right toward Batterley Drove and then first left.

PUBLIC TRANSPORT Buses run from Bournemouth to Verwood, or you can take a train to Poole and catch a taxi. Express Coaches travel between London and Ringwood, where you can arrange to be picked up by the owners.

OPEN All year.

THE DAMAGE 2 adults with tent or caravan £17 per night, dogs and under-4s, free 4–17yrs £4.25. Hook-ups £5 per night.

Thistledown is, quite simply, enchanting. More than just a beautiful campsite nestled among 70 acres of organic meadow and woodland, it is an inspirational place, too – a dream realised by Richard Kelly, who has nurtured Thistledown since 1993, when he began creating habitats for the wide range of local plants and wildlife. Richard now runs the site with his son Ryan, and neither could be more helpful or enthusiastic about the site, which is easy to find – just head towards a majestic wind turbine located 300 metres from the entrance. The turbine was one of the first to be erected by the increasingly popular Ecotricity, the UK's first provider of mainstream electricity produced from renewable sources. It's part of

the eco-vibe in this neck of the Gloucestershire woods, so if you've ever fancied living the sustainable *Good Life*, then this is probably the place in which to settle. Nearby Nailsworth and Stroud are the hubs of all things green and well worth a wander, especially for food. Nailsworth has the divine Hobbs House Bakery – home to TV's *Fabulous Baker Brothers* – and Stroud boasts a wonderful farmers' market.

In the meantime you can camp in three main areas at Thistledown. There's a choice of 80 pitches, but don't for a minute think that you will be crowded out. Richard and Ryan ensure that no one camps on top of one another, and the 70 acres here take in trees, undulating pasture, glades

thistledown

Thistledown, Tinkley Lane, Nympsfield, Gloucestershire GL10 3UH   01453 860420/07868 713180   www.thistledown.org.uk

of wild flowers, and lots and lots of space. The top field allows cars and offers camping in pitches individually mown into a pretty elderflower orchard, while the bottom two pastures are car-free and tranquil. For those with children, there's real freedom here; the pastures are flanked by woodland offering numerous opportunities for lengthy walks, nature-watching, or just some good old-fashioned hooning around. Richard and Ryan often run talks, walks and events, which are free for campers, from barbecues to bird walks and bat evenings. At dusk you can actually wander down to a spot where badgers come out to feed and, as long as the wind is in the right direction (so they can't smell or hear you), you'll be able to stay transfixed for ages.

All three camping areas have firepits, and in the evening, Richard whizzes by on his little off-road vehicle selling wood by the heaped barrowful. You can take your own, but are asked not to collect it from the woods as it provides shelter for creatures such as snakes and slow worms. Picnic tables and sawn logs are dotted around the site, so that you can make the most of this tranquil environment, its stunning views, the nature trails on offer and the stunning starlit sky. Streams spouting from Roman drainage systems gurgle in the background, and the rope swings near them offer great excitement. But the really magical thing about Thistledown is its colour. The trees, grassland and space are all green. Green in colour, and green in ethos, that is.

COOL FACTOR Camping under the stars in an ancient valley surrounded by nothing but wildlife.

WHO'S IN? Tents, groups, dogs (on leads) – yes. Campervans – yes (in elderflower orchard). Caravans – no.

ON SITE Campfires allowed in pre-dug firepits. There are 3 main camping areas on this 70-acre site: the elderflower orchard (20 pitches), where cars are allowed, and the car-free second (20 pitches) and third (40 pitches) pastures. Pitches are unmarked, but there's plenty of room (and we mean metres, not centimetres) to stretch out and play ball games. The elderflower orchard has the most basic facilities, with portaloos. The pastures have compost loos, hot showers and basins, plus washing-up sinks. The site has numerous walks, lakes and a birdwatching hide. You can borrow a wheelbarrow to transport your gear into the no-car zones, or pay £5 to be whizzed down in the off-road buggy, as long as the guys are available. Wood is available to buy and you're also welcome to bring your own, but nothing must be taken from the campsite and woodland, as it's a vital natural habitat. New for 2013 is the farm shop, selling farm- and locally-grown produce. No food miles here.

OFF SITE A walk through the woods from Thistledown will take you to the fascinating Woodchester Mansion and Park (01453 861541; see www.nationaltrust.org.uk). The house is an unfinished Gothic manor, so you can open doors that go nowhere and get an idea of the building process. Don't visit after dark though; it's haunted... The area surrounding Thistledown is also known for its burial mounds. The Neolithic Nympsfield Long Barrow (see www.english-heritage.org.uk) has internal burial chambers for viewing. Just along the ridge is the Uley Long Barrow (aka Hetty Pegler's Tump) – take a torch if you want to see inside. On the other side of Stroud is the beautiful Slad Valley, which formed the backdrop for the late Laurie Lee's novel, *Cider with Rosie*; there are lots of beautiful walks to be done here, perhaps stopping off at Lee's old local, The Wool Pack Inn, in the village of Slad, where they serve lunch and dinner.

FOOD AND DRINK There are plans to offer locally produced organic food boxes on site, so watch this space... Foodie heaven Nailsworth is only 3 miles away, and bread will never taste the same again once you've sampled the stuff at Hobbs House Bakery (01453 839396; www.hobbshousebakery.co.uk); or, for an upmarket deli, there's William's Foodhall (01453 832240; www.williamsfoodhall.co.uk). The award-winning Stroud farmers' market (6 miles away) is open every Saturday from 9am–2pm; you can buy everything there, from locally produced meat, bread and cheese to Thai takeaways. Good local pubs offering food include the Old Spot (01453 542870; www.oldspotinn.co.uk) at Uley, which has its own microbrewery, and the Black Horse (01453 872556; blackhorseamberley.co.uk) at Amberley. For a pub within walking distance of the site, try Nympsfield's Rose & Crown (01453 860240; www. theroseandcrowninn.com).

GETTING THERE From the M5 take the A419 towards Stonehouse. After a mile, take the third exit to Eastington at the roundabout and head on to Frocester. At the crossroads at the top of Frocester Hill go straight over and turn left after about 300 metres, towards Nympsfield. At the staggered junction go straight across to Tinkley Lane, signposted Nailsworth; after 1 mile, Thistledown is on your left. (If you reach the wind turbine you've gone too far.)

PUBLIC TRANSPORT Train to Stroud, then (twice-daily) bus 35 to Nympsfield, then a 15-minute walk.

OPEN March–late October.

THE DAMAGE Tents £10 per night plus charges per person: adults £6, children (over 4 yrs) £3, under-4s free. Dogs £1. If you camp in the elderflower orchard or arrive via public transport, foot or bike, the tent fee is reduced to £5. Booking in advance is essential, via the website www. thistledown.org.uk.

hayles fruit farm

Hayles Fruit Farm, Hailes, nr Winchcombe, Gloucestershire GL54 5PB   01242 602123   www.haylesfruitfarm.co.uk

So beautiful and tranquil is this campsite that people travel from as little as three miles away to stay here! It's also a great base for exploring the Cotswolds, with Cheltenham in one direction and the honey-coloured stone of Stanway, Stanton and Broadway in the other.

The site is pretty well equipped, with a great farm shop and café. But as Hayles is a family run fruit farm, you can also take the opportunity while you're here to do some PYO (pick your own), starting with strawberries and other soft fruits in May, plums in August and apples and pears through to October. The vibe is laidback in the extreme. There's a six-acre field where you're more or less free to pitch wherever you like, and everyone rubs along nicely, with plenty of fresh Cotswold air to breathe in and field space in which to throw a ball around, or just stretch out to read the paper. There's a slight slope to the field, but young fruit trees have been planted to create shade, shelter and interest, so all in all it's very pretty. At dusk, listen and look out for the locals – roe deer, muntjac and foxes – before stoking up the fire and doing a spot of stargazing. There are firepits, and wood is for sale from the campsite shop, which also sells all manner of excellent produce, including (natch) plenty of fresh fruit and really good local cider. As for the surroundings, they're glorious, with plenty to do, including easy access to the 100-mile-long Cotswold Way, which runs from Chipping Camden to Bath. The nearby Cotswold Farm Park is great for kids, but really the best way to experience Hayles Fruit Farm is to hang out here and do, well, not much at all.

COOL FACTOR A tranquil camping retreat in a beautiful rural location.

WHO'S IN? Tents, campervans, caravans, groups, dogs – yes.

ON SITE Campfires allowed. Plenty of tent pitches plus 15 electric hook-ups, 12 with hard-standing. 4 ladies and 4 gents toilets; 2 showers. 2 fishing lakes (bring your own equipment and licence).

OFF SITE Walkers love being close to the Cotswold Way. The hike up the hill to Farmcote Herbs (01242 603860; www.farmcoteherbs.co.uk) has great views, and Adam Henson's Cotswold Farm Park satisfies lovers of farm animals (01451 850307; www.cotswoldfarmpark.co.uk). There are also the striking ruins of Hailes Abbey (01242 602398; www.nationaltrust.org.uk/hailes-abbey), a 13th-century Cistercian monastery.

FOOD AND DRINK The Hayles farm shop is open every day and sells most things you might need, though they're happy to order in if there's something specific you want. The farm café also does a great cooked breakfast. Winchcombe, 3 miles away, has many food shops and several good pubs, including the excellent Lion Inn (01242 603300; www. thelionwinchcombe.co.uk). If you want a good old-fashioned Cotswold pub, try the Halfway House at Kineton (01451 850344; www.thehalfwayhousekineton.co.uk). There's also the Mount Inn in Stanton (01386 584316; www. themountinn.co.uk), just outside Broadway, which serves local Donnington ales (brewed in Moreton-in-Marsh), and food every day lunchtimes and evenings.

GETTING THERE Leave Winchcombe on the B4632 (towards Toddington). After about 2 miles take a right into Hailes and follow the signs.

OPEN All year.

THE DAMAGE Tent and 2 people £13, with electric hook-up £16.50. Extra people £6.50. Prices subject to change.

Discovery
£1-70 kg

WARWICKSHIRE
DROOPERS
£2.95 kg
EXELLENT JAM PLUMS!

holycombe

Holycombe, Whichford, Shipston-on-Stour, Warwickshire CV36 5PH   01608 684239   www.holycombe.com

The village of Whichford in Warwickshire is harbouring one of the county's best-kept camping secrets; but with its mash-up of the medieval, Middle Eastern and mystical, Holycombe is unlikely to stay a secret for too long.

The six-acre site is in the grounds of what used to be a Norman castle, the only legacy of which is a splendid moat that harbours carp among the bulrushes. Local mystics also have Holycombe (which takes its name from combe 'valley' and the nearby Holy Well spring) as a sacred Neolithic site, evidenced by six converging ley lines. Yet this rich heritage lay beneath a scrapyard until Sally and Andy Birtwell built their eco-home and house of healing and set up their campsite here. It's a perfect place for camping purists, and – with four furnished bell tents and a geodesic dome – for part-timers, too. There's also a magic new treehouse in a private section of the site (only open to couples) that is straight out of Middle Earth.

Holycombe has a natural beauty to match its rich history, adjoining Whichford Wood (a wildlife-filled Site of Special Scientific Interest). It's also handily located a short walk from the popular Norman Knight in the village of Whichford, a classic Cotswold pub. So after a long ramble, or a pint up the road, you can light a campfire as dusk settles on the valley, and banter long into the night about whether ley lines really do exist and whether it is indeed a galactic portal (as geomancers claim), or just ponder what might be lurking at the bottom of that mysterious moat.

COOL FACTOR Think *Countryfile* meets *Time Team*.

WHO'S IN? Singles, couples, campervans and families – yes. Dogs, groups, caravans, unaccompanied teenagers – no.

ON SITE Campfires allowed, and wood can be bought on site. Up to 20 pitches. One electricity hook-up for VW vans. Bell tents are equipped with rugs, eco lanterns and two single futon mattresses. The kitchen log cabin has a fridge, sink, electric cooker, and seating. There are 2 hot electric showers and 3 loos (2 compost, 1 flush).

OFF SITE Holycombe adjoins Whichford Wood, where you might see muntjac deer, polecats or kingfishers. There's also the Rollright Stones, 3 miles up the A3400 (www.rollrightstones.co.uk) and Happy Valley, a charming tree-shaded walk following a stream through fields. Or take home a handmade terracotta memento from Whichford Pottery (01608 684416; www.whichfordpottery.com).

FOOD AND DRINK It's a short stroll to the Norman Knight (01608 684621; www.thenormanknight.co.uk), where you can enjoy traditional ales and gastropub grub while the kids run free on the village green. Wyatts Farm Shop at Hill Barn Farm (01608 684835; www.wyattsgardencentre.co.uk), has a good selection of meat and veg. There's a village shop at Long Compton.

GETTING THERE Leave the M40 at jct 8; follow the A44, and turn on to the B3400 north. At Long Compton, turn right, signposted Whichford; after 2 miles take a right down a steep lane; Holycombe is at the bottom on the right.

PUBLIC TRANSPORT Nearest train station is at Moreton-in-Marsh, 5 miles away, from where it's a taxi.

OPEN May–September.

THE DAMAGE Flat rate fees for all campers of £10 per night, children (over 2) £5. In addition you pay £25 per night for bell tents, £40 per night for the geodesic dome, and £100 per weekend (2 nights) for the treehouse.

cotswolds camping

Cotswolds Camping, Spelsbury Road, Charlbury, Oxfordshire OX7 3LL   01608 810810   www.cotswoldscamping.co.uk

This relaxed and efficiently-run gem of a campsite is on the edge of the beautiful market town of Charlbury, with stunning views across the Evenlode Valley. It offers a couple of grass fields flanked by pine trees, with walks across open countryside that's accessible through a gate at the back. There's a bijou summerhouse for those seeking indoor space in inclement weather; the washing facilities are all housed in the yard next to the field, and there's a small modern kitchen. Everything's so clean that you could eat your free-range eggs (from the resident hens) off it, and the drop of your pulse rate is palpable as you settle down for the night to the soundtrack of the busy local wildlife.

It's a great springboard for visiting the Cotswolds, but it's a bit of a foodie place too. You can wander into Charlbury for its many pubs, or in the opposite direction to the little village of Chadlington for a community-managed shop at its best, complemented by a café that sprawls out on to the pavement a few doors down. You're not in the middle of nowhere here, but it feels like it.

COOL FACTOR Simple Cotswold site in a lovely location.
WHO'S IN? Tents, campervans, caravans, groups, well-behaved dogs – yes.
ON SITE Up to 20 pitches, most with hook-ups, and 2 wooden camping huts. Immaculate facilities include separate toilet blocks with free showers and shaver points. Kitchen with a fridge, toaster, kettle and washing-up sink. Field for outdoor games. No campfires, but BBQs okay. A second shower block with disabled facilities is planned.
OFF SITE Chadlington (2 miles away) has an excellent wooden adventure playground, and the picture-postcard town of Burford (9 miles away) boasts the Cotswold Wildlife Park (01993 823006; www.cotswoldswildlifepark.co.uk).
FOOD AND DRINK You can buy (and also collect) fresh eggs on site. Nearby Charlbury is home to the award-winning Rose & Crown (01608 810103) and the Bell Hotel (01608 810278), which serves local, seasonal food.
GETTING THERE From Charlbury go north on the B4026 towards Spelsbury. The site is on the right after a mile or so.
PUBLIC TRANSPORT Train to Charlbury, then bus X9 towards Chipping Norton, which drops you off at the gate.
OPEN April–October.
THE DAMAGE Tent and 2 adults from £17 high season; from £15 low season. Wooden huts £30–£35 per night.

northmoor lock paddocks

Northmoor Lock Paddocks, Appleton, Oxfordshire OX13 5JN   07974 309958   www.campingonthethames.co.uk

Hidden away to say the least, Northmoor Lock Paddocks is not a manicured site, but more reminiscent of the old days when your mum and dad used to take you camping back in the 1970s. Tussocky meadows shaded by mature willows are fringed by the soporific tumble of water from the nearby weir, while over the hedge there's nothing but cornfields and ploughed earth as far as the eye can see. David Walliams crawled shivering from Northmoor Lock after the first leg of his epic 2011 Thames swim, but you can be much more snug in one of their two timber log pods – simple affairs stocked with chopped wood outside to burn in the firepit and little else. The two camping fields offer either plenty of sunlight, or – among the willows – mottled shade. Both blaze in a riot of wildflowers come spring, the grass thick and bouncy and providing a naturally comfortable underlay. Bring a fishing rod and plant yourself by the river in the dappled sunlight, a blade of grass in your mouth like Huck Finn, and gaze out across the weir and lock as a crayon-coloured barge rolls by. Welcome back to your childhood!

COOL FACTOR Back-to-basics camping, 1970s style.

WHO'S IN? Tents, campervans, dogs on leads, families and small groups – yes. Caravans, large groups – no.

ON SITE 15–20 mainly camping pitches and 2 log pods; no electrical hook-up. No shower block on site, but over the river there's a public shower/toilet next to the lock-keeper's cottage. Fires are allowed (logs £6), so too is fishing (permits £6). Be careful with little tots wandering off to the river.

OFF SITE Blenheim Palace (01993 810530; www. blenheimpalace.com) is 30 minutes away. Alternatively there's the excellent Cotswold Wildlife Park (01993 823006; www. cotswoldwildlifepark.co.uk).

FOOD AND DRINK The welcoming Plough (01865 863535; www.theploughappleton.com) in Appleton is a short walk. The Rose Revived (01865 300221; www.rose-revived-inn-newbridge.co.uk) is a half-hour walk along the Thames Path.

GETTING THERE Take the A420 towards Swindon, turn off at Oaksmere and follow the road into Appleton, turn right then second left into Badeswell Lane as far as the last house on the right; take a road labelled 'Environment Agency' (confirmed bookings are given an access code) and you're there.

OPEN Camping March–September; pods all year.

THE DAMAGE £15 per tent and 2 people; log pods £35 per night (minimum 2 nights). Confirmed bookings only.

grange farm

Grange Farm, Grange Chine, Brighstone, Isle of Wight PO30 4DA   01983 740296   www.grangefarmholidays.com

The ultra-green, festival-hosting Isle of Wight has reinvented itself into a hip little island offering something for everyone today, with exceptional waves for surfers, as well as kite-surfing, paragliding, and summer events that attract new crowds every year. The isle is shaped a bit like a front-on cow's head. At its temple is, fittingly, a town called Cowes. At its respective ears sit the towns of Yarmouth and Ryde, both of which have regular ferry services to the mainland. And perched atop tall cliffs, behind the beach at Brighstone (about midway down the left of the cow's jawline), sits the charming Grange Farm campsite.

It's a lovely, unspoilt site situated in a beautiful part of the island. Two flat, grassy fields go right to the edge of the cliff, and there's an overflow field across the road, aptly christened the 'Cool Camping' Field. You'll need a sturdy tent for the winds blowing across the top of these fields, but the reward is a panoramic view across the sea and an easy scramble down to the beach below. It's also a family-run, family-friendly site – kids will love getting close to its Noah's Ark of farm animals, including llamas, kune-kune pigs, goats, water buffalo, and a variety of poultry. Plus there is a play area for ball games and a children's playground, with boats and trains, stepping stones and rope bridges, in case the beach should lose its appeal – though parents should be mindful of the cliff edge at all times. All in all, it's a friendly and wonderfully varied site that enjoys a marvellous location on this multi-faceted isle.

COOL FACTOR Cliff-top, adventurous camping with panoramic sea views.

WHO'S IN? Tents, campervans, caravans, dogs (in caravans) – yes. Groups – sometimes, by arrangement.

ON SITE Campfires allowed on the beach below. Two fields with 60 pitches, most with hook-ups; extra Cool Camping Field only open for 28 days in July/August. A heated block has 15 showers, a coin-operated bath, toilets, and washing-up sinks. Laundry, hairdryers, phone and drinks machine. They also offer self-catering in a variety of onsite barn conversions and static caravans.

OFF SITE Head out surfing/paragliding/kite-surfing, or take it easy exploring nearby Newport, whose Roman remains can be supplemented by the Roman villa at Brading (01983 406223; www.bradingromanvilla.org.uk), which has a visitor centre and museum.

FOOD AND DRINK The Blacksmiths Arms (01983 529263; www.blacksmiths-arms.co.uk), a little way inland near Newport, serves food and has a pleasant beer garden. See how far English wine has come at Adgestone Vineyard (01983 402503; www.adgestonevineyard.co.uk) in Sandown, one of the oldest vineyards in the UK, half a mile from the Roman villa at Brading.

GETTING THERE From Yarmouth, follow signs to Freshwater Bay, then take the A3055 for 5 miles. Grange Farm is on the right. Contact Wightlink (www.wightlink.co.uk) or Red Funnel (www.redfunnel.co.uk) for ferry info.

PUBLIC TRANSPORT From Yarmouth/Newport, take bus no. 12 to Brighstone. Alight at the Three Bishops pub and walk ¾ mile to the site.

OPEN March–November.

THE DAMAGE Standard tent £13.50–£20.50 (depending on season) per night.

stubcroft farm

Stubcroft Farm, Stubcroft Lane, East Wittering, Chichester, West Sussex PO20 8PJ   01243 671469   www.stubcroft.com

Bracklesham Bay runs from Selsey to the sand dunes at East Head and encompasses a glorious part of the Sussex coast, centred on the villages of East and West Wittering (collectively known as the Witterings). The area is known for having some of the best beaches hereabouts – lovely sandy affairs that are perfect for surfing or kite-surfing or just exploring the run of promenade alongside. The West Wittering blue flag beach, in particular, is the stuff of memorable family days – with beautiful dune-backed sands, sheltered waters and acres of space. Catch a sunny day here and you'll wonder why people bother going to Europe on holiday.

A walk or cycle ride inland from East Wittering, at Stubcroft Farm, owner Simon's day job is tending to his sheep farm and overseeing a growing bee-keeping operation. But he's both proud and passionate about the campsite too. Five flat camping paddocks are sheltered by recently laid hedges (keep a look out for blackberries, elderberries and sloes hidden inside), beyond which is pure countryside all around, thanks to the farm's secluded position at the end of a private lane. Don't be surprised to see deer, pheasants, buzzards, or some of the other 72 species of birds drawn to the area's tranquillity.

Work has started on a brand-new, state-of-the-art eco amenities block, which should be ready late in the 2013 season and should keep campers clean and happy. It's a busy place for sure, but the pitches are comparatively generous, and in any case that's the trade-off for choosing one of the few low-key countryside campsites along such a glorious stretch of coast.

COOL FACTOR Beautifully low-key camping, superbly located for 'the Witterings'.

WHO'S IN? Tents, campervans, caravans, dogs (on leads), well-behaved groups – yes.

ON SITE Campfires permitted in containers off the ground, which can be rented (or brought with you); logs also sold. There are 90 pitches across 5 paddocks, plenty of water taps, plus 8 hook-ups. Brand-new shower block; small shop,; bike hire available by the day.

OFF SITE Easy access to some of the UK's best beaches – head to Bracklesham Bay for surfing; walk along the East Head spit with 50 acres of *Lawrence of Arabia* sand dunes; or West Wittering beach has some of the cleanest water in the country. For kids, visit the Planetarium in Chichester or Old Windmill in Halnaker, or Portsmouth's Historic Dockyard (02392 728060; www.historicdockyard.co.uk) and impressive Blue Reef Aquarium (02392 875222; www.bluereefaquarium.co.uk).

FOOD AND DRINK For fresh fish to cook back at camp, seek out the little fish shack on the beach at the end of Shore Road in East Wittering. There are plenty of good places for fish and chips at Bracklesham Bay, or take dinner at East Wittering's 16th-century Thatched Tavern (01243 673087), which offers mouthwatering, locally produced dishes.

GETTING THERE Take the A286 towards the Witterings and Bracklesham. Go through Birdham village then left on to the B2198 (Bell Lane) at the mini-roundabout by a Total garage. After the Bell pub take the second right into Tile Barn Lane, then turn left and follow signs to the farm.

PUBLIC TRANSPORT A regular bus (Chichester–Bracklesham Corner), stops one stop past the Bell pub.

OPEN All year.

THE DAMAGE Tents £7–£8 per adult per night; child £3.50; dog £1; campervan/caravan and 2 adults £20–£25.

spring barn farm

Spring Barn Farm Park, Kingston Road, Lewes, East Sussex BN7 3ND   01273 488450   www.springbarnfarmpark.co.uk

43

Surely one of the prettiest towns in Sussex, Lewes is bursting at its timbered seams with history. Beer lovers will be delighted to know that Sussex's premier ale, Harveys, is brewed in town, and there are plenty of cosy pubs in which to sample it. Lewes is also famous for its Bonfire Night, which sees a cast of thousands parading through the streets in fancy dress before burning effigies in the nearby fields.

Located on the undulating South Downs, in a vista of buttery hills and widescreen skies, Spring Barn Farm is manna from heaven for kids, and perfect for campers who like a good walk. Let's start with the secluded campsite: it's basic – little more than a field with a loo block – but the views are fantastic. Look out over the downs, peer into the adjacent *Children of the Corn* maize field, and hear the myriad calls of animals from the adjoining farm. Kids love the farm park in the farm's central building, and the menagerie outside. If goats, rabbits and chickens are passé, then show them the cheeky Shetland ponies and South American alpacas. The maze is great fun, too; three acres of twisting turns in which to lose yourself.

COOL FACTOR History and great walks just beyond your tent flaps.

WHO'S IN? Tents, small groups – yes. Campervans, caravans, dogs – no.

ON SITE Pitches available with firepits. BBQs allowed off-ground. 32 pitches; mains cold water; no electricity; toilet block. For the kids: indoor slides, zip wire, pedal go-kart track, trampoline, swings, sandpit, pirate play ship, soft-play area and a maze. Campers get into the farm half price.

OFF SITE Lewes has its Norman castle (01273 486290) and the historic Anne of Cleves House (01273 474610).

FOOD AND DRINK The farmhouse kitchen is a cosy place to hole up for breakfast or a Sunday roast. In neighbouring Firle, the Ram Inn (01273 858222; www.raminn.co.uk) does wonderful Sunday lunches and has a pretty garden.

GETTING THERE Follow the A27 towards Lewes and, at the Kingston roundabout, take the exit for Kingston. Drive through the village to the T-junction opposite the garden centre and turn left. Spring Barn Farm is on the left.

PUBLIC TRANSPORT Take a train to Lewes, and then a taxi or 123 bus.

OPEN Late March–late September.

THE DAMAGE Prices vary; contact Spring Barn Farm for details.

firle

44

Firle Estate, Heighton Street, East Sussex BN8 6NZ   07733 103309   www.firlecamp.co.uk

The South Downs National Park is the UK's newest National Park, so it seems entirely fitting that a brand new campsite with a fresh approach has opened in one of its most beautiful areas. The owner, however, is far from new to this game – it's James from the much-loved Sussex site Kitts Cottage Campsite (p114). Firle is his latest venture, blazing a trail with a pop-up campsite concept in 2012, open just for popular summer weekends. Proper service commences in 2013 with a modest shower block replacing the portaloos, but don't expect huge changes here as the beauty of this site is in its back-to-basics simplicity. Two flat, hedge-edged fields are hidden behind an 18th-century stone barn; other than the proposed shower block, that's it: there's not much else to say. Except, look around – immediately beyond the hedges are the rolling South Downs, tempting you to leave your tent and walk straight off into this Area of Outstanding Natural Beauty (and there's a cracking country pub nearby to reward those that do). There are no marked pitches, but expect James to cluster families and non-families in separate groupings, each around the essential firepit, of course.

COOL FACTOR Beautiful green countryside, all around.
WHO'S IN? Tents, campervans, groups, dogs on leads – yes. Caravans, noisy groups – no.
ON SITE Campfires allowed. Around 40 tents max. Shower block under construction. There's a small shop in Firle village and a top-notch farm shop at nearby Middle Farm (01323 811411; www.middlefarm.com).
OFF SITE It's all about the walking here: you can access paths directly from the site and walk to Firle Beacon (1 mile), from where you can pick up the South Downs Way. Nearby, Firle Place estate (01273 858307; www.firle.com) is set to reopen in 2013 following renovations. The lovely county town of Lewes (4 miles) is also an easy trip.
FOOD AND DRINK There's a great pub 15 minutes' walk from the site: the Ram (01273 858222; www.raminn.co.uk), with a high-quality menu and a lovely garden. Families should try the Barley Mow (01323 811322; www.barleymowonline.co.uk) at Selmeston, which has a kids' play area.
GETTING THERE From the A27, 4 miles east of Lewes, turn on to Heighton Street, marked by a sign saying 'Ripe 3, Laughton 5'. Firle is 300 yards on the left.
OPEN April–October.
THE DAMAGE Adults/under-13s £10–£7.50 per night. Under-2s free. Minimum 2-night stay at weekends.

blackberry wood

Blackberry Wood, Streat Lane, Streat, nr Ditchling, East Sussex BN6 8RS   01273 890035   www.blackberrywood.com

45

You can stay at Blackberry Wood any number of times, but each visit is likely to feel completely different – partly because the secluded woodland changes with the seasons, but mainly because owner Tim is so focused on expanding his unique range of glamping accommodation, that there's no anticipating what weird and wonderful structures you might find each time.

But let's start with the 'proper' camping, which is the heritage of this site. The sought-after woodland pitches can be found behind the small glamping field. Follow one of the footpaths leading into the rambling straggle of trees and thicket to find twenty individual clearings, each comprising a firepit, some rudimentary seating and enough space for a medium-sized tent. With trees all around, each spot feels gloriously secluded, and with so few pitches in this part of the site anyway, there's a rare and special kind of peace in the woods here, enhanced each evening by the soporific soundtrack of campfires gently fizzing. Each pitch has its own personality and most have been named by previous campers, including Fruity in the shade of a crab apple tree, Minty with its gloriously fresh-smelling herbs, and the more eclectically christened Aroha ('love' in Maori, in case you're wondering). One of the recent developments at Blackberry Wood is the opening of another camping area during peak season, across the road from the main site. Again, it's woodland camping, but there's a 'no kids and no groups rule' on this side of the road, so it's great for couples looking for a peaceful escape.

Once you've finished exploring the woods, you can strike out across the Downs to discover miles of walking uninterrupted by roads or cars. The South Downs National Park is the newest in the UK, which means a lot of recent investment in the excellent paths and landscape. Depending on which direction you take from the site, a 45-minute walk can take you to the village of Ditchling; to the superb Jolly Sportsman pub with outstanding food and friendly ambience; or to the Black Cap viewpoint, a high point on the South Downs Way from where you can see eight miles across the Sussex countryside to the sea. Maps are

available at reception, marking all the walks, pubs and other attractions.

But no review of this site would be complete without a round-up of the glamping possibilities. A characterful 1960s caravan affectionately known as 'Bubble' and a brightly-painted gypsy wagon are fairly standard offerings, but there is now also a red routemaster double-decker bus, equipped with a kitchen/diner downstairs and a kids' soft-play area upstairs which handily converts into a bedroom. There's also a helicopter (we kid you not), a full-size chopper complete with rotor blades which sleeps four and comes with central heating.

All these contraptions can be found scattered around the first small field when checking in at the reception caravan. Of course, reception was in a caravan at the time of writing, but we hear that NASA is selling off de-commissioned space shuttles, so next year's check-in experience might be quite different…

COOL FACTOR Back-to-nature woodland camping – with campfires! And, er, a helicopter.

WHO'S IN? Tents, dogs (on leads at all times), well-behaved groups – yes. Motorhomes, caravans – no.

ON SITE Campfires allowed in the designated firepits; logs and BBQ coal are available from reception, as well as food essentials. 4 hot showers on the main site take 20p coins; there's also a fantastic alfresco shower on the adults-only side of the site. Plenty of toilets and washing-up sinks. Bike hire available on site.

OFF SITE The site provides route maps for lovely local walks. Chilled-out Lewes (see Spring Barn Farm, p98) is just 5 miles away, or it's 8 miles to the bright lights of Brighton, with its pier, pebble beach and pavilion.

FOOD AND DRINK There's a truly great pub within walking distance. The Jolly Sportsman (01273 890400) in East Chillington is fantastically snug and cosy, and serves up a changing menu of gastro delights. Visit the farmers' market on the second Friday of the month at Garden Pride Garden Centre (01273 846844) in Ditchling.

GETTING THERE From the M23 continue south on to the A23 for 14 miles. Turn left on to the A273 for about a mile, then bear right on to B2112 New Road for 2 miles. Turn right on to the B2116 Lewes Road and turn left on to Streat Lane after 2 miles. You'll see the site signposted on the right.

OPEN All year.

THE DAMAGE Camping charges per night are £5 per tent plus £5–£9 per adult (depending on the season); children (3–12) half adult price. 2-night minimum stay at weekends; 3-night minimum on bank hols. The Double Decker is £60 per night plus the same per-person charges. The gypsy caravan is £35 per night; the retro caravan is £25 per night; both plus the same per-person charges.

the secret campsite

The Secret Campsite, Town Littleworth, Barcombe, East Sussex BN8 4TD   01273 401100   www.thesecretcampsite.co.uk

46

The Secret Campsite is, of course, not really very secret at all. Nor does owner Tim want it to be. He wants people to know about it, to come and support his fledgling business and the economy of the rural community nearby. The real secret is just how unique and special this place is.

After arriving and parking at the reception and amenities area, occupying the various nondescript buildings of the now defunct garden centre previously located here, visitors grab a wheelbarrow, load up their gear and follow the grassy path up and over an old brick railway bridge. (The railway underneath has long gone, leaving a beautifully overgrown pathway to explore.) Accessing the site from the bridge makes it feel isolated, secluded – and just that little bit secret. From this vantage point, it's easy to take in the features of the place: just 15 hugely spacious pitches cut into the long grass of a secluded meadow, interspersed with a scattering of recently planted saplings and all encircled with a backdrop of ancient oaks and hornbeams. Wild flowers are bursting to show off their colours, while the woods beyond are ripe for exploration. In fact, the plan is for plants to be a big part of the site. Tim is a botanist and wants to turn this place into the UK's first 'edible campsite' – a planting programme is underway, with an increasing array of berries, edible shrubs and flowers growing freely, ready for campers to pick fresh and add to the saucepan.

In the meantime, there's something else growing quickly – and that's the reputation of the Secret Campsite. Secret? Not for very long.

COOL FACTOR A special hideaway, almost cut off from the world – and only an hour from London.

WHO'S IN? Tents – yes. Caravans, campervans, big groups, young groups, dogs – no.

ON SITE Campfires allowed. 12 large pitches in the main meadow; another 3 on the car-park side of the bridge. 3 newly-built showers occupy an old stable block along with new toilets; compost-loo shacks are nearer the pitches. Trolleys are available to transport your gear to the main meadow. No shop as such, but you can buy firewood at reception.

OFF SITE There's plenty to do in Brighton, 13 miles away, but don't overlook the delights of Lewes, a pretty market town nestled in the South Downs just 5 miles from the site. There's a farmers' market on the first Saturday of the month and an outdoor lido (www.pellspool.org.uk) for hotter days. You can walk there from the site – ask at reception for the route.

FOOD AND DRINK Tim, the owner, knows all the best places to get fresh, local produce, including the Holmansbridge Farm Shop (01273 401964; www.holmansbridgefarm.com) in Town Littleworth. Pub-wise, if all country pubs could be as good as The Griffin at Fletchling (01825 722890; www.thegriffininn.co.uk), with its delightful garden and exceptional food, the world would be a happier place.

GETTING THERE From the A275 between South Chailey and Cooksbridge, take the turning beside the Marco Pierre White-owned Rainbow Inn on to Deadmantree Hill. Follow the road for 2 miles to Holmansbridge Farm Shop. The campsite is the fourth turning on the right and shares a driveway with a house called 'Woodside'.

OPEN All year.

THE DAMAGE High/low season prices are £13/£10 per adult and £6.50/£5 per child.

dernwood farm

Little Dernwood Farm, Dern Lane, Waldron, Heathfield, East Sussex TN21 0PN   01435 812726   www.dernwoodfarm.co.uk

47

Dernwood Farm is hidden away down a rolling country lane among the patchwork fields of Sussex. Like a Russian doll-within-a-doll, the campsite itself is further secreted inside an eight-acre clearing in the middle of a coppice wood originally grown for charcoal burning. Isn't it fitting, then, that fires are a welcome addition to the earthy, authentic camping experience on offer here?

On arrival you make yourself known at reception, pick up your organic eggs and choose from a rich selection of fresh flavoursome beef (produced here) to roast on your barbecue. Then, armed with some logs, pop it all into one of the trolleys or wheelbarrows provided and make your hobbit-like journey through the woods to the fairy-tale field that truly earns its moniker of 'wild'.

'It's a kind of filter', says Amanda, your welcoming host, of the 10-minute walk through the woods, 'a real discovery as you shed your city skin and unwind. It also keeps away noisy campers looking for a quick fix.' There's no electricity here; this is a low-impact, eco-friendly campsite, so it's just you, your canvas, and delicious food cooked by your own fair hands over the firepits provided.

Come spring, the three adjoining semi-natural ancient woods are aglow with thousands of bluebells. When you take a walk through them keep an eye out for the small pits once dug for the mining of ore in centuries past.

This is a place to really lose yourself in for a few days, zone out from the urban noise you left behind, and tune into the wildlife around you.

COOL FACTOR As hidden and earthy as it gets.

WHO'S IN? Tents, dogs (on leads) – yes. Campervans, caravans, groups – no.

ON SITE Campfires allowed in designated pits. Well-equipped 5m bell tents in individual clearings and sleeping 4. Safari tent sleeps 6, has hot running water and 'proper' shower. Shop sells meat and eggs. There are 2 toilets for campers, cold washing-up area, standpipe, and log store (£5 per load), plus solar shower sacks. Wheelbarrows to transport your kit. Kids love to explore the fallen trunks while playing hide-and-seek in the endless expanses, and Amanda can show them the animals. The yellow trail is a 40-minute walk through the woods. The nearest road is 2 miles away – and that's a mere country lane.

OFF SITE The Cuckoo Trail, a spit from the site, is a great option for cycling or walks – weaving through woods, fields, and the best of Sussex countryside. Normans Bay, named after the conquerors who landed here a thousand years ago, is just 20 minutes away. Pop into the Observatory Science Centre (01323 832731; www.the-observatory.org) – on selected evenings you can stargaze through their telescope.

FOOD AND DRINK Stock up on steaks at the farm shop before heading to your pitch – they're hung for 21 days so are bursting with flavour. In Chiddingly, the Six Bells (01825 872227) comes highly recommended (voted Best Bargain Pub in Britain) for its tasty fare and shabby-chic decor.

GETTING THERE Head to Horam on the A267 and, just before the garage on your left, turn right down Furnace Lane. After a mile, take the first left to Chiddingly. Little Dernwood Farm is on your left, opposite Copfold Farm.

OPEN 1 April–late September.

THE DAMAGE Tent plus adult £8 per night; child (over 5) £5, under-5s free. Family (2 adults and 2 children) £26.

hop pickers wood

Hop Pickers Wood, Quarry Farm, Bodiam, East Sussex TN32 5RA 01580 831845 www.original-huts.co.uk

46

A secret, shady glade near an old castle may sound like the stuff of fairy tales, but Hop Pickers Wood Campsite is no fantasy. Opened in summer 2012, it's a tiny little grassy clearing of just ten pitches, surrounded by trees, wildlife and the soundtrack of British farmland in summertime. Due to its size and the fact that the owners want to keep it relatively secret and exclusive, campers need to book ahead rather than just turn up. You also won't know the exact location until you make a reservation, but let's just say it's not far from Bodiam Castle in East Sussex, hidden about half a mile down a private track. You'll probably be greeted and guided in by friendly owner Anna Eastwood, who also runs the adjoining Original Hut Company – indeed the stylish wooden wagons on offer might make you think twice about packing your own tent. After parking your car (quite possibly next to a tractor, as this is very much a working farm), you'll need to walk your gear down to the clearing, but it's literally only 10-20 metres to the pitches, so no great hardship. The facilities are in keeping with this low-impact place; the eco loos, hot showers and washing-up facilities are housed in a discreet shepherd's hut. There's also a handy sheltered area with an open fire which makes it ideal for communal gatherings – in fact, the entire site is perfect to hire out for groups of families or other groups looking for some privacy and seclusion. The 'whole site' rates are very reasonable for such a lovely little place in such a good location.

COOL FACTOR A lovely, private dingly dell – hire the whole place for even more privacy!

WHO'S IN? Tents, groups (by arrangement) – yes. Campervans, caravans, dogs – no.

ON SITE Campfires allowed; a box of logs and kindling is £4. Just 10 pitches in total on this very simple site; no fridge-freezing facilities and no electricity. There's a covered communal area with a fireplace and chimney; the loos, lovely hot showers and washing-up sinks are in a shepherd's hut for added novelty factor.

OFF SITE Bodiam Castle (01580 830196; see www.nationaltrust.org.uk) is a 15-minute stroll across undulating Sussex fields. Entry to the grounds is free, but the entry fee to the castle (adults £7/children £3.50) is worth it for the views from the top of the towers. The castle also plays host to various events throughout the year. Kids will love the Kent and East Sussex Railway (01580 765155; www.kesr.org.uk), an old steam train that chugs from Bodiam Castle to Tenterden. The huge sandy beach of Camber Sands is half-an-hour away (17 miles).

FOOD AND DRINK The Castle Inn (01580 830330) opposite Bodiam Castle offers good value food served in generous portions. The terrace overlooks a big field, which acts as a play area for kids. Buster's Farm Shop (01580 882020; www.bustersfarmproduce.co.uk) near Robertsbridge stocks some of the finest cuts of meat from pedigree Sussex cattle and sheep.

GETTING THERE The campsite is just outside the village of Bodiam, East Sussex; exact location and directions provided on booking.

OPEN All year.

THE DAMAGE Pitches £20 per night, plus £3 per adult and £2 per child. The whole site can be rented out for £200 per night, plus per person charges.

WOWO

Wowo, Wapsbourne Manor Farm, Sheffield Park, nr Uckfield, East Sussex TN22 3QT   01825 723414   www.wowo.co.uk

49

Lovingly sculpted in the late 1700s by the visionary landscape architect, Capability Brown, Sheffield Park is arguably one of the country's finest gardens. With the famous four lakes forming its centrepiece, the rich array of surrounding horticulture exudes vibrant explosions of colour at almost any time of the year. In autumn, black tupelos blend with the rusty reds of the maple and deep scarlet leaves of the oak. Spring brings a lively riot of daffodils and iconic Sussex bluebells. In summer there are flashy splodges of pink rhododendrons and the soft, magenta tones of the rampant azaleas, while an early morning winter circuit around the lake, the grounds blanketed in snow, gives the whole setting an otherwordly quality. Cricket fans might also care to know that the park's pitch was the venue for the very first home tie between England and Australia in 1884.

Nowadays the easy-going nature of this fabulous manor farm campsite is worn proudly on its sleeve. Wapsbourne Manor Farm, or 'Wowo', as it's affectionately known by a growing band of regulars, is a rare and beautiful thing – a great campsite within two hours' drive of London. It's light on unnecessary rules and regulations, and big on fun and freedom. With smoky campfires (facilitated by a firewood delivery-man who appears at dusk on his little tractor), old rope swings and free camping for performing musicians, this is not a site for the Nanny-State obsessed. But go with the flow and this rural wonderland is the perfect outdoor adventure playground.

This magical spot always seems to have something new to reveal: another field hidden behind the thicket, a secret pathway, a yurt nestled among the trees. And while the 40 pitches in the camping fields come with plenty of surrounding space for game playing, there's a whole separate site that you might not see unless you go looking: the premium woodland camping pitches, otherwise known as the Tipi Trail. These eight pitches (christened with such delightfully spacey names as 'Hobbit', 'Woodland' and 'Little Owl') are secreted away in their own exclusive woodland setting, ideal for celebrities, politicians, and newlywed royal couples looking for seclusion. What's more, they offer a fairy-tale-like setting for games of hide-and-seek. Two new additions to the site include the fully-equipped shepherd's huts and a couple of roomy bell tents. There's always something fun going on during summer weekend evenings, too: soup suppers; pizza making and plenty of mingling.

Children's entertainment is strictly of the old-school variety: climbing trees, swinging on tyres, rolling around in ditches, making camps in the undergrowth. In fact, the entire 150-acre site is a huge, natural adventure playground extending well beyond the four main camping areas. Saturday night is music night: free camping for musicians in return for an 'open campfire' policy allowing all-comers to join in a sing-song around the fire. It's a hippified rule alright, but fitting for mildly bohemian Wowo.

With the evening air scented with campfire smoke, the soft murmur of sociability and perhaps a musical soundtrack, this wonderful woodland hideaway just oozes back-to-basics appeal. Leave the rules at home. Let the kids roam free.

COOL FACTOR A cracking, chilled-out atmosphere and 'to-your-tent' firewood delivery.

WHO'S IN? Tents, campervans, dogs – yes. Caravans, motorhomes, groups of unsupervised under-18s – no.

ON SITE Campfires (in designated firepits) and BBQs off ground are allowed. 40 standard pitches with firepit trivet and benches plus 8 'Tipi Trail' secluded woodland pitches (each with benches, picnic tables and chairs, and a trivet for your fire); 4 yurts and 2 luxury shepherd's huts. 2 bell tents in camping fields for hire with covered cooking area. There are 2 flushing compost toilets and 1 shower in the Tipi Trail area; 4 compost toilets in Lower Moat field plus 2 basic but clean and free-to-use shower blocks with 8 showers, 8 toilets and 1 family wet room with accessible toilet and shower (no shaving/hairdryer points). A communal barn has a ping-pong table and (of course) a piano; free communal fridges and freezers; wi-fi; an honesty bookshelf; coin-operated laundry. An onsite shop stocks a plethora of organic food goodies plus artisan bakery goods. A particularly nice touch at Wowo is the complimentary soup and freshly baked bread served on Saturday nights in the communal area, often with accompanying acoustic music. It's a great opportunity to meet other campers and help cultivate a communal atmosphere. Ask also about their weekend Apache and night bushcraft/foraging/basket making activities – it's all going on at Wowo! Bear in mind this is a busy site in the summer, so won't suit everybody, but for a fun, buzzy atmospheric campsite where it's easy to meet fellow campers, it's hard to beat.

OFF SITE Go for a wander around the beautiful National Trust-run Sheffield Park (01285 790231), just a mile or so up the road. Kids can run about, feed the swans and ducks by the lake and enjoy the children's trail. The Bluebell Railway is practically next door (01825 720800; www.bluebell-railway.com) and chugs from Sheffield Park to Kingscote. With a big collection of steam locomotives, it's perfect for a *Thomas the Tank Engine*-inspired day out. You could also try walking some, or all, of the picturesque 42-mile Ouse Valley Way.

FOOD AND DRINK Wowo's reception sells home-produced eggs, veg, herbs and locally sourced organic goodies – including ice cream. Avoid the overpriced tea rooms at Sheffield Park (though do call in to pick up some delicious organic cider, real ales and sparkling wines from the Vineyard & Nursery tucked behind the walled garden). A few miles up the A275, Trading Boundaries (01825 790200; online.tradingboundaries. com) is a delightful café and eclectic furniture/antiques shop (see p117). The family-friendly Sloop Inn (01444 831219; www.thesloopinn.com) is a 40-minute walk away through shady woodland and serves up hearty food and local ales. For foodies, there are 2 excellent gastropubs close by: the Coach and Horses at Danehill (01825 740369; www.coachandhorses.co) and the Griffin Inn (01825 722890; www.thegriffininn.co.uk) in Fletching, which boasts a magnificent beer garden and equally impressive views across the adjoining countryside. Both are less than 10 minutes' drive or a longer scenic trek along the Ouse Valley Way.

GETTING THERE Follow the Bluebell Railway signs along the A22. Pass the railway on the right and Wowo is the second entrance on the right.

PUBLIC TRANSPORT The nearest station is Haywards Heath, from where a taxi costs about £15.

OPEN Tipi Trail and yurts open all year; camping March–October.

THE DAMAGE Adult £10 per night; child £5, under-3s free. Firewood £5; one-off charge for dogs (£4.50) and cars (£5). Tipi Trail pitches an extra £10 per night except during winter. Yurts £112–£250 per 2-night stay. Musicians free by prior arrangement. There is a minimum stay of 2 nights; this is a very popular campsite, so early booking is essential!

kitts cottage

Kitts Cottage Campsite, Freshfield Place Farm, Sloop Lane, Scaynes Hill, West Sussex RH17 7NP 07733 103309 www.kittscamp.co.uk

50

James, the manager of both the local affiliated gastropub, the Sloop, and Kitts Cottage campsite, is a wry chap; he looks as if he might have been a highwayman or pirate in a former life, so we're not sure whether or not to believe him when he points to the campsite's eastern treeline and says there's a ghost of a lady who sometimes walks through there from the woods. Certainly it's an atmospheric spot, and on creepy nights, as the north wind wraps its teeth around your guy pegs and whistles at your door, you might wish that we'd never mentioned it. To be honest, though, there's nothing faintly spectral about Kitts Cottage – indeed the story (coupled with James himself) just adds to the site's charm.

Sandwiched between Lewes and Haywards Heath, the 18-acre site takes its name from a house that used to stand here hundreds of years ago. There are no style awards or glamping brownie points being won here. Kitts is all about bowling up with your tent and doing all the hard stuff like pitching up and cracking open your cool box, as well as stoking the flames on one of the many designated firepits. Essentially it's a huge meadow bookended on two sides by alluringly ancient woods and bordered by sheep-grazing fields; there's an area for families shaded by mature oaks, a section for groups further away, and the remainder is left for couples and singles. The eastern treeline is always kept free and uninterrupted for aesthetic purposes – an arboreal canvas that might have come from the brush of John Constable.

James runs it this way to keep things in balance, just like the unspoken eco-agreement with the nearby forest critters. Your side of the bargain is not to gather logs, or any kindling whatsoever – it's provided to you on arrival. And, in return, the creatures leave you alone. Fires are positively encouraged, though, as part of the site's back-to-basics ethos.

The site sits on a slight elevation, giving great views from the top of the hill. Gazing across the woolly backs of sheep and rusted ploughs, you have to pinch yourself when you remember you're less than an hour from London. The surrounding woodlands are criss-crossed with public footpaths, one of which leads directly to the much-celebrated Bluebell Railway, which provides a journey into yesteryear with a fully working steam railway system. With its old-fashioned stations peppered with nostalgic signs, octogenarian conductors, and steam billowing from *Thomas the Tank Engine* funnels, it's a delight for even the weariest cynics. The footpaths from the site are perfect for getting back to nature and, if you don't fancy walking, then bring your bike to explore the woody glades, sunburned fields and pretty hamlets.

The local Cuckoo Trail is a cyclist's paradise – 11 miles of disused railway track, choking on wildlife and woodland as it meanders gently through quiet hamlets, monuments, and the best of Sussex countryside. It starts in Polegate and zigzags through Hailsham, Horam and Heathfield. There are plenty of places en route to stop for a cheeky cool pint or a snack, as well as various sculptures in wood and steel to look out for. In May, keep an eye out for the Orange-tip butterfly, and orchids growing near the path.

COOL FACTOR Back to basics, camping au naturel. Ditch the iPod speakers and lace up your walking boots – there's proper countryside to discover.

WHO'S IN? Tents, well-behaved dogs (on leads), groups, all folk – yes. Caravans are not welcome, however this is prime ground for campervans.

ON SITE Campfires are positively encouraged in the firepits. Pick up all your wood and kindling on arrival, then James will direct you to the appropriate pitch to suit you, with young families in one general area, older families in another, while quiet couples and adult groups each have a corner too. Although Kitts is acutely eco-conscious, there are now proper flushing loos and showers housed in the brand new field barn (separate sides for boys and girls). There's also a new covered dishwashing area to replace the old alfresco facilities, which comes equipped with sinks, draining boards and hot and cold water. There are no rubbish disposal facilities on site, so campers are requested to take all their rubbish with them (there are recycling facilities nearby).

OFF SITE There's plenty to do if you're looking for organised activities: Sheffield Park and Garden (01825 790231) features 18th-century ornamental gardens laid out by Capability Brown, bursting with azaleas, rhododendrons, monkey trees, and views to set the soul alight – plus soothing lakes and a nice little tea room to quieten the groaning belly. Just 20 minutes' walk from Kitts, the Bluebell Railway (01825 720800; www.bluebell-railway.com) is a heritage steam railway running between Sheffield Park and Kingscote, and a real journey back through time. The old boys that operate it are charming and take you back to another era as they doff their caps, wrinkle their leathery faces, and guide you on to the glorious old carriages, with smoke billowing from the funnels as if you were off to Hogwarts School. Bring on the lemonade and slamming doors, the cucumber sandwiches, and the *Famous Five* – this is a rare and evocative slice of olde England. A little under half-an-hour away lies the Ashdown Forest (01342 823583; www.ashdownforest.org). It's great for exploring on 2 wheels along the Forest Way cycle route and you can hire a bike from Deers Leap Bikes (01342 325858; www.deersleapbikes.co.uk) for £20 per day. The Weir Wood Reservoir is an excellent spot for walking, taking a boat out or doing some trout fishing.

FOOD AND DRINK Apart from campfire food cooked by yourself you'll have to seek warming fare at your local tavern – the Sloop Inn (01444 831219; www.thesloopinn.com), a welcoming gastropub with organic meats from local butchers, seasonal produce, and prices to match the affable atmosphere. Nearby, too, at the end of Ketches Lane on the A275, is the Trading Boundaries (01825 790200; www.tradingboundaries.com) – a group of wonderful shops containing treasures from around the world, grouped around an old house and courtyard. The café there sells light lunches all day, and there's a lovely garden in which to sit and eat on a warm day. A small children's playground will keep younger kids entertained. Both places can be reached by public footpaths and the campsite actually has access to 3 separate footpaths that meet in Long Kitts and can take you to the south, west and east.

GETTING THERE Take the A22 through East Grinstead and Forest Row, 100 metres after the Wych Cross crossroads turn right on to the A275 towards Lewes. When you reach the church at Danehill, turn right following signs to Freshfield (2 miles). Stay on that road past Brickworks and a mile after that you'll see the Sloop Inn on the left. Half a mile beyond, turn left into Butterbox Lane and the campsite entrance is 300 yards down on the left.

OPEN 1 April–late October.

THE DAMAGE Tent plus adult £12.50 per night; children (under 15) £7.50 per night; infants camp free. There is a minimum stay of 2 nights at weekends.

eco camp uk

Eco Camp UK Beech Estate, Netherfield Hill, Battle, East Sussex TN33 0LL 07779 979823 www.ecocampuk.co.uk

51

There's camping, and then there's off-grid camping. Eco Camp UK Beech Estate is most definitely the latter – no electricity, no mobile phone signal, wheelbarrow your gear to the tent, eco toilets – you even have to light a fire to heat up your own shower. If that all sounds like too much effort, then please turn the page for something more suitable. If it sounds like the perfect escape, you're in for a real treat. Beech Estate is the second campsite from off-grid specialists Eco Camp UK (the first being a bell-tent-only affair in West Sussex) and this location has one major advantage – you can bring your own tent. The pitches are spaced out in individual clearings in the woodland of 1900-acre Beech Estate. If that doesn't sound like camping heaven already, then just wait for the punchline: the 500 acres of woodland on which the site is located is for the exclusive use of Beech Estate guests to walk, mountain bike and generally run wild. Additional non-woodland pitches are available on a hill overlooking the surrounding countryside; pre-erected bell tents are also available, and it's fair to say these are functional rather than luxuriously appointed. Just what you'd expect in this off-grid, back-to-basics paradise.

COOL FACTOR Pristine woodland camping.

WHO'S IN? Tents, groups, 'whole campsite' bookings – yes. Caravans, campervans, dogs – no.

ON SITE Campfires permitted. There are 8 woodland camping pitches, and 2 hilltop pitches. The 5 bell tents accommodate up to 2 adults and 3 children and have beds, coffee table, lantern, cool box and everything for cooking. A wood-fired shower and eco toilets are also provided.

OFF SITE Historic Battle (1066, and all that) is 3 miles away. Hastings, home of the cool new Jerwood Gallery (www.jerwoodgallery.org) is just a short drive. A few miles down the A271, you'll find the historic village of Herstmonceux, with its Observatory Science Centre (www.the-observatory.org) and Tudor Herstmonceux Castle (www.herstmonceux-castle.com).

FOOD AND DRINK An outdoor shack on Hastings seafront serves freshly cooked fish. Closer to the site, the White Hart Inn (www.whitehartnetherfield.co.uk) has a great garden with countryside views; for good pub food, try the Netherfield Arms (www.netherfieldarms.co.uk).

GETTING THERE Beech Estate is between Netherfield and Ashburnham; exact location given on booking.

OPEN August until early September, plus selected dates.

THE DAMAGE Adults/children (3–6yrs) £15/£7 per night. Bell tents start at £150 for 2 nights.

woodland camping

52

Woodland Camping, Ashwood Farm, West Hoathly Road, East Grinstead, West Sussex RH19 4ND   01342 316129
woodlandcampingeco.wordpress.com

This woodland escape in the very heart of the Ashdown Forest is nothing short of magical. Its owners, Wendy and Patrick, are fiercely eco-minded and their sense of respect for the land resonates throughout the site.

On arrival, plant your bags in a wheelbarrow and make your way past the fairy knoll and maze to the enchanted woodland area – a sanctuary of oak and silver birch at the source of a river. There's every encouragement for you to get reacquainted with nature here – build a fire, recline, relax and listen to the breeze. There aren't any mod cons, just one of the best locations in wild Sussex to get in touch with your inner bushman. In the centre of the wood there's a maypole for pagan festivities, and the trees are strung in brightly hued ribbons and trinkets – fortunately there are no wicker effigies with burning policemen inside.

On a warm night, sit around the fire, strum your guitar or shoot the breeze with your fellow eco-people by the nearby tipi. There's a compost loo in the wood, but for showers you'll have to pop back to the block by reception. In order to keep things natural there are no electric hook-ups.

COOL FACTOR Hidden-away pitches in an ancient forest.

WHO'S IN? Tents – yes. Dogs, groups, campervans – no.

ON SITE Campfires allowed – collect wood from the forest, £5 per firepit, per night. There are 10 pitches, a compost loo and a canvas shelter for communal dinners. Water vats are brought to the clearing every morning. Owner Patrick can ferry you and your gear on his tractor (£5 each way) or else use the wheelbarrows. Shower block by reception; pigs and ducks, plus a kids-only fairy knoll.

OFF SITE The fabulous gardens at Sheffield Park (01825 790231) are a short drive away. Deers Leap Bikes (01342 325858) are around the corner from the site (£20 per day) – head for pretty Weir Wood Reservoir or the Ashdown Forest.

FOOD AND DRINK Organic eggs, milk and bread is for sale at reception. Nearby, the Old Mill (01342 326341) is a homely gastropub in a 15th-century building.

GETTING THERE From East Grinstead, take the A22. Turn right on to the B2110 (Turners Hill Road), then right again on to Saint Hill Road, then left to West Hoathly Road. Ashwood Farm is about 1/3 mile up, on your right.

PUBLIC TRANSPORT Train to East Grinstead, then a cab.

OPEN 1 April–late October.

THE DAMAGE Adult £12 night; child (up to 13 yrs) £6; reductions for carless campers.

forgewood

ForgeWood Barn, Sham Farm Road, Danegate, nr Tunbridge Wells, Kent TN3 9JD   07720 290229   www.forgewoodcamping.co.uk

One of a bright young generation of new campsites, ForgeWood has taken *Cool Camping* principles and applied them beautifully. The site opened fully in 2010 after a low-key try-out the previous season, and has proved to be an instant hit, with that killer combination of campfires, woodland pitches, a tents-only rule (with the exception of the odd vintage campervan) and a laid-back approach.

ForgeWood – like Bedgebury (see p124) and Wowo (see p110) in East Sussex – is a solid example of the new breed of simple yet contemporary campsites – sites that totally 'get' that people want to let their kids roam around woods making camps and dens and getting dirty. They understand, too, the importance of the campfire, and provide a generous hoard of chopped wood and marshmallows, and they agree that a camping trip is about being out amid nature, immersed in the experience of the wild. Oh, and they totally get that today's tent campers don't want to share these magical pockets of nature with shiny white caravans sporting satellite dishes on their roofs. Banning caravans is always a popular move among the tent fraternity.

What ForgeWood and others are doing is putting the unassuming tent camper back at the centre of things. With an attractive mix of ancient woodland and open fields, this site gives tenters space and freedom. But the pitches within the woodland are the ones that stand out – surrounded by a sprawling, undulating thicket, unkempt and scattered with fallen branches, and left to the influences of weather, nature and time. It's a beautiful place to camp. If truth be told, it's not entirely untouched – a regular visit from the tree surgeon ensures that all potentially dangerous overhanging branches are removed before they fall on an unsuspecting camper's head. But don't let small details get in the way of the romantic – it looks untouched, and you do (sort of) feel like you're camping out in the wilds.

Such splendid surroundings are a result of the fact that ForgeWood is situated in a quiet corner of the vast Eridge Park Estate, a gorgeous 3000-acre expanse of countryside and farmland incorporating Britain's oldest deer park. The countryside site has been preserved since the 11th century, when William the Conqueror gave the estate to his half-brother Odo, a man of vast wealth and questionable morals who ended up in prison for embezzlement. Today the estate belongs to the Marquess of Abergavenny and, although it's not open to the public, there are rights of way along parts. Venison from the estate is available at ForgeWood in the form of sausages, burgers and steaks – ideal for grilling over the campfire. Firewood, marshmallows and all the basics are also sold at the new onsite shop, as are handy little cooking thingamajigs, which allow you to use your pots and pans on the fire instead of the gas burner, so there's no doubt this place supports a strong campfire culture. In case this site needed anything else to recommend it, then the fact that there's a pub and a station nearby would seem to top it all off nicely. So for London-based campers, it's possible to get here in just over an hour, including a stop for a pint of Badger at the Huntsman.

COOL FACTOR Expansive ancient woodlands and a campfire culture.

WHO'S IN? Tents, occasional vintage campervans, dogs – yes. Caravans, motorhomes, groups of under-21s – no.

ON SITE Campfires encouraged. Pitches available in the woods or the fields. Many pitches are inaccessible by car; campers are encouraged to leave their cars in the car park. Rope swings and random kids' shelters can be found in the woods, which are used as a giant playground for young campers. At weekends and in the school holidays, kids can learn a diverse range of woodcraft skills with the ForgeWood Forest Crafts workshop. There are also art retreats and bushcraft courses for the adults. Portakabins are used for the facilities and reception – part of the plan, the managers say, to provide a truly low-impact environment. Without permanent buildings, this entire site can disappear out of season and be returned to nature with no sign that a summer campsite exists. The facilities include free hot showers, washing-up sinks, disabled facilities, and ice-pack freezing. There is a brand new shop selling all the basics including milk, bread, eggs and meat from the Eridge Park Estate. Fire grills (from £5 per night) and cooking equipment are available to rent or buy; firewood, marshmallows, and other bits and bobs are also available at the shop. At the other side of the car park is a restaurant/tea room, open daily in summer, which serves snacks, afternoon teas, light meals and dinner options in the evening.

OFF SITE Walks through the Eridge Park Estate start from the campsite and will take you variously to historic ice caves, a Victorian folly and a Saxon fort. Maps are available at reception. A trip to nearby Groombridge Place (01892 861444; www.groombridge. co.uk) is a very worthwhile excursion, with its renowned formal gardens and the excellent Enchanted Forest attraction for kids, which includes treetop walkways, birds of prey and huge swings. Further afield, but equally worthwhile, is Bewl Water (www.bewlwater. co.uk), a huge, picturesque reservoir with an activity centre, kayaking, sailing, a zip wire and a big playground for children. Kids can also go 'Hydroballing' – walking across water in a giant, transparent bubble. The historic spa town of Tunbridge Wells is only 4 miles away, and has castles, gardens and aged houses to explore, as well as the pretty colonnaded Pantiles area with its shops, restaurants and cafes.

FOOD AND DRINK The Huntsman pub (01892 864258; www.thehuntsmanpub.com), next to Eridge station, has a pleasant beer garden, ales from the Badger Brewery, and a changing menu with an emphasis on locally sourced, seasonal produce. Head into Tunbridge Wells for a host of options including, for something a bit special, Thackeray's (01892 511921; www. thackeraysrestaurant.co.uk) on London Road – a modern French restaurant in a beautiful 17th-century weather-boarded villa.

GETTING THERE Eridge Park is just off the A26, between Tunbridge Wells and Crowborough, although the campsite is not accessed via the main entrance to the estate. Instead, take the turning on the south side of the A26, towards Rotherfield and Mayfield. This is Sham Farm Road. Follow the road for a mile or so and look out for the campsite on the left.

PUBLIC TRANSPORT Direct trains run from London Bridge to Eridge station in as little as 50 minutes; other connections are available via East Croydon. From Eridge station, it's about half an hour on foot (about 2 miles), or 5 minutes in a taxi. Tunbridge Wells station is 4 miles from the campsite and, although slightly further away, has better taxi connections.

OPEN April–October.

THE DAMAGE There is a simple per-person tariff. Adults (over 16 yrs old) are £12.50 per night; for families, the rates are £10 per adult and £5 per child over 3 yrs old. Minumum 3-night stay on bank holiday weekends.

bedgebury

Bedgebury Camping, Pattenden Farm, Goudhurst, Cranbrook, Kent TN17 2QX 01580 213487 www.bedgeburycamping.co.uk

You can instantly tell that more than the average amounts of thought and love have gone into Bedgebury Camping. It's the little extras: a communal tipi for campfire gatherings and general hanging-out; the cute little wooden compost toilet blocks, hand-built by owner Jim; the campfire starter packs, which include straw bales to sit on in addition to logs, kindling and marshmallows. All those little extras add up to big effect, the result of which is a well-tended, well-run place to camp in a really beautiful location.

The approach from Goudhurst is dramatic; as you leave the pretty Kentish village, the road immediately plunges from the elevated ridge down into the Weald of Kent, it's a rollercoaster ride that affords great views across this sandstone landscape. If you're driving, though, you won't have an opportunity to enjoy the view; you'll be focused on the winding country lane, looking for the sudden sharp turn into Bedgebury. A quick right on to the campsite road, then after a few formalities at the reception hut, it's off along the dirt track to the camping field, a very gentle slope of green nestled in the shallowest of valleys. It's a tranquil, picturesque spot, well away from the main road and, although camping is restricted to four acres, there are another 20 acres to explore, including woodland and a small stream. You might catch the occasional glimpse of a traditional oast house beyond the trees – these distinctive buildings serve as a reminder of the hop-farming heritage of the area.

Bedgebury itself was a hop farm in times gone by, but now the rows of old hop-drying huts have found another use as perfectly proportioned cycle storage sheds. There's a good reason for that – just up the road is Bedgebury Forest, with over 13km of challenging single-track mountain bike trails, including the infamous 'Cardiac Hill'. If that sounds a bit too much like hard work, you might want to opt for one of the gentler family cycle routes through the 2000-acre forest, stopping off for a lakeside picnic half-way round. There is a cycle-hire shop at the start of the trails, as well as some handy showers – for both bikes and riders!

There are also gentle rides around nearby Bewl Water, a huge reservoir set in 800 acres of countryside. Watersports on offer include sailing, windsurfing and canoeing, but many visitors come on sunny days for a gentle amble, an ice cream, a run around the playground, or just to sit by the lake.

After action-packed days out, you'll be wanting to head back to the communal tipi to swap stories of downhill speed or sailing prowess – it's a great place to mix with fellow campers and a good under-cover hangout in the event of rain. On most weekends, the owners arrange for local acoustic musicians to provide entertainment, sometimes accompanied by food from local producers – another nice touch on a campsite that goes the extra mile.

COOL FACTOR Spacious, chilled-out camping with plenty of outdoor attractions nearby.

WHO'S IN? Tents, campervans, dogs – yes. Caravans – no. Well-behaved groups – yes (separate field for large groups).

ON SITE Campfires allowed; starter pack including 2 hay bales, logs, matches, kindling and marshmallows £25. The main, L-shaped camping field is largely flat in the areas where camping takes place, although other bits slope slightly. 8 compost toilets; clean showers and WCs in a portaloo cabin; and washing-up sinks next to the bike-storage huts. Atmospheric communal tipi open 24/7; tea and cakes served in the afternoon. There are 20 acres of woodlands and pasture to explore on site, plus children's bushcraft courses on Saturdays and Sundays (from £6).

OFF SITE This is a fantastic area for walking and cycling, with both Bewl Water and Bedgebury Forest an easy drive away (see above). There is also Sissinghurst Castle (01580 710701; see www.nationaltrust.org.uk), with its remarkable gardens, 8 miles away. Maps detailing local footpaths are also available at reception.

FOOD AND DRINK The stylish Globe & Rainbow (01892 890803) at Kilndown serves excellent seasonal food sourced largely from Kentish farms – a 45-minute walk/10-minute drive from the site. This is also wine country – 3 renowned vineyards are close by. The nearest is Lamberhurst Vineyard (01892 860000), the oldest vineyard in the UK, where wine tastings and guided tours take place regularly.

GETTING THERE Take the A21 towards Hastings. After Blue Boys services turn left at the next roundabout on to the A262. Turn right at Goudhurst village pond, follow the road down into the valley, then look out for Bedgebury Camping on the right.

OPEN For 28 days during July and August only.

THE DAMAGE Adult/child (3 to 14 yrs) £8–£12/£4–£6 per night. Vehicles £5 for the duration of your stay. Pets £3.

welsummer

Welsummer Camping, Chalk House, Lenham Road, Kent ME17 1NQ   07771 992355   www.welsummercamping.com

Named after an old (and sadly long-since departed) rescue hen called Welsummer, Med and Laura Benaggoune's campsite is the epitome of laidback cool – not something, admittedly, that you immediately associate with Kent. A multicoloured windsock hangs from a tree, chickens roam free, and acoustic instruments and fireside singalongs are the order of the day or, rather, the night.

The range of camping experiences on offer at what is quite a bijou site is pretty impressive. Traditionalists can pitch in one of two cosy fields, where there's a range of small and large pitches, all with campfire spots. Backwoods types can set up their tent (as long as it's not too big) in the small wood and enjoy a more rugged, 'wild camping' feel. Those with no canvas home to call their own should head to the top field. Here, campers can choose from one of six bell tents, which come either non-equipped or equipped with a choice of add ons, such as a sturdy campfire grill. There's also a wide-open space where kids can play ball games and fly kites.

The owners' organic garden produces veg which is for sale in the small onsite shop, as well as free-range eggs. Campers can also pick up basic supplies such as locally sourced apple juice, bacon and sausages and at weekends this may even include a loaf of homemade bread or some scrumptious dish fresh from the oven. Meanwhile, the site's eco-credentials are bolstered in the washrooms, where water for the showers is heated by a wood-burning stove.

But it's the woodland life here that sets this campsite apart from most others. Laura used to camp among these same trees as a child, and it was her desire to let others share this experience that led her to open this smallholding as a campsite. This is a campsite made by campers, for campers. You won't find an extensive rulebook, and there's hardly any signage, so there's a much greater sense of freedom. Campers must park their cars in an adjacent field, which makes it feel like you're in your own little pocket of camping bliss. Grown-up campers can settle down and unwind, while their little campers can roam free, making dens in the woods and trying to catch butterflies as they dance through the branches.

There's a path leading out of the woods, straight on to Kent's Greensand Ridge: a 40-mile walk which extends as far as Leighton Buzzard in Bucks. Along the way, you can spot heather, gorse, common lizard and nightjar on the heaths; and bluebells, woodpeckers, buzzards, and – if you're really lucky – muntjac deer in the woodlands. Should you wish to explore further afield then Leeds Castle, which sits majestically across two adjacent islands on the River Len, is one of the must-visit attractions in the area. Set amongst 500 acres of beautiful grounds, there's something for every garden enthusiast (and kids will love losing themselves in the yew maze).

Med and Laura have worked hard to make Welsummer a wonderfully welcoming campsite. And, with so much to do in the local area, it's no surprise that most of the campers are returning visitors who love the site so much that they keep coming back year after year. We certainly know that we'll be joining them.

COOL FACTOR Something to suit every sort of cool camper.

WHO'S IN? Tents, dogs (maximum of 3 on site at any one time) – yes. Campervans, caravans, big groups, young groups – no.

ON SITE Campfires allowed. There are 20 pitches plus there's the option to camp in the woodland area or on the fields (try to get one of the woodland pitches for the most authentic camping experience). Most pitches have their own firepit, and firewood and kindling can be bought on site. There are 4 loos and 3 hot showers, as well as a washing-up point. Kids are free to climb the trees and explore the woods. The tiny shop sells the smallholding's free-range eggs, plus local bacon and sausages, and serves hot drinks and snacks all day. The distant murmur of the M20 can be heard – but that's the only downside.

OFF SITE Check the blackboard for daily offers and ideas for local trips out. Leeds Castle (01622 765400; www.leeds-castle.com), less than 4 miles away, is every child's dream of an ancient stronghold and has a fantastic play area for kids, too, as well as a maze and regular boat trips to take you there. Grown-ups may prefer the castle estate's 9-hole golf course, and may wish to reward themselves afterwards with a visit to the Biddenden Vineyards (01580 291726; www.biddendenvineyards.com), which is open throughout the year and runs free tours and tastings every day; their sparkling wines are particularly good. Take a trip also to Badgers Hill Farm (01227 730573) in Chilham, which has a shop, garden emporium and tea room set on an old cider farm. Here, grown-ups can stock up on delicious homemade ciders, while children spot the wallabies, donkeys, chickens, Patagonian maras, Indian runner ducks, geese and goats, and the village itself is one of Kent's most picturesque. Canterbury is less than 20 miles away and has a range of sights, but must-see attractions include the Cathedral (01227 762862; www.canterbury-cathedral.org) and St Augustine's Abbey (01227 767345; www.english-heritage.org.uk). Plus you could do worse than go for a punt on the river (07786 332666; www.canterburypunting.co.uk).

FOOD AND DRINK The food at the nearby Pepperbox Inn (01622 842558) comes highly recommended (no under-14s inside the pub, but there is a beer garden). The King's Head pub in Grafty Green is a gentle 1½ mile stroll through the woods and country lanes and has a treehouse in the garden, which is popular with children. The small and rather appealing market town of Lenham boasts traditional family butchers, GB Lister (01622 858220; www.lenham-butchers.co.uk), as well as Pippa's Tea Rooms (01622 851360), which serves good breakfasts and lunches. Further afield, Canterbury has plenty of good pubs and restaurants, including the excellent British food at Deeson's (01227 767854; www.deesonsrestaurant.co.uk) and the delicious wood-fired pizzas and authentic Italian dishes at Osteria Posillipo (01227 761471; www.posillipo.co.uk).

GETTING THERE Are you sitting comfortably? Then listen carefully. From the M20 (junction 8), head towards Lenham on the A20. After 1 mile, turn right on to Chegworth Road towards Kingswood, Ulcombe and Grafty Green. At the crossroads, turn left on to Lenham Road, and Welsummer is a mile or so down on the right, before Elmstone Hole Lane and Platts Heath. Look out for the double wooden gate, and a small sign marked Welsummer.

PUBLIC TRANSPORT Take a train to Lenham, 2 miles away, then cycle, walk or taxi to the site (costs about £7 with Streamline or Express Cabs, 01622 750000 and 01622 690000 respectively).

OPEN April–October.

THE DAMAGE Price per dwelling: small tent £12 per night; large tent £20; bell tent from £45 empty (with extra add-ons). In addition, adults are £3 per night; children (3–13yrs) £1. Booking strongly advised.

palace farm

Down Court Road, Doddington, nr Faversham, Kent ME9 0AU   01795 886200   www.palacefarm.com

The cockerel may crow or the goats may mutter as you enter, but that's as noisy as it gets here. It's a quiet old place, off the beaten track (but not far from some very worthwhile places to visit), with a 10pm quiet rule that's largely respected.

It's a simple set-up: a flat, grassy field holds up to 25 tents around its hedgerow edges, with an adjoining field left free for games or general haring around. Two pre-erected bell tents provide the slightest hint of camping glamour, but this is good, honest Kentish camping with no pretensions to be anything else. Don't confuse quietness with strictness, though. Campfires are allowed, campers can help themselves to plums from the orchard or blackberries from the old hedgerows around the farm, and edible mushrooms grow prolifically across the site in the autumn (make sure you're with someone who knows their puffballs from their death caps!). While you're hunting and gathering, have a forage at the honesty shop, where zero-food-mile courgettes, pumpkins and other seasonal veg are available fresh from the farm.

The site is a great base to explore this under-rated part of the country. Nearby Leeds Castle is a good place to start, a spectacular moated Tudor structure in a beautiful parkland setting. Foodies will want to head to Whitstable to sample the fresh oysters and explore the restaurants, while sightseers will be off to Canterbury for a good look at the cathedral or a punt down the River Stour.

Busy days, quiet nights. Life is very good at Palace Farm.

COOL FACTOR Unpretentious camping in an under-rated part of the country.

WHO'S IN? Tents, campervans, dogs (pre-booked, on leads), well-behaved groups – yes. Motorhomes, caravans – no.

ON SITE Campfires allowed (in firepits); 25 pitches plus 2 bell tents with a wooden shower block (3 showers, 3 toilets including family/disabled room). Tourist info and walking maps available at reception. Honesty shop. Reduced noise after 10pm and no noise after 11pm.

OFF SITE Lots to explore including Leeds Castle (01622 765400; 10 miles), Challock Forest (10 miles), Canterbury (14 miles), and Whitstable (16 miles). Leeds Castle is well worth a visit; as well as the castle itself, there's a decent children's playground, a maze, an underground grotto and perhaps the world's only museum of dog collars!

FOOD AND DRINK The local butcher in Doddington, S W Doughty (01795 886255), has recently been named 'the UK's Best Butcher' by the Countryside Alliance; there's also a deli counter and a good selection of fruit and veg. The Chequers Inn (01795 886366), also in Doddington, serves good pub food and is just a short walk from the campsite. The George Inn (01795 890237) in Newnham doesn't have as much character, but does beat the Chequers in the food stakes, with a good selection of interesting dishes.

GETTING THERE From the A2 turn south at Teynham, signposted Lynsted. Go through Lynsted, over the M2, then take the second right into Down Court Road. Palace Farm is on the left.

PUBLIC TRANSPORT Train to Sittingbourne, then a bus to Doddington (up to 4.30pm), or hop in a taxi for about £12.

OPEN April–October.

THE DAMAGE Adult £8/night; child (3–15) £4. Bell tent £50/night, £250/week. Firepits £2.50/night; logs £4/bag.

town farm

Town Farm, Ivinghoe, Leighton Buzzard Bedfordshire LU7 9EL   07906 265435   www.townfarmcamping.co.uk

Whipsnade Zoo; hot-air ballooning above the Chilterns; the Grand Union Canal; parks aplenty; and endless cycling, walking and riding trails – with the area offering all this, surely the BBC's *Room 101* was wrong to consign Leighton Buzzard to the bin?

The sheep-rearing Town Farm family-owners have enjoyed living here for generations regardless, and have opened their land to campers looking to extol this part of Bedfordshire, too. Expect a warm welcome from Charles when you arrive on site.

The site has an informal layout, but no matter where you choose to camp, the views are magnificent. Tents can be pitched at the foot of Ivinghoe Beacon, where the famous Ridgeway Walk starts its journey to Wiltshire, or overlooking the Vale of Aylesbury. Ignore the pylon wire running along the right of the site, and head left towards the Chilterns, past a hip, new, chalet-style washblock, to pitch at the far end.

Frazzled parents looking for activities to wear out their brood have plenty of choice on their doorstep to ensure that everyone will sleep soundly at night (plus there's a no noise after 11pm policy, just to make sure). Onsite there's a large play park, tennis court, and a pick-your-own farm (summer only) where campers can collect fruit and veg to feast on back at the tent. Whipsnade Zoo and Woburn Safari Park are both under half-an-hour away, and the pretty market town of Tring, with its array of shops and fortnightly farmers' market, is just a 10-minute drive away.

Room 101 obviously wasn't thinking about parents; we think Leighton Buzzard is a keeper.

COOL FACTOR An ideal trial location for first-time campers and Londoners not wanting to stay far from home.

WHO'S IN? Tents, campervans, caravans, obedient dogs (that won't bother sheep), groups – yes. Noisy groups – no.

ON SITE Campfires allowed in onsite firepits (rented for £5; wood bundle £5) and barbecues on blocks. A total of 50 pitches, with 12 hook-ups for caravans/motorhomes. The facilities block has 2 showers, a washing machine (£3.50), tumble-dryer (50p/8 mins), freezer, wi-fi and electricity points. There is a distant hum of local traffic.

OFF SITE Whipsnade Zoo (01582 872171; www.zsl.org) is 10 miles away, and the elephants and tigers at Woburn Safari Park (01525 290407; www.woburn.co.uk/safari) are 30 minutes' drive. The Natural History Museum in Tring (020 7942 6171; www.nhm.ac.uk/tring) is perfect for a rainy day. Take a boat trip down the Grand Union canal, or use 2 wheels to explore The Chilterns Cycleway (www.chilternsociety.org.uk).

FOOD AND DRINK It's a gentle 15-minute walk to the Rose and Crown (01296 668472; www. roseandcrownivinghoe.com) which serves good-value and top-notch pub grub from a seasonal menu. Stock up on goods from the Mead & Sons Farm Shop (01442 828478; pemeadandsons.co.uk), which sells a wide range of local produce including sausages, pies and ice cream. There's a farmers' market in Leighton Buzzard on the third Saturday of every month (01895 632221), which is very popular with locals and producers alike.

GETTING THERE Town Farm is just off the B489 between Ivinghoe and Dunstable (on your right if travelling west).

PUBLIC TRANSPORT Train to Tring, then a taxi (£10).

OPEN All year.

THE DAMAGE Adult £8–£10 (depending on length of stay); child (6–18 yrs) £5. Under-5s and dogs free.

bouncers farm

Bouncers Farm, Wickham Hall Lane, Wickham Bishops, Essex CM8 3JJ   01621 894112   www.operaintheorchard.co.uk

If you've been searching in vain for a campsite that offers its own pony-and-trap taxi service, then search no more. Get within a few miles of Bouncers Farm – to Witham station, say – and, for a small fee, Ann Bishop will take you clip-clopping down narrow country lanes to her lovely woody site in the bucolic Essex countryside.

The campsite occupies a wonderful spot on Ann's smallholding. Cars aren't permitted, but you can move all your stuff on the trolleys they leave at the entrance. There is a gypsy camp, with a bender tent sitting room and kitchen, and two gypsy caravans, perfect for a group of four friends or a family. Beyond are two camping fields with ten pitches for tents, two two-person gypsy wagons and the 'Buccaneer', a regular caravan with a pristine 1960s interior. The woods are a rural heaven for children, who can make dens and swing on the branches, while grown-ups can sling up a hammock between the trees. Dogs are welcome, and can hang out with Ann's gentle Irish wolfhound and feisty Jack Russell. Finally, the Bouncers Farm Opera, held every second Saturday of July in the garden, has become something of a local institution.

COOL FACTOR A fabulous rural idyll – in Essex!

WHO'S IN? Tents, dogs – yes. Campervans, caravans, groups – no.

ON SITE Numerous firepits for campfires; 10 pitches; a wetroom with double shower and loo; portakabin with 2 loos and a woodburner-heated shower; and a fridge-freezer.

OFF SITE Sessions can be arranged at a local riding school or try a canal cruise along the Chelmer and Blackwater Navigation (01245 225520; www.papermilllock.co.uk).

FOOD AND DRINK The Du Cane Arms (01621 891697; www.theducane.co.uk) in Great Braxted is highly regarded for its food. Or give Ann a shopping list in advance and a local shop will deliver.

GETTING THERE Leave the A12 at junction 21. Take the B1389 into Witham and turn right on to the B1018 towards Maldon; the road goes back under the A12; after ½ mile turn right on to Wickham Hall Lane.

PUBLIC TRANSPORT Take a train to Witham and arrange collection with Ann.

OPEN Easter–October and 4 weeks over Christmas and New Year.

THE DAMAGE Small tent and 1 person £12 per night; larger tents £24; extra adult £4; child £3. Gypsy wagons from £40 a night.

swattesfield

Swattesfield Campsite, Gislingham Rd, Thornham Magna, Suffolk IP23 8HH   01379 788558   www.swattesfieldcampsite.co.uk

Deep in the wilds of north Suffolk, keen camper Jonathan set up this seven-acre campsite with his dad in 2011. It's a simple site exuding a *Cool Camping* vibe, with two grassy fields – one for camping, the other for glamping – separated by a small lake with some adjoining woodland to explore. The position is perfect for bucolic strolls across the well-marked paths and bridleways of nearby Thornham Walks and for exploring the historic Walled Gardens on the estate, which has recently been restored and is open on weekends.

It's a great place to do nothing and get into nature. You can pitch your tent in the bottom field or the woodland beyond, or take up residence in a boutique bell tent or a well-equipped caravan complete with its own outside decking and cooking area. Plus there's a log cabin for let as two separate units – ideal for a family or small group. They have some ingeniously suspended firepits for cooking, and some of Jonathan's mates recently built him a fabulous outdoor pizza oven out of recycled materials.

Overall, it's a site with a lovely chilled-out atmosphere situated in a very special location.

COOL FACTOR Wonderfully tranquil, with not a jot to do but walk, cycle or just sit and think.

WHO'S IN? Tents, small campervans, dogs – yes. Caravans, big groups, young groups – no.

ON SITE Campfires allowed off the ground. 12 pitches, 3 bell tents, 1 caravan, plus 2 double rooms in the log cabin. No hook-ups. Simple but clean toilet block, with 2 showers, 6 sinks and 6 toilets. Small shop sells camping equipment and food essentials. Gislingham village shop is a 15-minute walk away.

OFF SITE Thornham Walks – 12 miles of waymarked footpaths accessible from the site (open daily 9am–6pm April–October; shorter hours outside this period).

FOOD AND DRINK The Thornham Estate's Forge Tea Room and Thornham Coach House are a 15–20-minute walk away and serve lunch and dinner. Try also the Four Horseshoes pub in nearby Thornham Magna, which serves breakfast, lunch and dinner and is about a 25-minute walk.

GETTING THERE Heading north up the A140, take a left by the White Horse Inn and, after half a mile or so, turn right by the Four Horseshoes; Gislingham Road is on the left.

PUBLIC TRANSPORT The nearest station is Diss (6 miles).

OPEN Easter–end of October.

THE DAMAGE Tent pitches £10–£12 for 2; £15–£18 for 4; extra people £3–£4.

karma farm

Karma Farm, 8 Fen Bank, Isleham, Cambridgeshire CB7 5SL   01638 780701   www.karmafarm.co.uk/camping.html

Will Taylor bought the land here a generation ago and built his farmhouse from scratch: a carbon-neutral, turf-roofed dwelling that must have seemed quite revolutionary at the time. The low-impact eco-house sets the tone for the rest of Karma Farm, which straddles the Suffolk-Cambridgeshire border. The campsite occupies a pretty spot by the side of the river Lark, with 40 unmarked tent pitches – visitors can simply stroll around and choose the nook they most fancy. There is also a yurt and a tipi, both basic enough to challenge the use of the term 'glamping', and a better-equipped three-berth cabin. In keeping with the rustic vibe, campfires are permitted, with wood available at the farmhouse. There's a games field and covered shed for rainy days, plus decent if basic washroom facilities, including a large shower pod into which you could fit your whole family (or a very friendly group). But perhaps the best thing about Karma Farm is its location right by the river. A track follows the river for seven miles to Prickwillow, while in the other direction a path takes you to the Jude's Ferry Inn about two miles away – choices to be considered over a breakfast of Will's free-range sausages and bacon.

COOL FACTOR Farm camping at its eco-friendly best – in the heart of the Fens.

WHO'S IN? Tents, campervans, caravans, groups, dogs – yes.

ON SITE Campfires allowed. Facilities include 2 toilets, 1 solar shower and 1 propane-powered shower pod, plus a portacabin with extra toilets and washbasins. Bikes available, for a donation.

OFF SITE As well as the walks and cycle rides along the river, and birdwatching on site, both Wicken Fen and RSPB Lakenheath are a short drive away.

FOOD AND DRINK The village of Isleham is a 20-minute walk and has shops and 2 pubs, the Griffin (01638 780447) and the Rising Sun (01638 780741), both of which do reasonable food. There's also a relatively upmarket restaurant, the Merry Monk (01638 780900), which Will says is good. You can also walk to the Jude's Ferry pub (01638 712277), a lovely 2-mile walk along the river.

GETTING THERE Take the A14/A11 and, roughly halfway between Newmarket and Barton Mills, take the B1085 north (signposted Freckenham) to Isleham. Drive through the village, bearing left down Sun Street past the post office, and make a left down Waterside; the site is a mile down the track.

OPEN April–October.

THE DAMAGE £2 per berth (tent or van), plus £4.50 per person. Yurt £40.

west lexham

West Lexham Manor, West Lexham, Norfolk PE32 2QN   01760 755434   www.westlexham.org

West Lexham Manor, and the beautifully rural 21-acre Breckland Estate that surrounds it, is being developed by celebrated garden designer and festival entrepreneur Edmund Colville as a 'creative social enterprise'. Plans include developing an ecosystem of businesses, tourist attractions, venues and events – while also providing local jobs and building a sense of community. A noble goal, indeed – 'but what of the camping?!' we hear you cry. Never fear, camping is at the very heart of this venture, with magical camping pitches hidden among the estate grounds. There are also three beautifully constructed treehouses in the woods, along with several yurts and so-called 'hobbit homes' – low-impact, one-room dwellings constructed to blend into the landscape. All the pitches are wonderfully private, and you can be as separate as you want from the main buildings of the complex, which has three delightful holiday cottages and a swimming pool. There's also a small lake with couple of rowing boats. Overall, it's a wonderful spot for old-fashioned holidays with the kids, an idyllic place that still has the feel of somewhere 'discovered' – hard to get to, but even harder to leave.

COOL FACTOR A beautiful old complex of farm buildings set around woods and a lake.

WHO'S IN? Tents, children, dogs – yes. Campervans, caravans – no.

ON SITE Campfires allowed. 17 tent pitches, including bell tents; 3 treehouses, 3 'hobbit homes' and 2 yurts. Each pitch has a firepit, outdoor seating area and BBQ; plus there are 3 communal firepits, 2 cob ovens and a fab outdoor kitchen. Treehouses and hobbit homes have their own facilities; otherwise there are 5 showers and 8 toilets.

OFF SITE It's just a couple of miles to Castle Acre, where you can visit the medieval church of St James, along with the fabulous ruins of the Norman Priory and Castle.

FOOD AND DRINK The Ostrich in Castle Acre (01760 755398) serves excellent pub food. In Swaffham, the Strattons Hotel (01760 723845) serves great food – well worth the trek.

GETTING THERE West Lexham is just off the A1065, midway between Swaffham and Fakenham, and is signposted to the right if you're heading north.

OPEN All year (from April 2013).

THE DAMAGE Tent pitches £30–£60 a night; treehouses from £140 a night; bell tents from £300 (per weekend); yurts from £400; hobbit homes from £500 (also per weekend).

deepdale

Deepdale Backpackers and Camping, Burnham Deepdale, Norfolk PE31 8DD   01485 210256   www.deepdalebackpackers.co.uk

Come mid-September, most people of sound mind put any thoughts of camping to rest – not just because the days start to turn colder but because there aren't that many campsites that stay open once the leaves begin to drop. Nudging the north Norfolk coastline, Deepdale Farm in Burnham Deepdale is a rare exception.

Some believe there is no better time to visit Norfolk than autumn – the hedgerows are pregnant with blackberries and the county is a vision of russet-coloured forests and blush-coloured clouds – and Andrea and Louise's site is a great place to come to if you do, with around 80 pitches and six tipis and yurts. These are not tipis awash with Indian silks and ethnic blankets, but they don't need to be. They are well-maintained and equipped with a cast-iron chimenea for heat, including kindling and fuel for the fire, foldaway chairs, a barbecue and a lantern. Sleeping in the round, with the wind whispering softly above you, is enchantment enough.

There's often an enthusiastic programme of events at the farm, with everything from organised stargazing to cookery classes with local produce. But in any case there are diversions aplenty in and around Burnham Deepdale. Kick-start the morning with a coffee at the café next door, and stock up on necessities at the nearby supermarket or onsite camping shop before hiring a bike or pulling on your walking boots. You are so near to the coastline here that a stroll down to the water's edge is a must. Their insistence on post-10pm 'quiet time' means that loud and drunken tomfoolery is not tolerated – a good thing if you want to get out and about early.

COOL FACTOR Lovely site, well run and friendly – perfect for exploring the beautiful North Norfolk Coast.

WHO'S IN? Tents, small campervans, dogs – yes. Caravans, big groups, young groups – no.

ON SITE There are 5 eco-friendly hot showers, 2 male toilets and 2 urinals, 3 female toilets, a unisex toilet block plus washing-up facilities. The water is heated by solar panels, with an oil burner back-up. There's an onsite camping shop and café. No campfires.

OFF SITE Grab your mac and wellies and revel in the muddy marshes and rockpools of the beach at Brancaster Staithe. Or escape to the posh boutiques of Burnham Market; it's not called Chelsea-on-Sea for nothing. Further afield, there's the huge, pine-backed expanse of sand at Holkham Bay, and the honest seaside town of Wells-next-the-Sea just beyond.

FOOD AND DRINK The excellent Deepdale Café next door serves everything from quality English breakfasts to chunky homemade soups (including evening meals in summer). The White Horse (01485 210262; www.whitehorsebrancaster. co.uk), a 5-minute walk west, is a buzzy gastropub serving local fish and shellfish, including cockles, mussels and oysters from the 'beds' at the bottom of the garden.

GETTING THERE The site is on the main road – the A149 – which runs through Burnham Deepdale.

PUBLIC TRANSPORT Burnham Deepdale is reachable using the Coasthopper bus service between Cromer, Sheringham and King's Lynn, all of which have train stations.

OPEN All year.

THE DAMAGE Tent camping is charged per person per night: adults £4.50–£9 and children £2.50–£5, depending on the season. Tipis/yurts £40–£114/£50–£145 per night, depending on the time of year and the number of people. Hostel beds start at £15 a night; rooms from £30.

overstrand

Overstrand Campsite, Beach Close, Overstrand, Norfolk NR27 0PJ   01507 343909   www.overstrandcampsite.co.uk

The east coast of Norfolk is often overlooked in favour of trendier North Norfolk, but in some ways it's hard to see why. Admittedly, there are one or two blackspots, yet the beaches of the east coast are generally larger, sandier and more accessible than those in the north, and the shoreline as a whole is often more remote and less dominated by a busy coastal road. The villages, too, are pleasant, unpretentious places that feel slightly more untouched by the modern world.

The pretty village of Overstrand, a few miles south of Cromer, is one such place, sitting atop cliffs that overlook a wide and beautiful stretch of child-friendly sandy beach. From its perch on the edge of the village, Overstrand Campsite makes the most of this location, with pre-pitched tents in a line along the back of the site and unmarked pitches for tents across the rest of the small, flat field. You can climb out of your tent in the morning and race down to the beach or go for a walk in either direction along the shore — either to Cromer, two miles to the north, or south towards the slightly larger resort of Mundesley.

Overstrand village itself was something of a destination in its own right once, with some Lutyens-designed buildings and a garden that was the work of plantswoman Gertrude Jekyll. But for the most part it's a sleepy place, with a good pub, a well-stocked shop and post office, a lovely beach café, a children's playground (right next door to the site), and; best of all, the glorious beach at the foot of the cliffs.

COOL FACTOR For location, this one's hard to beat.

WHO'S IN? Tents, dogs, groups – yes. Caravans, campervans – no.

ON SITE No campfires. 2 toilets, 2 showers, 4 basins in the ladies; the same in the gents; 4 washing-up sinks in a separate room. No hook-ups, but they do freeze ice and have sockets for phone charging. The café serves breakfast, lunches, evening meals, drinks and ice creams and also stocks a few grocery items. There's a games area with table tennis and table football.

OFF SITE The Peddars Way runs right by the site; it's a 40-minute walk to the seaside town of Cromer. The National Trust's Fellbrigg Hall (01263 837444) and Sheringham Park (01263 820550) are also nearby.

FOOD AND DRINK The White Horse (01263 579237), 5 minutes' walk away on Overstrand's High Street, dishes up Thornham oysters, Morston cockles, and other locally sourced fare at lunchtimes and in the evening. Or there's the excellent, and closer, Clifftop Café, which does a great line in crab sandwiches and other snacks and has seats overlooking the sea. Stock up on delicious fresh crab or lobster from the sheds on the path down to the beach.

GETTING THERE Take the A140 towards Cromer; just before you reach the town, turn right at a roundabout (signposted Overstrand). Continue into the village then follow signs to the long-stay car park; the site is just past this, on the right.

PUBLIC TRANSPORT There are regular trains, usually 2 an hour, to Cromer from Norwich, from where it's a short ride on bus 35 to Overstrand.

OPEN Open July and August only.

THE DAMAGE Regular pitches £15 per night, including 2 people; larger pitches £22 per night, including 2 adults and 2 children. Ready-pitched tents start at £117 for 3 nights, sleeping 4–6 people.

clippesby hall

Clippesby Hall, Clippesby, Norfolk NR29 3BL   01493 367800   www.clippesby.com

Clippesby Hall in the Norfolk Broads achieves the near impossible – managing to make a large campsite feel friendly, non-commercial, peaceful, and, well, lovely. Set in the manicured grounds of John Lindsay's family manor house, the site forms its own little self-contained canvas village. The facilities are extensive, with 115 pitches (many with electric hook-ups), a small outdoor swimming pool, tennis courts, mini-golf, archery courses, children's play areas, a tree house in the woods, a games room, bike hire, shop, café, pine lodges, even an onsite pub. You might assume that this place is about as quiet and peaceful as a night on the hard shoulder of the A12. But somehow John and his family have managed to incorporate all these amenities into the grounds of their home, while still retaining its unique character and personality. The result is an exceptionally appealing camping park with a relaxed, family atmosphere.

Campers have been coming here since the 1970s. It has evolved at its own pace over the years and today the pitches are divided across several camping areas, each landscaped and spacious enough to avoid any feeling of overcrowding, and named according to their individual characters. Pine Woods is a dog-free space almost entirely surrounded by conifers, The Orchard has plenty of tree cover, while The Dell is hidden away in a quiet corner with woodland pitches just for tents. Rabbits Grove is a favourite among younger campers, and the Cedar Lawn has pitches spread out over a gently sloping sweep of lawn beneath a huge cedar, complete with rope swing. There is plenty of space between pitches and some interesting little nooks and crannies mean that even in busy periods you can still find a relatively secluded space to call your own. They have had some issues with drainage over recent summers, and as a result they have adapted a few pitches to hard-standing, but they've done it sensitively, and there's no loss to the overall feel of the place.

Clippesby Hall is also the perfect location from which to explore the Broads National Park, a network of rivers and lakes that forms Britain's largest protected wetland. Although the rivers are natural, the lakes are man-made, the result of 400 years of enthusiastic peat digging that resulted in a stunning waterscape that can be explored by canoe, day boat or bike. The CanoeMan will pick you up at the site for a nature-spotting canoe trail through beautiful waterways inaccessible to motor-powered boats. If you'd rather explore the local area by pedal power, Clippesby also hires out bikes along with circular route maps, helmets and locks.

Don't be surprised when you are personally guided to your pitch on arrival – it's all part of the service, along with the deliberate decision not to put large, obtrusive pitch markers and unnecessary signs everywhere. After all, this is John's home and garden. It's been in the family since his grandfather bought the hall back in 1945, and he doesn't want to ruin it by making it look too much like, well, a campsite. Which is exactly the point: Clippesby is a large, well-appointed site with great facilities; but being here is more like camping in the delightful grounds of a stately home.

COOL FACTOR Great facilities combined with a peaceful, relaxed, family atmosphere in a beautiful rural location.

WHO'S IN? Tents, campervans, caravans, dogs – yes. Big groups, young groups – no.

ON SITE Some 115 pitches (with and without hook-ups) spread out in separate glades (some of which have tent-only areas). There is plenty of entertainment and things to do on site, including an outdoor heated swimming pool, grass tennis courts, mini-golf, archery, children's play areas, a games room, bike hire, shop, café, and even an onsite pub. The facilities blocks are dotted around the place and have modern showers, toilets, basins, and washing-up sinks with draining boards outside. There's even a family room with a bath. Plenty of staff members on site mean that everything is kept clean and well maintained. No campfires permitted.

OFF SITE The Broads National Park (www.enjoythebroads. com) is Britain's largest protected wetland, and Clippesby Hall's welcome pack includes a booklet all about discovering the area, including lots of ideas for days out on foot, and bike, boat or canoe. One of the best means of exploration is in a Canadian canoe with knowledgeable 'CanoeMan' Mark Wilkinson (0845 4969177; www. thecanoeman.com), who runs all sorts of wildlife-spotting and bushcraft tours. Or, for something bigger, head for Potter Heigham – 'the Blackpool of the Broads' as Mark likes to call it – 4 miles north of the campsite, where there are boatyards hiring out all sorts of vessels by the hour or day (including canoes), as well as pleasureboat trips. There are glorious dunes and sandy beaches at Winterton-on-Sea, about 6 miles away, and then at Horsey, a few miles north, where you'll also find the 19th-century Horsey Windpump (01263 740241; www.nationaltrust.org.uk/horsey-windpump). Climb its 5 flights of steep steps for views over the coast and broadlands landscape, then walk along the dyke to Horsey Mere; or hike across the fields for half an hour or so to the dunes and beach, where you will almost certainly see members of the local grey seal colony.

FOOD AND DRINK You don't actually need to leave the site for anything. Susie's Coffee Shop serves hot drinks and croissants for breakfast, and sandwiches and cakes throughout the day. You can order freshly baked bread or pizza to take away, and the shop sells local and fair-trade produce. Susie also sells ice cream from her summerhouse by the pool on sunny days. The campsite pub, the Muskett Arms, serves meals with local ingredients, and local real ales and ciders. Off site, the Lion Inn (01962 670796) in nearby Thurne village is a decent pub, there's also a good pub in nearby Winterton-on-Sea, The Fisherman's Return (01493 393305), which serves food, and the Nelson Head (01493 393378) in Horsey village, is a good spot for a pint of locally brewed 'Wherry' and a hearty lunch after a seal-spotting trip. In the other direction, south towards Acle, the Ferry Inn (01493 751096; www.ferryinn.net), right on the river in the pretty village of Stokesby, does great food lunchtimes and evenings, and is the perfect spot to down a pint of ale while checking out the traffic on the river. In Acle itself, right on the main road into the village, The Hermitage (01493 750310; www.thehermitageltd.co.uk) is a legendary local fish restaurant, serving up everything from regular fish and chips to superb scallops and mussels, all locally sourced – sometimes by the chef himself.

GETTING THERE Take the A47 from south of Norwich, and then the A1064 going north at Acle. After a mile or so, turn left on to the B1152 and the site is signposted on the left.

PUBLIC TRANSPORT It's easy to reach Acle station by train on the Wherry Line from Norwich, though from there it's either a long walk or a short taxi ride.

OPEN All year.

THE DAMAGE Prices range from £12.50 per night in low season for a tent, car and 2 people to around £33 in high season. Extra adults cost £6, children £3, under-3s free; dogs £4; hook-ups £4.

wing hall

Wing Hall, Wing, Oakham, Rutland LE15 8RY   01572 737090   www.winghall.co.uk

The 100 acres of garden and fields surrounding the manor house at Wing Hall make for a near perfect camping spot. Sitting just outside the pretty Rutland village of Wing, the site overlooks a colourful collage of woods and rolling fields of wheat and rape, and just a mile down the road is the lovely 3100-acre reservoir, Rutland Water. Created by flooding in 1974, the water and surrounding area now provide both a haven for wildlife and sport and leisure opportunities, with the 25-mile track around its perimeter making a beautiful cycle route. Surrounding the reservoir, a major nature reserve and wildfowl sanctuary spans some thousand acres and has several pairs of resident ospreys, which can sometimes be spied from one of more than 30 birdwatching hides dotted around the water. Robin Curley's great-great-grandfather built Wing Hall in 1891, and she has lived here all her life, long before England's tiniest county, Rutland, regained its independence from Leicestershire in 1997. The campsite used to be a basic, fiver-a-night-type stop, but Robin and her five (now grown-up) children have created something rather more sophisticated here over recent years.

Son Lyndon has transformed the onsite shop into a delectable deli, stocked with locally-sourced organic produce, artisan breads and a wide selection of wines and ales alongside the usual campers' basics. The shop also has maps of local walks, and onsite bike hire is a recent innovation. Daughter Zia runs the Veranda Café, serving up breakfast, lunch, afternoon teas and evening meals, including local treats like local rib-eye steak and roasted goats' cheese with homemade salsa. Enjoying one of her cream teas on the lawn, you can easily forget you're on a campsite – it feels more like the grounds of a stately home. The campsite has four camping fields, with around 250 pitches across the whole site, of which just 20 are for caravans. A large, flattish field on the left as you enter the site is for tents only. A second field on the right of the long, tree-lined entrance drive has wonderful views across the surrounding countryside and is for tents, caravans and mobile homes. A third field has a handful of pitches overlooking the valley and the resident free-range chickens, while a fourth field has swathes cut through wheat to provide more pitches and some of the best views. A short walk down through another wheat field takes you to the three fishing lakes at the bottom of the estate. There are acres in which to play or cycle around the site, and a large tree in the middle of the second field, with a couple of swings slung from its branches, provides a focal point for kids.

Despite the site's wide range of facilities, the general ambience of this place is far away from the holiday-park atmosphere you might expect. And the no-music policy, which is particularly popular with families, helps to maintain an air of peace and tranquillity. As night falls, parents swiftly sweep up their offspring in compliance with one of the few onsite rules – unaccompanied kids back under supervision after dark – and tranquillity returns. In any case, if splendid isolation is required, there are plenty of nooks and crannies and hideaway pitches to hole up in.

Sunday
Roast
Book now
To Avoid
Disappointment
From 12 - 2·30

Come In
WE'RE
OPEN

COOL FACTOR If you aren't to the manor born this is a great place in which to pretend you are.

WHO'S IN? Tents, caravans, dogs (on leads) – yes. Groups of young people/single-sex groups/groups of 3 tents or more – by arrangement only.

ONSITE Campfires allowed in firepits – bring your own or rent them for £2 per night. The shop also sells bags of firewood. 4 large camping fields spread out over a large part of the 100-acre estate, with only 20 of the 250 pitches allocated for caravans. Although there is no playground, a large tree in the centre of one of the camping fields has a couple of rope swings and low branches ideal for climbing on. The family are gradually upgrading the washing facilities each year to ensure that 'real camping' doesn't equal uncomfortable camping. 7 new showers have joined 5 older ones and all have free hot water; there are 6 covered alfresco washing-up sinks; and 3 blocks of toilets. The site shop opens from mid-March to the end of September and the café-restaurant also opens throughout the summer from April to September (serving breakfasts and evening meals at the weekend and lunches and afternoon teas all week). Campers can fish (and birdwatch) on the 3 lakes at the bottom of the estate for a daily fee of £7. There's also onsite cycle hire that rents bikes for £15 per day or £10 for half a day.

OFFSITE Come rain or shine, head to nearby Rutland Water for indoor and outdoor activities. Near the village of Edith Wesston, Normanton Church Museum (01572 653026) charts the history of the reservoir. *The Rutland Belle* (01572 787630; www.rutlandwatercruises.com) cruises around the shoreline from Whitwell, where you'll also find the Rock Blok outdoor adventure centre (01780 460060; www.rockblok.com), offering high ropes, climbing, abseiling and trampolining. In the same place, Rutland Water Sports has have-a-go sailing, windsurfing, kayaking and power boating sessions for kids (01780 460154; www.angliawater.co.uk).

FOOD AND DRINK From April to September, the Veranda Café has breakfast, lunch, afternoon teas and evening meals on offer at the weekend and opens from 11am to 5pm on spring and summer weekdays for lunch and afternoon tea. If you want to venture off the site, the 17th-century Kings Arms (01572 737634; www.thekingsarms-wing.co.uk) in Wing is a short walk away and has real ales and excellent local seasonal food. The Horse and Jockey at Manton (01572 737335; www.horseandjockeyrutland.co.uk) is on the cycle route around the reservoir, or a 40-minute walk away along footpaths and bridleways from the campsite. If you really want to push the boat out, Hambleton Hall is 3 miles away and offers gourmet dining and stunning views across Rutland Water (01572 756991; www.hambletonhall.co.uk). We also love the Olive Branch at Clipsham (01780 410 355; www.theolivebranchpub.com), a couple of miles north of Rutland water, whose high-end gastropub fare is well worth the short drive. In the opposite direction, the restaurant of the Lake Isle Hotel (01572 822951; www.lakeisle.co.uk) in Uppingham is fab, and not as pricey as you might think, with a good, wide-ranging lunch menu of light dishes including omelettes and sandwiches, and posher fare in the evening.

GETTING THERE From the A47 take the A6003, on the outskirts of Uppingham, towards Oakham. At Preston, turn right after the village pub, signposted Wing. Follow the road up the hill to Wing and turn right into the campsite at the top.

PUBLIC TRANSPORT Train to Oakham then either the Rutland Flyer bus towards Corby, which passes through Wing once a day in one direction and twice in the other (Monday–Saturday), or a taxi (around £10).

OPEN All year.

THE DAMAGE Adult £7 per night; child (under 14) £3.50 per night.

brook meadow

Brook Meadow Camping, The Wrongs, Welford Road, Sibbertoft, Leicestershire LE16 9UJ   01858 880886   www.brookmeadow.co.uk

People seem to fall in love with Brook Meadow – particularly the staff! Fishing bailiff Mick had been coming to the site for years with his wife Pam before taking on his current role; and site manager Vanessa chose the campsite as the venue for her wedding reception before returning to work and live here with her family.

It does feel like a special place to camp. Perhaps it's the sunsets over the lake? The cattle grazing peacefully in the neighbouring fields? The hundreds of stars to gaze at on a clear night? Or perhaps it's the philosophy of farmers Jasper and Mary, who want people to come and enjoy their land. This even extends to providing free camping for groups of young people hiking and camping towards their Duke of Edinburgh awards.

It's a peaceful, secluded site with 50 pitches over 15 acres with a five-acre fishing lake. Ducks waddle around and you might catch a glimpse of the resident wildlife – deer, hares, red kites – or hear owls hooting in the night. It feels (and is) very spacious. Some of the best pitches are around the fishing lake on the lower of the two fields (shared with three holiday chalets), although families with kids tend to opt for the top field for The Mound, which kids love to scramble on.

The site has a couple of high-adrenaline neighbours: Avalanche Adventures next door, where you can hire quad bikes or try your hand at clay pigeon shooting and other outdoor activities; and the Gliding Centre at Husbands Bosworth Airfield just down the road, where you can get a birds-eye view of the site as you drift by overhead.

COOL FACTOR A secluded campsite to fall in love with.

WHO'S IN? Tents, campervans, caravans, dogs, groups (by arrangement) – yes.

ON SITE Campfires allowed if contained and off the ground. Around 50 pitches (including 17 hardstanding and 8 grass with hook-ups) including several next to the lake. Fishing lodge houses 2 unisex toilet and shower rooms, 2 washing-up sinks, a kettle, microwave and freezer, and a laundry room with washing machine and dryer, a further 2 toilets and baby change facilities. Showers are free and solar-powered, and the fishing lodge facilities will soon be joined by a new toilet block. Fishing is £8 per day.

OFF SITE For outdoor activities there's Avalanche Adventures (01858 880613; www.avalancheadventures.co.uk) and the Gliding Centre at Husbands Bosworth Airfield (01858 880521; www.theglidingcentre.co.uk) both bookable in advance. More sedate alternatives include Cottesbrooke Hall (01604 505808; www.cottesbrookehall.co.uk) and Althorpe House (www.althorpe.com).

FOOD AND DRINK The Red Lion in Sibbertoft (01858 880011; www.redlionwinepub.co.uk) does great food and is just a mile away. The CAMRA-recommended Wharf Inn at Welford (01858 575075; www.wharfinn.co.uk), can be reached by footpath from the site.

GETTING THERE Leave the M1 at junction 20 and follow the A4304 towards Husbands Bosworth. Midway between Husbands Bosworth and Welford on the A5199, take the Sibbertoft turn. The farm entrance is 1½ miles on the left.

PUBLIC TRANSPORT County Connect operates an on demand bus service for pre-booked journeys made as little as an hour and up to a week ahead (Monday–Saturday).

OPEN All year.

THE DAMAGE Flat rate of £14 per pitch per night (free to Duke of Edinburgh groups).

eastnor castle

Eastnor Castle Deer Park, Ledbury, Herefordshire HR8 1RL   01531 633160   www.eastnorcastle.com

You know you're in the heart of the country when you can crawl from your tent in the morning and find yourself gazing into the eyes of a young stag – not the bleary-eyed groom-to-be variety, but a real red deer. Camp at the top of Eastnor Castle's 23-acre camping field – right next to their deer park – and there's every chance it could happen to you.

If you time your arrival right, there are some pretty fantastic places to pitch at the foot of the field. Veiled in trees on the slopes opposite, Eastnor Castle itself is a fairy-tale confection built in the early 19th century. There's a maze and a great playground for kids with a mock wooden castle and suspension bridge and tractor. The absolutely unmissable experience, though, is climbing the hill through the deer park to the obelisk at the summit. It offers an even better view of the Malvern Hills than that afforded at the campsite, so take a camera along.

The absence of toilets and showers at Eastnor explains why there are more caravanners than campers here. So, why not even out the numbers and bring a tent, your own portable chemical toilet and, if you can cope with alfresco ablutions, a solar-powered shower? Not many showers boast a castle view – reason enough to visit!

COOL FACTOR Red deer for neighbours plus castle views.

WHO'S IN? Tents, campervans, caravans, dogs (on leads), big groups, young groups (with an organisation) – yes.

ON SITE Few facilities on the 23-acre site – just some standpipes and a CDP and, most importantly no loos; campers are obliged to bring their own. Fishing in the lake is free. The castle has its own gift shop and café. No campfires.

OFF SITE The castle holds events such as open-air theatre, and is very child-friendly. Campers can get a family ticket (2 adults, 3 children) for half-price (£12.50).

FOOD AND DRINK Ledbury is home to swish café-deli Cameron & Swan (01531 636791; www.cameronandswan.co.uk), and also the timber frame hotel, The Feathers (01531 635266; www.feathers-ledbury.co.uk), which has a welcoming brasserie and restaurant.

GETTING THERE Leave the M50 at junction 2 and take the A417 into Ledbury before following the Eastnor Castle signs to the A449 (signposted Worcester and Malvern). After a mile turn right on to the A438. The castle is on the right.

PUBLIC TRANSPORT Train to Ledbury then a taxi ride or walk (it's only 2 miles).

OPEN End of March–end of September – check the website.

THE DAMAGE Caravan, campervan, trailer or family tent £8.50 per night (concessions available); small tent £3.

meredith farm

Meredith Farm Camping, Llancloudy, Herefordshire HR2 8QN   07813 027670   meredithfarmcamping.blogspot.co.uk

With its wide-open skies that seem to go on for ever, hills in every direction and a gently sloping meadow tumbling down to a wood of cherrywood and mystical oaks, 10-acre Meredith Farm is as rugged and magical a site as you could hope for. Run by the amiable Neil who, with his thick blond beard and weather-seasoned face looks like an extra from the pages of *Moby Dick*, Meredith is all about peace and quiet. Music lovers should go elsewhere unless they have headphones on, for here the only sound is the rustle of the breeze and the chirrup of kids in the site's little play area.

Campers can pitch up close to the hedge that splits the two meadows of the campsite or, for more remote camping, head down the hill to the babbling stream that runs through the wood. It's good for kids, too, with a petting zoo – if you're into pigs you'll love friendly pot-bellied Elvis, or the cute guinea pigs – and there are gorgeous walks to be done in every direction – Charlie has bags of routes he can keep you busy with and he may even give you a lift to the starting point if you need it.

COOL FACTOR Rugged site in a lovely location.

WHO'S IN? Tents, campervans, caravans, dogs on a lead, families – yes. Noisy groups – no.

ON SITE There are 6 pitches by the wood, 10 pitches up in the field. Basic shower block with 1 hot shower and electricity point, cooking facilities and a fridge-freezer. £1 honesty cupboard with basics. Fresh eggs on demand. Electricity hook-ups, free firepit range, kids' play area, petting zoo. Campfires encouraged.

OFF SITE Skenfrith Castle (www.nationaltrust.org.uk/skenfrith-castle) is just over 3 miles away, while 7 miles away at Symonds Yat is the Wye Valley Butterfly Zoo (01600 890360; www.butterflyzoo.co.uk) and Goodrich Castle (01600 890538; www.gooodrichcastle.co.uk).

FOOD AND DRINK Closest pub is the welcoming Royal Arms (01989 770267), or treat yourself at the excellent Bell at Skenfrith (01600 750235; www.skenfrith.co.uk).

GETTING THERE From the south take the A466 from Chepstow through Monmouth. After approximately 5 miles you'll find a sign to Meredith Camping on your left.

PUBLIC TRANSPORT The site is 2 minutes' walk from a bus stop on the Monmouth to Hereford route.

OPEN All year.

THE DAMAGE Campervans £7, tents £7 (includes 2 people); additional people £2.

penlan

Penlan Campsite, Brilley, Hay-on-Wye, Herefordshire HR3 6JW   01497 831485   www.penlancampsite.co.uk

Western Herefordshire feels lost in some distant time, the sort of place where you could expect to turn a corner and bump into a buxom milkmaid. Penlan Campsite, a mere half-mile from the Welsh border, draws repeat campers time and again for its royal views: to the far right the iconic Brecon Beacons, next to them the hulking Black Mountains, untamed by the gentler Herefordshire hills to the east; the drop down a field or two and look to the left and there are the Malverns. On a clear day you can even pick out the village of Birdlip on the edge of the Cotswolds, some 60 miles away. Look higher, still, and you might be lucky enough to catch a red kite riding the thermals.

The camping area is a gently sloping, cutlass-shaped swathe of tended greensward. The caravan pitches are at the back, while campers get the pick of the front-row seats and enjoy the additional advantage of the shelter afforded by a low beech hedge. As evening draws on horseshoe bats living in the farm's ancient barns take flight. Finally, as night falls, the woods behind the campsite are haunted by the calls of tawny owls.

COOL FACTOR So perfectly bucolic it should be bottled.

WHO'S IN? Tents, campervans, caravans, dogs (on leads) – yes. Groups – no.

ON SITE 10 touring pitches and 10 pitches for tents. Immaculately clean shower block (1M, 2W), with 2 electric showers, games shed, fridge-freezer and a PYO fruit area. No campfires but the owners have BBQs that can be borrowed.

OFF SITE Hay-on-Wye, with its second-hand bookshops and famous literary festival, is just 7 miles away. Paddles & Pedals in Hay (01497 820604; www.canoehire.co.uk) does bike and canoe hire.

FOOD AND DRINK The Sun Inn (01544 327677; www.thesuninnwinforton.co.uk) at Winforton is recommended for food. Erwood Station Craft Centre and Gallery (01982 560674; www.erwood-station.co.uk) has a good café.

GETTING THERE From Leominster, follow the A44 west to Kington. A mile after the second roundabout, turn left (signposted Kington Town Centre). Take the second right (to Brilley); after 4 miles turn left into Apostles Lane. Penlan is the first farmhouse on the right.

OPEN Easter–end of October.

THE DAMAGE Advance booking only. Tents – adult £7, child (5–12 yrs) £4, under-5s free. Caravan/campervan £15. Hook-ups £3, dogs £1.50.

monstay farm

Monstay Farm, Burrington, Ludlow, Shropshire SY8 2HE   01584 318007   www.monstayfarm.co.uk

Some say that Britain's decline as a world power is directly attributable to the dearth of campsites offering facilities for campers who want to bring their horse along. If that's so, no one can blame the owners of Monstay Farm, whose stables are ready and waiting (though will need to be pre-booked). Opened in 2009, the 100-acre sheep-and-cattle farm's campsite sports two slightly sloping fields, one with a gorgeous view west to the Cambrian Mountains, while the other looks south over a flock of sheep and Mortimer Forest. The nearby facilities are basic but clean. And the whole shebang is up a very long track and thus away from traffic noise. Kids intent on hiding-and-seeking, den building, or just getting away from their fuddy-duddy parents for a while will delight in the woods adjacent to the site. Off-road cyclists of all ages, meanwhile, can take off on the trail that runs through the farm or head for the paths that cross Mortimer Forest. The River Teme, which flows a few miles to the north, is a hit with wild-swimmers, while those who prefer the dryness of footpaths can enjoy a pleasant circular walk down to the church at Burrington

COOL FACTOR Want to take your horse camping? Trot right up.

WHO'S IN? Tents, campervans, caravans, dogs, big groups – yes. Motorhomes, young groups – no.

ON SITE Communal fire circle and fire bowls for hire (£5), plus kindling/firewood for sale. Pitches: 20 for tents; 5 for caravans; 6 hook-ups. 3 'rustic' loos and 2 showers. The owners will freeze ice packs, and groceries can be ordered in advance.

OFF SITE A mountain-bike trail runs across the farm and there are more in Mortimer Forest, which is also home to numerous bridleways as well as the Herefordshire Trail and the new Mortimer Trail (www.ldwa.org.uk).

FOOD AND DRINK There are 2 really good pubs in the area: the Riverside (01568 708440; www.theriversideinn.org) at Aymestry, with posh nosh and beer garden; and the Royal George (01544 267322) at Lingen.

GETTING THERE Follow directions to Whitcliffe and Monstay Farm is 2 miles further up the road.

PUBLIC TRANSPORT Train to Ludlow, then a taxi (£6).

OPEN Easter–late October (weather dependent).

THE DAMAGE All fees per person: adult £6, child (5–16 yrs) £2, under-5s free; hook-ups £4.

foxholes castle

Foxholes Castle, Montgomery Road, Bishop's Castle, Shropshire SY9 5HA   01588 638924   www.foxholes-castle.co.uk

To wake up feeling literally on top of the world, or on top of Shropshire, at least, makes a truly invigorating start to any morning, and that's the feeling you get when you greet the day at Foxholes, whose expansive grassy plateau is surrounded by far-reaching views of magnificent hills, which wistfully beckon campers on to the Shropshire Way running through the campsite, and deep into their bucolic embrace.

There can be few campsites in England that enjoy such a vista: the foothills of the Cambrian mountain range, the famous bulk of the Long Mynd, Stiperstones – in whose Roman lead mines Wild Edric is said to be buried with his soldiers, ready to fight should England ever be endangered – and a cornucopia of other bumps, knolls and mounds that make up part of the 139-mile loop that is the Shropshire Way. With almost a 360-degree panorama, it's as near to heaven as a hillophile is ever likely to get.

Four sprawling, natural camping areas are spread out among 10 acres. A sloping field at the back accommodates tourers and caravans; a cosy half-acre enclave suits tents requiring shelter; above that is the field that feels like a hilltop Iron Age fort (only without the ramparts); and there's a further, more out-of-the-way field, which has been largely left to meadow. Campers arrive and pitch up in all weathers, but less hardy souls can book the comfy, clean bunkhouse in the farmyard that sleeps six and costs a bargain £10 per bed per night.

Owners Chris and Wendy bought the property in 2006 and opened for business the following year, and they are experienced, easy-going hosts – just as long as you don't attempt to throw anything away that can be recycled. How else would they be able to make their castellated-roof tin knight, plastic recycling bin guard or papier-mâché notice board? They will readily invite visiting conservationists and the occasional camper into their kitchen for a cuppa and a chat, and their eco-friendly stance affects everything they do, with new eco-facilities that feature solar-powered showers and loos that are flushed by rainwater.

Pass by the metal sculpture of a fox skulking around a hedge, down towards the path that leads to the nearest town, Bishop's Castle, to find a little Buddha under the trees, collecting coins for the local air ambulance (Shropshire's roads are too windy and narrow to receive emergency vehicles quickly). Each year the town plays host to a May Fair (the weekend after the first May Bank Holiday); a walking festival (the second week of June); a stone-skimming championships (the last Sunday in June); a carnival (the first Sunday in July); and a beer festival (the weekend after the carnival) among others. Phew! Or merely leave the crowds behind by tackling a section of a long-distance footpath. The Offa's Dyke Path, Wild Edric's Way, and the Kerry Ridgeway are all within striking distance, the last of these doubling as a cycle route if you're a peddler rather than a plodder. Meanwhile, at basecamp, wildlife is nurtured, and the hedgerows left to grow freely, which pleases the birds that thrive here, and adds to the morning welcome. Just pack earplugs!

COOL FACTOR Views, views and more views.

WHO'S IN? Tents, campervans, caravans, dogs ('must be well-behaved, but we love them'), big groups, (well-mannered) young groups – yes. Non-recyclers – no.

ON SITE Fires permitted in drums rented on site. Roughly 100 pitches, but the site is never allowed to get too busy. No hook-ups. There are separate family/accessible wet rooms. Additional toilet and shower-block with 3W, 3M showers and 4W, 3M toilets; plus 9 solar-powered showers and 10 toilets using rainwater for flushing. There's plenty of space to run around and the top field is especially good for kite flying. Ice packs can be frozen. A brand new washing-up area is planned for 2013.

OFF SITE With The Long Mynd, Kerry Ridgeway, Wild Edric's Way and Offa's Dyke Path on your doorstep, a good pair of sturdy hiking boots is essential; this is great walking country by any standards. If walking isn't your thing, it's worth knowing that Bishop's Castle town hosts a carnival and beer festival in the summer (01588 630144), among other events – indeed the 10-minute walk downhill to Bishop's Castle for groceries is easy enough, though climbing back up will earn you an extra treat. Bishop's Castle itself is a bohemian, arty hangout with a few pleasant independent shops and a chilled-out vibe. Further afield, you're just a short drive from Stokesay Castle (01588 672544; www.english-heritage.org.uk), just outside Craven Arms, which is reckoned to be the finest fortified manor house in the country, dating originally from the 13th century. A few miles further down the A49, the market town of Ludlow has its own, rather impressive castle (01584 873355; www.ludlowcastle.com), and a long-standing foodie reputation that belies its diminutive size, with any number of great pubs and places to eat, busy shops and a thriving annual food festival held every September (www.foodfestival.co.uk) that brings all the best local producers to town.

FOOD AND DRINK The Three Tuns in Bishop's Castle (01588 638797; www.thethreetunsinn.co.uk) is a good local that serves its own real ales (brewed around the corner) along with decent food – excellent steaks and high-class pub grub. The very nice restaurant at the friendly Castle Hotel (01588 638403; www.thecastlehotelbishopscastle.co.uk) has a reputation for excellent dishes created from locally sourced produce, and lovely gardens at the back. There's a farmers' market in Bishop's Castle town hall every third Saturday of the month, and an ordinary fruit and veg market there every Friday. Sol Delicatessen (01588 638190), at the top of the High Street, is full of delicious nibbles and lush liquids with which to wash them down. If you want the full-on foodie experience, make the short journey to Ludlow for dinner at the frankly brilliant Mr Underhill's (01584 874431; www.mr-underhills.co.uk), the town's only Michelin-starred restaurant; or plump for the more pubby but excellent food at the Unicorn (01584 873555; www.unicorn-ludlow.co.uk). For a proper village pub experience, try the friendly Kangaroo Inn in Aston-on-Clun (01588 660263; www.kangarooinn.co.uk), where owners Michele and Simon will make any campers extremely welcome.

GETTING THERE You approach Bishop's Castle along the A488, which runs just to the east of the town. Turn west along the B4384 (Schoolhouse Lane) and then first right up the B4385 (Bull Lane). Foxholes Castle is about half a mile along here on your left. There are lots of signs to the campsite in the vicinity so, if in doubt, follow the fox.

PUBLIC TRANSPORT You can either take the train to Church Stretton and a shuttle bus from there to Bishop's Castle (April–September); or take a train to Shrewsbury and then bus 552 or 553 to Bishop's Castle. From there it's a short (uphill) walk.

OPEN March–October.

THE DAMAGE Adults £7, children under 13 £3, dogs £1. Fire drums £3, wood £3 a bundle.

bank house farm

Bank House Farm, Hulme End, nr Hartington, Buxton, Derbyshire SK17 0EX   01298 84441   www.bankhousefarmcamping.co.uk

Cycling and walking trails abound around these parts, and after a hard day's pedalling or rambling, sometimes you just want to sit and relax. Which is where Bank House Farm comes in – a pretty near-perfect spot for camping. Its riverside pitches are just the ticket for resting weary legs and simply admiring the views over the Manifold Valley and distant hills. And if the thought of even a short walk to the nearest pub or shop makes your heart sink, no problem! The village pub is just across the road for a quick pint or something more substantial, and the village shop is right next door. Here you can stock up for your campfire cooking or enjoy a refreshing cuppa.

In the heart of the Peak District, and in the middle of the pretty hamlet of Hulme End, the River Manifold winds its way around the campsite, forming the main attraction for kids who are camping here. Rope swings are slung from tree branches and there's even a tiny beach along the river's banks. The main camping field is near the farmhouse (and the main facilities) and there are pitches set along the riverbank and in the adjacent fields. A second field runs on a freestyle or pitch-where-you-like basis and is where owner Wayne, who recently took over the site with his wife Alexa, directs larger groups.

The nine-mile Manifold Valley cycle and walking trail starts just 200 yards from the site and follows the old route of the disused Leek and Manifold Light railway to the village of Waterhouses. And you can join the Tissington Trail, which runs from Ashbourne to Parsley Hay, two miles away in Hartington.

COOL FACTOR Riverside camping in the heart of the Peak District with en-suite village pub and shop.

WHO'S IN? Tents, campervans, caravans, dogs, groups (in the second camping field) and large groups (by arrangement only) – yes. Young, unaccompanied groups – no.

ON SITE Campfires allowed – as long as they are off the ground in a firepit or similar container. 2 camping fields provide around 70 pitches, some with electric hook-ups and lots by the riverbank. You can fish from the site for £5 per day. The toilets and (free) showers are well maintained and kept clean and there are 2 washing-up sinks and a drainer – the second field is a short walk from these.

OFF SITE Thor's Cave (near Wetton) is a former home to stone-age dwellers and has magnificent views over the surrounding area. For more adventurous climbers, The Roaches rocks also have stunning views.

FOOD AND DRINK The Manifold Inn (01298 84537; www.manifoldinn.co.uk) is just across the road and has a more interesting menu than the average pub; plus there are 2 good pubs in Hartington, both serving food – the Charles Cotton Hotel (01298 84229; www.charlescotton.co.uk) and the Devonshire Arms (01298 84232; www.devonshirearms. co.uk). Also in Hartington, the Old Cheese Shop (01298 84935; www.hartingtoncheeseshop.co.uk) sells more than 70 types of cheese.

GETTING THERE From Ashbourne take the A515 towards Buxton, through the village of Newhaven, and take the first left (the B5054). Continue through Hartington to Hulme End and the campsite is on the right opposite the Manifold Inn.

PUBLIC TRANSPORT Bus 442 from Buxton to Ashbourne stops in Hulme End.

OPEN March–October.

THE DAMAGE From £15.50 per night for 2 people with a tent and car.

shallow grange farm

Shallow Grange Farm, Old Coalpit Lane, Chelmorton, nr Buxton, Derbyshire SK17 9SG   01298 23578   www.shallowgrange.com

It can be a nightmare finding a decent working sheep farm in which to camp in the middle of the Peak District National Park. Luckily Shallow Grange, three miles south of Buxton, manages to combine both sheep (around 600 ewes and lambs to be precise) and tents amid 110 acres of grassy farmland and rolling hills.

To stay here is to be in noble company, historically speaking – we're not still baahing on about sheep – since the battalions of the Sherwood Foresters used the land as their summer camp back at the beginning of the last century. But those days are long gone and it's been functioning as a campsite for a couple of decades, run by Ed and Marilyn, who've worked hard to make the site a pleasant and highly eco-friendly experience.

You'll find a comprehensive recycling system; a renovated shower block with thermostatically controlled underfloor heating system (and Dyson hand dryers, no less); toilets with low-volume, harvested rainwater flushes; and solar panels providing hot water for the showers and sinks. The Merry Men would be jealous indeed. The site's large camping meadow is slightly sloping, well-drained and bordered by low stone walls. It has space for 30 tents (with generously sized pitches), and there's a separate touring field for caravans, which has electric hook-ups that can be used by those staying in tents (if they pay the caravan tariff) as well as an occasionally used rally field. It's a simple sort of place, despite the jazzy eco-facilities. There's a pond, where you can fish for perch, carp and bream. And as it sits in the Peak District Dark Skies area, it's a great spot for stargazing, too.

COOL FACTOR An eco-friendly spot where you can get away from it all.

WHO'S IN? Tents, dogs – yes. Campervans, caravans, groups – by arrangement.

ON SITE Campfires are allowed if raised off the grass. 30 pitches, plus more in the caravan field. Showers and toilet facilities are modern, well-equipped and environmentally friendly. Freezer available for ice packs in the laundry room, which also has a washing machine and dryer. Electric hook-ups must be booked in advance.

OFF SITE Nearby Chatsworth House (01246 565300; www.chatsworth.org) and Haddon Hall (01629 812855; www.haddonhall.co.uk) are grand but very different houses with wonderful gardens. Arbor Low Stone Circle – the 'Stonehenge of the Peak District' – is a Neolithic henge surrounded by unspoiled countryside, with fantastic views over Derbyshire (about 5 miles south west of Bakewell). The traffic-free, 8½-mile Monsal Trail between Chee Dale and Bakewell is now fully open to walkers, cyclists and horse riders.

FOOD AND DRINK The Church Inn (01298 85319; www.thechurchinn.co.uk) at Chelmorton serves good-quality British pub lunches and home-cooked meals, while the Bulls Head (01629 812372; www.thebullsheadmonyash.co.uk) in Monyash offers good food in a refurbished dining room.

GETTING THERE The site is located off the A5270 (Old Coalpit Lane), accessed from the A6 and A515.

PUBLIC TRANSPORT Trains run hourly to Buxton from Manchester. Buses will drop you off outside the farm gates on Old Coalpit Lane by prior arrangement. Services include the TransPeak (TP) between Manchester, Derby and Nottingham, and the 193 (between Buxton and Tideswell).

OPEN March–October (and out of season by arrangement).

THE DAMAGE Tent, 2 people and car from £14 per night.

the royal oak

The Royal Oak, Hurdlow, nr Buxton, Derbyshire SK17 9QJ   01298 83288   www.peakpub.co.uk

The biggest challenge for those staying at the Royal Oak isn't fishing around for coins (the hot showers are free), or being kept awake by fellow campers (it's quiet after 10.30pm), or finding things to do (it's slap-bang in the middle of the Peak District). No, it's chomping your way through one of the award-winning pies sold at the onsite pub. You could probably actually camp in one of these monsters – they're that big. Packed with fine ingredients, they make for a well-deserved reward after a day's play in the Peaks, especially if accompanied by the excellent local ale.

There are two camping fields here, one sloping and one flat, with space for around 40 pitches (bring strong pegs for the rocky ground in the upper field), and there's a converted stone barn with comfortable bunks if the weather's wreaking havoc. Surrounded by farmland, with the 13-mile Tissington Trail passing right next to it and the Limestone Way actually cutting through some of the site, this is a great base for those interested in walking and cycling. If you didn't bring your own bike, Parsley Hay Cycle Hire is two miles away and has a range of bikes for adults and kids, including tandems.

COOL FACTOR Who ate all the pies? We did.

WHO'S IN? Tents, campervans – yes. Caravans – no. Dogs, groups – by arrangement.

ON SITE Small campfires allowed if contained and off the ground. 2 camping fields (the lower one is flatter) with good washing-up facilities, free hot showers, and toilets in a refurbished barn.

OFF SITE Bakewell (famous for its puddings), Ashbourne and the spa town of Buxton are all short drives away.

FOOD AND DRINK The Royal Oak – definitely your local – serves real ales and excellent pub grub. Good fry-ups are available at Old Smithy Tea Rooms (01629 810190; www.oldsmithymonyash.co.uk) in Monyash. Piedaniels (01629 812687; www.piedaniels-restaurant.com) in Bakewell serves fine French and English cuisine.

GETTING THERE Head towards Ashbourne on the A515 and, after 5 miles, take the right-hand turn signposted Hurdlow, Crowdecote and Longnor. The pub and campsite are 400m down on the right.

PUBLIC TRANSPORT The nearest station is Buxton (6 miles away). There's no direct bus service but the 42 (42A or 442 on Sun) will stop on the main road, half a mile away.

OPEN All year.

THE DAMAGE £16 per pitch, per night; £24 per large pitch.

bushey heath

Bushey Heath Farm, Tideswell Moor, Tideswell, Buxton, Derbyshire SK17 8JE   01298 873007/07710 163376 (9am–9pm only)
www.busheyheathfarm.com

Rod and Lisa run Bushey Heath Farm with a decidedly no-frills, back-to-nature and environmentally-friendly approach to camping. When *Cool Camping* visited, they'd just spent the previous night sleeping in the back of a van at a nearby folk festival!

This small, quiet campsite has an away-from-it-all feel, with views over Tideswell Moor and sheep, hens and alpacas roaming the nearby fields. The camping field slopes slightly towards a very minor road, and a rope swing and surrounding woods provide natural, low-key play opportunities for kids. The facilities are very basic. There are no washing-up facilities and no-hot water taps; and although a wind turbine provides electricity, there are no power points and no hook-ups. Which all adds to the charm and means that small tents win out here – caravans and motorhomes just don't fit in. Keen walkers will be pleased to find that two long-distance footpaths pass nearby: the 46-mile Limestone Way is about ¾ mile away as it passes from Castleton on its way to the Dove Valley at Rocester; and hardy folk on the 1000-mile-plus route from Land's End to John O'Groats often pitch up here for the night.

COOL FACTOR Get away from it all on a simple, back-to-nature site with resident farm animals.

WHO'S IN? Tents, small campervans, dogs, groups – yes. Caravans, motorhomes, extra-large tents, parties – no.

ON SITE Maximum 80 campers, plus a couple of small camping huts. Facilities consist of a water tap, a toilet and shower block with 2 toilets (flushed with harvested rainwater) and 2 hot showers. Small shop sells basics. No campfires.

OFF SITE Eyam's Museum, 5 miles away, tells the tale of the famous plague village (www.eyammuseum.demon.co.uk). Castleton Caves are a good rainy day option (www.castleton.co.uk/caverns); as is Chestnut Centre Wildlife Park at Chapel-en-le-Frith (01298 814099; www.chestnutcentre.co.uk).

FOOD AND DRINK Vanilla Kitchen in Tideswell (01298 871519) for coffee and cake; the George in Tideswell (01298 871382) or the Red Lion at Litton (01298 871458; www.theredlionlitton.co.uk), for real ales and good food.

GETTING THERE Off the M1 (junction 29), take the A617 to Chesterfield then the A623 towards Chapel-en-le-Frith. Continue past the Tideswell turning, then take the next right.

PUBLIC TRANSPORT Bus to Tideswell, then a 30-min walk.

OPEN Easter (weather permitting) to October.

THE DAMAGE £7 per person 13 yrs and over, £2 per person 3–13 yrs, under-3s free. Bothys £20 per night.

clumber park

Clumber Park, The Paddocks, Clumber Park, Worksop, Nottinghamshire S80 3BQ   01909 506581   www.nationaltrust.org.uk

Fancy following in the footsteps of Robin Hood and camping out in Sherwood Forest? Then head to Clumber Park, northern gateway to the home of the green-clad one – although you'll hopefully find it a rather more stylish experience than he would have done. Despite his best efforts to rob from the rich and give to the poor, the campsite sits in the midst of The Dukeries, the former pleasure-belly of the Midlands' aristocracy and a concentration of wealth in its day.

The site is surrounded by a massive 3800 acres of gardens, parkland and woods on the former country estate of the Dukes of Newcastle. Its chapel, pleasure ground, lake, walled garden and double avenue of lime trees all stand testament to its grand past, while contemporary art installations highlight little-known stories of extravagance and eccentricity: the fourth Duke, Harry Pelham-Clinton, bought himself a leopard from India in 1820; while the seventh Duke travelled around in a touring caravan with its own portable wine cellar.

The National Trust runs a great campsite, and this one is no exception. The flat camping field has plenty of space, there's a no-noise-after-10pm rule, and the facilities are clean and well maintained – all making for a relaxed, family-friendly atmosphere. But what makes this campsite really special is that, when the park closes its gates to visitors for the day, campers have all those acres of country estate on their tent-step to themselves. And even when you have to share it, with more than 20 miles of cycle routes and countless walking trails, it's easy to lose the crowds.

COOL FACTOR Family-orientated camping in the heart of a National Trust country estate.

WHO'S IN? Tents, campervans, dogs – yes. Caravans, large groups, and unaccompanied under-21s – no.

ON SITE Campfires allowed if contained. Camping field has 39 tent pitches as well as 3 wooden wigwams (which sleep up to 5) and 3 pods (which sleep up to 4). For kids, there's outdoor Connect 4, Jenga, giant chess, a volleyball net, and orienteering kits to borrow. A small shop sells things you may have forgotten, and has details of what's on at the local cinema in case you hit bad weather.

OFF SITE There's an adventure playground and indoor discovery centre a 15-minute stroll away; ranger activities; cycle hire; and fishing on the lake. Waymarked cycle and walking trails throughout the park.

FOOD AND DRINK Barkers Restaurant (01909 544925), a 5-minute walk away, serves morning coffee, afternoon tea, lunch and Saturday evening meals. Its real ales are brewed at the microbrewery in the park. There is also a National Trust café and a shop selling local produce.

GETTING THERE Clumber Park is 4 miles south-east of Worksop and there are a number of entrances. From the A1 take the A614 towards Nottingham; after 400m turn right on to Lime Tree Avenue and take the second left to White Gates crossroads. Turn left and the campsite is on the right.

PUBLIC TRANSPORT The nearest train station is Worksop. The Sherwood Arrow bus between Worksop and New Ollerton stops on the edge of the park on the B6034, from where it's about a 20-minute walk to the site.

OPEN March–October.

THE DAMAGE Tents £12 low season, £15 mid season, £22 high season. Prices include entrance to park (£5.80). Pods from £100 per weekend and the larger wigwams from £140 for a weekend.

lincolnshire lanes

Lincolnshire Lanes, Manor Farm, East Firsby, Market Rasen, Lincolnshire LN8 2DB   01673 878258   www.lincolnshire-lanes.com

This campsite has a good old-fashioned feel to it. It's in a peaceful, rural spot, with 20 pitches, including five in a secluded and quiet, adult-only area, and a couple of log cabins hidden among a grove of Christmas trees. There are two adjoining flat fields, separated by and surrounded by hedges, with plenty of space for games and family fun, and a couple of swings and a small animal area with rabbits and guinea pigs for the kids. Situated in their own enclosure at the bottom of the second camping field are two fully-equipped, comfy tipis with real beds, duvets and pillows (bring your own bedding if you are here three nights or less). There's also a fully-equipped gypsy caravan that sleeps up to four people – though this was in need of (and awaiting) some TLC when we visited. Site-owners Rosemary and Robert keep the site shipshape and maintain its air of tranquillity by enforcing the no-noise-after 10.30pm rule. Rosemary also welcomes the tipi and caravan dwellers with eggs and bacon or flapjacks and elderflower cordial, and Robert is an avid recycler. Please make him happy by putting aluminium, glass, plastic and paper in the right containers!

COOL FACTOR Old-fashioned family fun on a child-friendly campsite in rural Lincolnshire.

WHO'S IN? Tents, campervans, caravans, groups, dogs – yes.

ON SITE Campfires allowed in firepits outside tipis. Pitches for around 20 tents, campervans and caravans across 2 large, flat camping fields; 15 hook-ups. 2 toilet and shower blocks, with 2 showers each and washing-up sinks. Disabled and baby changing facilities, and laundry room with a washing machine and dryer. Bike-hire £6 a day.

OFF SITE Lincoln, with its cathedral and castle, is about 12 miles away.

FOOD AND DRINK The Inn on the Green at Ingham (01522 730354; www.innonthegreeningham.co.uk) is easily the best place to eat nearby.

GETTING THERE Head north for 12 miles on the A15 from Lincoln. Take a right (Cliff Road) into the village of Spridlington and a left on to Owmby Road.

PUBLIC TRANSPORT Lincolnshire Council's CallConnect buses will run to the site if booked in advance (Mon–Sat).

OPEN All year – although the tipis and the gypsy caravan are not available in winter.

THE DAMAGE From £12 a night for 2 adults and 2 children in a tent. Tipis £50 per night; gypsy caravan £35 per night.

three horseshoes

Three Horseshoes, Shoe Lane, Goulceby, Lincolnshire LN11 9WA   01507 343909   www.the3horseshoes.com

Ian and Denise, the team behind the pop-up summer site at Overstrand in Norfolk (see p142), now have a permanent home for their latest venture, behind the Three Horseshoes pub in the village of Goulceby. In the heart of a relatively unexplored Area of Outstanding Natural Neauty (AONB), the Lincolnshire Wolds, the site has spaces for just seven tents alongside two fully-equipped bell tents and a yurt. It's a great spot for sitting and admiring the Wolds scenery and sunsets and, when you're ready for a little exercise, the 147-mile Viking Way passes by on its way from the Humber Bridge to Rutland Water.

This is definitely a get-away-from-it-all destination for campers. But, if you do find yourself in need of some retail therapy, then England's antiques capital, Horncastle, is about six miles away. Louth (eight miles to the north) is the main hub of the Wolds and was recently voted Britain's favourite market town, with independent shops and cafés galore. The quiet seaside town of Sutton-on-Sea, with sandy beaches – but without the kiss-me-quick atmosphere of the busier Lincolnshire resorts – is about a 40-minute drive away.

COOL FACTOR Small is beautiful – and so are the views.

WHO'S IN? Tents, dogs – yes. Caravans, motorhomes campervans and groups – by arrangement.

ON SITE Campfires allowed. 7 pitches with hook-ups and 2 fully-equipped bell tents and a yurt. 2 unisex shower and toilet washrooms with free hot showers and more toilets in the pub. Cycle hire £10 per day.

OFF SITE Rand Farm Park (01673 858904; www.randfarmpark.com) is a working farm with animals to touch. Further afield, Gibraltar Point Nature Reserve extends 3 miles along the coast (01507 526667; www.lincstrust.org.uk).

FOOD AND DRINK The pub does food and has a shop. There's also the Bluebell in Belchford (01507 533602; www.bluebellbelchford.co.uk) and Melanie's Restaurant in Louth (01507 609595; www.melaniesoflouth.com).

GETTING THERE Heading north on the A153, turn left as the road bears right, just before Scamblesby and Cawkwell. At the junction, turn left and then left again into Shoe Lane.

PUBLIC TRANSPORT CallConnect services 6H (to Horncastle) and 51F (to Louth) stop 300m from the site (Monday–Saturday).

OPEN All year.

THE DAMAGE From £15 per pitch for 2 people in a tent with a car. Bell tents and the yurt £50 for the first night then £35 for each extra night.

wyreside farm

Wyreside Farm Park, Allotment Lane, St Michael's-on-Wyre, Garstang, Lancashire PR3 0TZ   01995 679797
www.wyresidefarmpark.co.uk

Here at Wyreside, in the green flatlands of rural Lancashire, life bumbles along quietly by the peaceful waters of the River Wyre, and initially nothing looks that radical. There's a lovely old redbrick farmhouse with a thatched roof that dates back yonks, and the usual cast of animals noodling about looking for something to eat. Then you notice that the hens wandering around are a bit hippy-looking, and discover that some lay blue eggs, others green (though they taste the same as 'normal'-looking ones), and it dawns on you that this is no ordinary campsite. What's more, the Badger Face Welsh Mountain sheep don't exactly belong in this part of Lancashire. Then you meet the effervescent owner, and it all becomes clear. Penny is wild about wildlife and its preservation; she's created conservation areas between the two camping fields, as well as 'butterfly bars' (Buddleia plants) to help with a healthy insect population.

But it's not all about flora and fauna. Should campers tire of watching the weird hens, badgers masquerading as mutton, or browsing butterflies, there are plenty of other distractions around, including microlighting, parachuting, cycling the lost lanes of north Lancashire, or exploring historic Lancaster or Garstang, Britain's first classified fair-trade town. And, just beyond, the Bowland Fells rear up challengingly. Alternatively, the saucy – and nowadays somewhat cool – seaside town of Blackpool is only a dozen miles away and the perfect place for a stick of rock, a ride on the bumper cars and a trip up the tower in a kiss-me-quick hat, or indeed a bit of late-night bar-and-club activity.

COOL FACTOR A rural riverside retreat with colourful eggs.

WHO'S IN? Tents, campervans, caravans, certain breeds of dog (nice ones, not too big – please check first) – yes. Groups – no.

ON SITE 12 pitches with electric hook-ups, generously spread out so there's plenty of wriggle-room. Modern toilets with free showers. Contained campfires and barbecues are allowed.

OFF SITE This is an intriguing area, with the valleys and moorland of the Forest of Bowland on the doorstep and a seemingly undiscovered stretch of coastline on the Lune Estuary a few leisurely bike miles away.

FOOD AND DRINK The Grapes pub has closed, so it's a choice of bulls – the White Bull (01995 640324; www. thewhitebull.co.uk) in St Michael's or the Black Bull (01995 670224; www.the-black-bull-great-eccleston. co.uk) 3 miles away in Great Eccleston. Or there's the Great Eccleston Fish Bar (01995 670862), which is licensed, so you can enjoy wine with your chips. For fine dining, the magnificent Grade I-listed Art Deco Midland Hotel (01524 424000; www.midlandhotel.org) in Morecambe has a great restaurant with marvellous views and does afternoon teas.

GETTING THERE The site lies between junctions 32 and 33 of the M6. Turn off the A586 as you come through St Michael's on to Allotment Lane, a narrow, hard-to-spot left-hand turn, then look out for the entrance to the Oaks and it's the next left.

PUBLIC TRANSPORT There's a regular train service to Blackpool, from which there's a bus service (42) to St Michael's.

OPEN March–October.

THE DAMAGE Tent plus 2 adults with hook-up £17 per night; extra adult £5; child £2; pre-arranged dog £1.

gibraltar farm

Gibraltar Farm, Hollins Lane, Silverdale, Lancashire LA5 0UA   01524 701736   www.gibraltarfarm.co.uk

Morecambe Bay is a classic sweeping stretch of coast, with an extended shoreline incorporating towns from Fleetwood to Barrow-in-Furness, a winding road trip of about 70 miles. Both beautiful and dangerous, the landscape may look like the stuff of beach dreams on a hot sunny day, with its expansive golden sands and gleaming sea in the distance, but the erratic tidal patterns and swampy sands can hold some hidden dangers, so it's best not to venture out too far. One of the best places from which to enjoy the sands of Morecambe Bay at a safe distance is the Gibraltar Farm Campsite, near Silverdale. Coming through the farm gates, you're greeted with a panoramic view of the bay with the camping area lying down an access track through a lovely field beyond the trees. So you can pitch your tent in the large grassy area set around a rocky protrusion on the seaward side of the farm and enjoy the sight and sound of the capricious curls of Morecambe Bay's waves just beyond the walled perimeter. If Morecambe Bay tires you out, then you're less than a mile away from Jenny Brown's Point, a popular viewpoint and birdwatching spot overlooking the bay.

COOL FACTOR Farm camping with wide bay views.

WHO'S IN? Tents, campervans, dogs (on leads) – yes. Groups can hire the woods for £120 per night (10 tents).

ON SITE 60 tent pitches; 30 caravan pitches with electric hook-up. Showers (5W, 5M), toilets (12W, 5M). Onsite shop with homemade ice cream. BBQs if off ground and extinguished after use, but no campfires.

OFF SITE The Wolfhouse Gallery (01524 701405) has paintings, ceramics and a café. The nearby Leighton Moss RSPB reserve has nature trails and a visitor centre, and the southern Lake District is only a short, scenic drive away.

FOOD AND DRINK March down to the Woodlands Hotel (01524 701655) for excellent real ales. For BBQ inspiration have a butcher's at F&W Burrow & Sons (01524 701209).

GETTING THERE From the A6 take the B5282 to Arnside and follow the signs to Silverdale. Go through the village, follow Hollins Lane for less than a mile, and the road turns sharp left; the site entrance is on your right.

PUBLIC TRANSPORT Trains run to Silverdale from nearby Carnforth and there's a shuttle service bus to the site.

OPEN All year, but best to phone ahead out of season.

THE DAMAGE Adult on foot with tent £7; 2 adults £10. 2 adults plus car and tent £10–£17, depending on size of the tent. Dogs £1.

low greenside farm

Low Greenside Farm, Greenside Lane, Ravenstonedale, Kirkby Stephen, Cumbria CA17 4LU   01539 623217   rosie@lowgreenside.f9.co.uk

'Camping as it used to be', says Rosie, who farms a flock of Swaledale sheep on the Howgill Fells, which rise behind her farmhouse a few miles out of Kirkby Stephen. The handwritten sign on the gate, and the notice on the door inviting you to pitch your tent if no one's around, all tend to back her up on this, as do the limited-if-adequate facilities. It's not quite the proverbial farm field and water tap, but it's not far off, with a single toilet and shower housed in a weathered caravan on the edge of the site. But Rosie keeps these spotless, while appreciative campers enjoy the other services she provides, from local walk and outing suggestions stacked in the caravan lounge to the wheel-rim campfire sites by each pitch. We say pitch – we mean five-acre meadow with lush, soft grass where you're free to spread out, until around 30 people are on site, at which point Low Greenside is full. There's a curve, almost a dome, to the field, so if you head for the edges, the other tents miraculously disappear, and all you can see are the big skies and distant hills of the encircling Howgills and Pennines.

COOL FACTOR Simple farm-field camping in glorious off-the-beaten-track countryside.

WHO'S IN? Tents, campervans, dogs (on leads), groups (by arrangement) – yes. Caravans, sybaritic lotus-eaters – no.

ON SITE Campfires and BBQs allowed – firewood available. Usually 8–10 pitches; 1 electric hook-up. Caravan facilities include 1 hot-water shower (free), 1 toilet, and changing room with power point, plus hot-water sink and fridge. There's another toilet at the farm.

OFF SITE The walk around Smardale Gill National Nature Reserve is a favourite. There's also trout fishing, horse riding and pony trekking, and walks straight from the farm gate.

FOOD AND DRINK Ravenstonedale, a 10-minute walk away, has 2 good pubs, both rated for their food – the King's Head (01539 623050; www.kings-head.com) and the Black Swan (01539 623204; www.blackswanhotel.com). The Black Swan also hosts the village shop, and there's a farm shop at the nearby trout farm.

GETTING THERE From Kirkby Stephen, drive south on the A685 for 4 miles, turn left for Ravenstonedale, go past the King's Head and look for the left turn to Greenside.

OPEN End March–end October.

THE DAMAGE Adults £6 per night, 4–11-year-olds £3; electric hook-ups £3 per night.

turner hall farm

Turner Hall Farm, Seathwaite, Broughton-in-Furness, Cumbria LA20 6EE   01229 716420   www.duddonvalley.co.uk

If you're looking for a truly remote wilderness camping experience, pitch up at Turner Hall Farm in the Lake District's lesser-visited Duddon Valley. The most spectacular way to arrive is over the Wrynose Pass, a tortuous zigzag of a road making for an exhilarating journey that matches some of the best Lake District walks, view for view. Even if you take the longer, winding road via Broughton Mills you have to stop to open and close gates, an action loaded with the symbolism of leaving civilisation behind.

Turner Hall Farm is tucked into the folds of the fells between the mountains of Scafell Pike to the north-west, and the Old Man of Coniston to the south-east. It's a basic campsite set up for walkers and climbers, the attraction being its location and outlook rather than the facilities, which run to a couple of toilet and shower blocks, but that's about it. But the surrounding fells provide an unforgettable backdrop that makes for a fine, inspiring vista.

It's a raw, boulder-strewn, long-grassed site, with private corners for sheltered pitching in among the crags and drystone walls. Weathered and worn, beaten and torn, the site merges seamlessly into the rugged landscape around. It's all pretty low-key: just turn up, pitch your tent, and someone will be round to collect your money in the morning or, if you're an early-bird walker, just drop by the house. It's as far off the beaten track as you can get, but thankfully you don't need a 4x4 to get here. Just remember to close the gates behind you as you journey back to civilisation.

COOL FACTOR A glorious wilderness among rocky crags and famous fells.

WHO'S IN? Tents, campervans, dogs, groups – yes. Caravans – no.

ON SITE Modern, clean facilities – separate toilet blocks (3W, 2M) and hot water for showers (3W, 3M – £1 for 4 minutes) and washing-up. You can buy eggs at the farmhouse; there's a post office and general store (01229 716255, www.ulphavillagestores.co.uk) 3 miles away in Ulpha. Bring midge repellent, sunscreen and waterproofs – it's not unusual to need all 3 in one trip. Off-ground BBQs fine; no campfires.

OFF SITE We suggest you enjoy some car-free time and just walk, walk, walk – the Dunnerdale Round (park near the old bridge in Ulpha) is a half-day circuit of the lesser-trodden local peaks. If you don't mind braving the zigzag Hardknott Pass, drive over towards Eskdale and visit the always-open Hardknott Roman Fort for some spectacular views and a bracing picnic site.

FOOD AND DRINK The Newfield Inn (01229 716208; www.newfieldinn.co.uk), 10 minutes' walk down the road in the hamlet of Seathwaite, has real ale, a real fire, and real hearty food. The nearest village is Broughton-in-Furness, 8 miles south, which, as well as pubs, a butcher and a greengrocer, has the excellent organic Broughton Village Bakery and Café (01229 716284; www. broughtonvillagebakery.co.uk), a finalist on TV's *Britain's Best Bakery*, no less.

GETTING THERE From Little Langdale, continue over the Wrynose Pass, and turn left for Seathwaite and the Duddon Valley. Turner Hall Farm is signposted on the left.

OPEN March–November, weather permitting.

THE DAMAGE Adult £6 per night; Duke of Edinburgh students £5; child £2; car £1; dog £1.

low wray

Low Wray, nr Ambleside, Cumbria LA22 0JA   01539 463862   www.ntlakescampsites.org.uk

A night or two next to England's largest lake is, we think, simply unforgettable. Low Wray sits on the quieter western shore of Lake Windermere, away from the fleshpots of Ambleside and Bowness and, if the weather holds, it can feel like the most relaxing place on earth.

As you'd expect from a National Trust site, it's well organised with good facilities, but it's not overly regimented. There are several camping areas, including an elevated meadow (open for a month only in summer) with big views, another patch in a clearing surrounded by trees, and – best of all – a spot right on the shore with sweeping views across the water. There's a surcharge for the lake-shore pitches (and a slightly longer walk from the car) but you'll go to sleep to twinkling stars and lights across the water and wake up with the promise of a bracing dip just steps from your tent. Glampers can also choose pods (book with the site) or yurts and tipis (outside providers), while children have the run of the woodland trails, an adventure playground and shallow lake-shore bays. Adventuring hereabouts is pretty much about the lake – lots of campers bring their own kayaks and inflatables – but a stroll up to wonderful Wray Castle is a must.

COOL FACTOR Unforgettable lakeside camping.

WHO'S IN? Tents, small campervans, dogs – yes. Caravans, groups – no.

ON SITE 110 tent pitches; 9 campervan pitches (no hook-ups); and 9 pods. Plentiful facilities in 3 blocks plus hot-water wash-up areas and laundry. Good site shop, gourmet food van, kids' playground, bike rental. BBQs off the ground; no campfires.

OFF SITE Wray Castle (see www.nationaltrust.org.uk), a short walk away, is great for families, and boats go from there to the Lakes Visitor Centre at Brockhole (01539 446601; www.brockhole.co.uk), and the terrific Treetop Trek (01539 447186; www.treetoptrek.co.uk).

FOOD AND DRINK Visit the foodie-fantastic world of Lucy's in Ambleside (01539 432288; www.lucysofambleside.co.uk) or the gastro-brewery heaven of the Drunken Duck (01539 436347; www.drunkenduckinn.co.uk).

GETTING THERE From Ambleside take the A593 to Clappersgate, turn left on the B5286, left again at the sign for Wray, and the site is on the left.

PUBLIC TRANSPORT Bus 505 from Ambleside drops you at the Wray turn-off, a mile from the site.

OPEN Easter–October.

THE DAMAGE Tent, adult and car from £8.25; extra adult £5.50; child £2.50; dog £1.50. More for lake-view or lake-shore pitches. Camping pods £30–£50.

great langdale

Great Langdale Campsite, Ambleside, Cumbria LA22 9JU   01539 463862   www.ntlakescampsites.org.uk

The perfect tonic for overwrought town-dwellers is an excursion into the serene valley of Great Langdale, overseen by two distinctive peaks – Pike O'Stickle and its neighbour Harrison Stickle, together known as the Langdale Pikes. They create a distinctive backdrop, forming part of a picture-perfect Lakeland scene as you twist and turn further into the valley; just as the road looks as if it might taper off into a narrow footpath, you'll find Great Langdale Campsite. This glorious National Trust site is set in a wooded glen at the head of the valley and consists of several small, grassy camping areas. It's typically well-organised, and includes a separate family field and children's playground.

Other private operators have glamping options on site (yurts and shepherd's huts), but Great Langdale rents out its own wooden pods – there's also a decent shop, a bread oven (for fresh bread and croissants in the morning) and a very handy drying room to stash walking clothes and boots. Cars aren't allowed in the camping areas, but none of the pitches is far enough for that to be a problem. As you would expect, the walking from here is first-class – you feel like you're in the true heart of the Lake District.

COOL FACTOR A tranquil treasure in the heart of classic Lake District scenery.

WHO'S IN? Tents, trailer-tents, campervans, organised groups, dogs – yes. Caravans, large parties – no.

ON SITE 220 tent pitches and 5 pods. 2 large shower-and-toilet blocks. Well-stocked shop; laundry facilities. Off-the-ground BBQs fine, but no campfires.

OFF SITE Easy walks around the valley shown on a map available from reception, while many visitors conquer the Langdale Pikes – the starting-point for which is just a few minutes' walk from the campsite.

FOOD AND DRINK Closest pub is the Old Dungeon Ghyll (01539 437272; www.odg.co.uk), famous for its Hiker's Bar. There's also the New Dungeon Ghyll (01539 437213, www.dungeon-ghyll.co.uk), and the Sticklebarn Tavern (01539 437356), the only National Trust-run pub in the country.

GETTING THERE From Ambleside take the A593 (Coniston Road) and veer right at Skelwith Bridge for Langdale, passing through Elterwater and Chapel Stile. The campsite's at the end of the road.

PUBLIC TRANSPORT The 516 bus from Ambleside stops a 5-minute walk from the site.

OPEN All year.

THE DAMAGE Pitch for 1 tent, 1 adult, 1 one car from £8.25; extra adult £5.50; child £2.50; dog £1.50. Pods £30–£50..

baysbrown farm

Baysbrown Farm Campsite, Great Langdale, Ambleside, Cumbria LA22 9JZ   01539 437150   www.baysbrownfarmcampsite.co.uk

Tourist traffic jams can be a bit of a problem in beautiful places, especially when the place is as enchanting as the Lakes. Fortunately, there is some respite from this mayhem in the lake-free valley of Great Langdale, at the heart of which serene Baysbrown Farm nuzzles up against a steep fell on one side while the other overlooks three generously sized camping fields that gently slope down to the valley's river.

The entire site lies beneath the humbling rocks of Crinkle Crags, Bowfell and the Langdale Pikes, which seem to swallow up your tent, the farmhouse, and distant Chapel Stile village, and give a sense of scale rarely found in the Lakes. Peering out each morning at the mist-shrouded peaks is worth the entrance money alone. You and your tent will be at the centre of an 800-acre farm. Baahs float over the lichen-drenched walls from the resident flock of sheep and chickens run amok around your guy ropes, much to the kids' delight.

Life is so much simpler here – as is the camping style. The site doesn't have any designated pitches; just rock up and find your corner of tranquillity. Then, when you're done putting up your tent, just walk up to the farmhouse to announce your arrival through the ever-open kitchen door and hand over your fee. There's no such thing as booking in advance here; it's not that kind of place. And, just like all Lake District sites, Baysbrown won't leave you short of things to do; grab a bike, put your boots on, or lie on the grass and stare at the peaks, thankful you're not stuck in the traffic for the Lakes.

COOL FACTOR Blissful Lake District chilling, minus the lakes and the congested roads.

WHO'S IN? Tents, small motorhomes/campervans/caravans (narrow site entrance with hump bridge so anything large or low won't fit), dogs (always under control) – yes. Large, loud groups – no.

ON SITE Approximately 200 first-come, first-served pitches. Facilities: solar-heated showers (5W, 5M), and separate toilet block (9W, 8M). Battery charging at the farm. It's a family-friendly place – no music, no noise or BBQs after 10.30pm. BBQs off the ground allowed. No campfires.

OFF SITE If you're not into hardcore hiking or valley strolls, you're probably staying in the wrong place – though even the resolutely unfit can manage the walk up the head of the valley to the Hiker's Bar at the Old Dungeon Ghyll inn (01539 437272; www.odg.co.uk). Otherwise, Ambleside and its many tea rooms, shops and attractions are a 20-minute drive away.

FOOD AND DRINK Open fires and real ales at the Langdale Estate's Wainwrights' Inn (01539 438088; www.langdale.co.uk), under a mile from the site; or another half-mile down the valley, at pretty Elterwater, the Britannia Inn (01539 437210; www.lakedistrictinn.com) is a classic Lakeland pub with good food and real ales.

GETTING THERE Take the A591 to Ambleside, then the B5343 to Chapel Stile. The campsite is signposted a mile past Wainwrights' Inn, on the left just outside Chapel Stile, form where it's a 5-minute drive down a largely unmade track. With satnav, use LA22 9JR.

PUBLIC TRANSPORT From Ambleside bus 516 will get you to Chapel Stile, ¼ mile walk from the site.

OPEN March–October.

THE DAMAGE Adult £5 per night; child £3, under-3s free; cars/campervans £2.50; dogs free. No credit cards.

wasdale head inn

Wasdale Head Inn, Wasdale Head, Gosforth, Cumbria CA20 1EX   01946 726229   www.wasdale.com

The only way you could actually camp closer to the Wasdale Head Inn would be to pitch your tent in the bar – they'd probably object to that, but the small wedge of green field just across the lane and over the stone wall is pretty good going. Time from tent flap to bar? Maybe 30 seconds – and it's not just any bar, either. As the historic birthplace of British mountaineering, the inn is a famously rugged and remote salute to all things daring and outdoorsy. Climbers and walkers head here year-round for a crack at England's most dramatic mountains, and the keenest of all have long eschewed the inn's cosy rooms (heating, beds, tea-making facilities? Pah!) for a first-come-first-served pitch at the back-to-basics campsite (previously run by the adjacent outdoor-gear-and-supplies Barn Door Shop, but now operated by the pub). It is what it is – a smallish section of field where you pitch where you can – but everyone squeezes in somehow, except perhaps on bank holiday weekends when there might be, literally, no room at the inn. Since the pub took over, camping facilities have been given a boost, namely the provision of three sparkly new toilets, a shower and a water-and-wash-up area, around the back of the inn. You can also get a bacon buttie and a cup of tea in the morning, and great meals in the evenings, but that's as far as it goes – families and glampers really should stay further down the valley at the nearby National Trust site. Here at the inn, everyone's tucked up in bed by 10pm, ready for the next day's assault on the stupendous tracks and peaks of Wasdale and beyond.

COOL FACTOR Awesome mountains, amazing pub – how many more facilities does a campsite need?

WHO'S IN? Tents (and small tents at that), well-behaved dogs – yes. Campervans, caravans – no.

ON SITE Variable number of pitches – there are no reservations, and the site's always open (well, it is just a field), but don't expect any of that six-metres-between-tents malarkey at busy times. Pitch up, then pay at the hotel reception; make sure you're out by 11am or you have to pay for another day. Facilities are new and modern: 2 toilets (1W, 1M), plus 1 disabled-access toilet with shower (hot showers £1); and there's a small washing-up area. No campfires, no BBQs.

OFF SITE Great big mountains (the Scafells, Great Gable, Lingmell, Pillar) are what you're here for, as well as England's deepest lake, Wast Water, whose headwaters lie a mile or so down the road from the inn.

FOOD AND DRINK Your own personal pub is right next door – the public bar at the Wasdale Head Inn (01946 726229; www.wasdale.com) is known as Ritson's Bar, after the pub's first landlord, and is a real climbers' and walkers' haunt, open every day of the year for weary walkers. As you might expect, meals are hearty affairs – all good home-cooked stuff, and with great local lamb and mutton when available – or you can go a bit more upmarket in the hotel dining room. The Barn Door Shop, next to the pub, sells hiking gear and supplies, including those crucial mountain nibbles – Kendal Mint Cake and fruit pastilles.

GETTING THERE From the A595, follow the signs for Santon Bridge or Gosforth, and then the signs for Wasdale Head. When you get to the inn, at the end of road, stop. You're there!

OPEN All year.

THE DAMAGE £5 per person per night.

wasdale campsite

Wasdale Campsite, Wasdale Head, Seascale, Cumbria CA20 1EX   01539 463862   www.ntlakescampsites.org.uk

England's highest mountains may not be on the scale of the Alps or the Himalayas, but they are majestic in their own understated way. They also have the advantage of being readily accessible and, in most seasons, relatively easy to conquer with the help of a pair of decent walking boots, clement weather and a thermos of hot tea.

Several of the country's highest mountains are clustered around the northern end of Wast Water in the Lakes, where the National Trust has thoughtfully sited a camping ground at Wasdale Head. It's not actually a lakeside site (though the water's not far away) – more the kind of place where you can lie in a sleeping bag, head poking out as the dawn mists clear, surveying the encircling slopes. It's a handy base for England's highest mountain, Scafell Pike, and you'll get plenty of advice at the site, where there's a small shop for walking maps and any gear that you might have forgotten – oh, and plasters. Three small fields scattered with trees provide plenty of flat grass for pitching and, with cars restricted to the parking areas, it's a peaceful site with a great family feel.

COOL FACTOR Wilderness location with breathtaking views of the high fells.

WHO'S IN? Tents, campervans, dogs (on leads at all times) – yes. Caravans, groups – no.

ON SITE About 100 tent pitches (4 with hook-ups); 8 campervan pitches with hook-ups; 7 pods with electric heaters and lighting. Timed barrier system for arrivals (8–11am; 5–8pm), though with an advance reservation you can get in any time. Hot showers, flush toilets, disabled facilities, washing machines and dryers. Small shop selling food and camping essentials. No campfires, no disposable BBQs.

OFF SITE Great family days out on the Ravenglass & Eskdale Railway (01229 717171; www.ravenglass-railway.co.uk) or at nearby haunted Muncaster Castle (01229 717614; www.muncaster.co.uk).

FOOD AND DRINK The Wasdale Head Inn (01946 726229; www.wasdale.com) is the hikers' and climbers' favourite; otherwise it's the Strands Inn (01946 726237; www.strandshotel.com), 5 miles back down the road to Gosforth.

GETTING THERE Approaching on the A595, turn right at Holmrook for Santon Bridge and follow signs to Wasdale Head.

OPEN All year.

THE DAMAGE Tent plus adult and car £8–£21. Extra adult £5.50; child £2.50; dog £1.50. Hook-ups £4. Pods £35–£50.

lanefoot farm

Lanefoot Farm, Thornthwaite, Keswick, Cumbria CA12 5RZ   01768 778097   www.stayinthornthwaite.co.uk

There's a pitch to suit all tastes at Lanefoot Farm. Love views? Park yourself in the big open field with a stonking vista of Skiddaw. Taking the kids? Head for the cosy family field. Seen the weather forecast and fancy a bit of shelter? Pop round the back of the farmhouse and find yourself a quiet spot among the wildflowers and trees.

Wonderfully amiable owners Gareth and Helen took over this campsite, in its little corner near Keswick, a few years ago and injected it with new life (and some free-range chickens). The facilities (constantly being upgraded) are the sort you'd be happy to eat your dinner off; there's a little shop on site, chickens roaming free, and a friendly atmosphere. Cyclists are well catered for – the site is bang on the C2C route and there are mountain bike trails aplenty in nearby Whinlatter Forest. And if you've turned up to discover you've forgotten to pack your tent (we've all done it!) there's a shepherd's hut for hire, as well as a couple of tree-shaded pods. Finally, for pub quiz devotees, nearby Bassenthwaite Lake is home to the vendace, Britain's rarest fish. Next question please, landlord!

COOL FACTOR Brilliant views, and wet-weather accommodation, too.

WHO'S IN? Tents, campervans, caravans, dogs (on leads), family groups, young groups (activities) – yes.

ON SITE Campfires allowed. Pitches: 50 tents, 12 caravans; 15 hook-ups. Good clean loos (3W, 3M) and 3 bright showers, washing-up area, drying room. Tiny shop sells basics and meats. There is some traffic noise.

OFF SITE Walks include popular local routes up Grizedale Pike and Skiddaw, while there's mountain bike rental and world-class trails at Whinlatter Forest (01768 778469; www.visitlakelandforests.co.uk).

FOOD AND DRINK The Coledale Inn (01768 778272; www.coledale-inn.co.uk) in Braithwaite is best for a post-Grizedale pint. If you scrub up nicely enough, there's classy dining not far from the site at the Pheasant Inn (01768 776234; www.the-pheasant.co.uk).

GETTING THERE From Keswick take the A66 west, turn left ½ mile after Braithwaite turning. The site is on the left.

PUBLIC TRANSPORT Train to Penrith, then bus X5 to just beyond Thornthwaite, then a couple of minutes' walk.

OPEN March–December (except Christmas week).

THE DAMAGE Adults £7.50–£8.50 per night, child £3.50. Shepherd's hut and pods £35–£40 per night.

side farm

Side Farm Campsite, Patterdale, Penrith, Cumbria CA11 0NP   01768 482337   andrea@sidefarm.fsnet.co.uk

Side Farm Campsite just might be one of the most scenically sited campsites on the planet. Located on the eastern side of the Lake District, it's comfortably sandwiched between the steep slopes of Place Fell and the restful shores of Ullswater – the second largest (after Windermere) but possibly most enchanting of the region's lakes. The view is one of the most compelling and beautiful sights in England, and simply to be able to open your tent every morning and look out is reason enough to stay a substantial while at Side Farm.

The family-run, working farm site is a decent, friendly place – simple, small and quiet, says the owner; so for lots of us, hanging out with a book, a beer – or both – and soaking up the magnificence of the surroundings is enough. However, others have something different in mind, from lake-larking on alluring Ullswater to bounding across the high fells. Plenty of people turn up with their own kayaks or dinghies, or – if you'd rather not get wet – you can take to the steamers that have been plying the waters here for well over a century. Piers at Glenridding, Howtown and Pooley Bridge let you plan one-way cruises and return walks, like the popular route from Howtown to Patterdale that would plonk you right back at the campsite. Or you might be tempted by the slopes of Helvellyn; all the routes up this 3000-foot monster are inspiring, but the one that everybody should attempt at least once is the nerve-jangling dance across the top of Striding Edge. Then you can return back to the flat, safe bounds of Side Farm – the simple site with one hell(vellyn) of a view.

COOL FACTOR Scenically perfect lakeside campsite with a phenomenal selection of nearby walks.

WHO'S IN? Tents, campervans, small motorhomes, dogs – yes. Caravans, large groups (unless pre-arranged) – no.

ON SITE Roughly 70 pitches spread out across the lakeside grass. 1 toilet block and 2 shower blocks (each with 2W, 2M), plus a washing-up area, 2 washing machines and 2 dryers. You can get a cuppa and a cake at the onsite tearoom. BBQs allowed off the ground. No campfires.

OFF SITE Lake cruises on Ullswater with Ullswater Steamers (01768 482229; www.ullswater-steamers.co.uk); the nearest pier is a mile or so up the road at Glenridding. Ullswater itself is ringed with attractions, from Aira Force waterfall to the Dalemain stately home (01768 486450; www.dalemain.com), while there's bike and boat rental at nearby St Patrick's Boat Landings (01768 482393, www.stpatricksboatlandings.co.uk).

FOOD AND DRINK The nearest pub to the farm (a 15-minute walk) is Patterdale's White Lion (01768 482214; www.thewhitelionpatterdale.co.uk), a straightforward hikers' pub (Patterdale is on the Coast-to-Coast walking route) with bar meals. Most other places are in Glenridding (a 20–30-minute walk or 15-minute kayak ride), including the bar and restaurant of the Inn on the Lake (01768 482444; www.lakedistricthotels.net/innonthelake).

GETTING THERE From junction 40 of the M6 take the A66 west, then the A592 along the shore of Ullswater, through Glenridding and Patterdale; after passing the White Lion, turn left for Side Farm.

PUBLIC TRANSPORT Both Penrith and Windermere have train stations. The 108 bus from Penrith runs through Glenridding to Patterdale. There's also the summer-season 508 to Patterdale from Windermere.

OPEN March–October.

THE DAMAGE Adult £8, child £3; car £2; no credit cards.

sykeside

Sykeside Camping Park, Brotherswater, Patterdale, Cumbria CA11 0NZ   01768 482239   www.sykeside.co.uk

Sykeside is one of those campsites that are all about the views. Situated in the midst and mists of the Lake District's Dovedale Valley and surrounded by the fells of Dove Crag, Hart Crag and Fairfield, it offers glorious mountain panoramas wherever you decide to pitch. Not only that, the Lakes themselves are enticingly close by, with unsung Brotherswater a short walk away and serpentine Ullswater four miles further away down the road.

Innumerable campers have been spilling into Sykeside's friendly embrace for over 35 years now. The current owners have been running the place for more than a decade and know a thing or two about how to run things efficiently. The valley campsite is hidden away down a private drive below the roadside Brotherswater Inn, and is fastidiously cared for, with neatly trimmed and well-nourished grass. If it sounds too manicured, one look up at the encircling fells puts everything into perspective – there's still a reassuringly natural, outdoorsy vibe, and as tent pitches are unmarked campers can choose their very own patch of grass on which to throw their canvas when they arrive.

The best place to pitch is on the terrace on the left-hand side of the site. As it's higher up it gives better views and stays relatively dry all year round (it's the only part of the site open to tents in the winter months), and as you can't take cars up the bank it's often quieter there in summer, too. (A word of warning, though: it's very occasionally reserved for the use of a school group.) Otherwise, you'll be able to park wherever you pitch – though after heavy rain the owners prefer to keep cars off the grass.

There's a wider-than-usual range of facilities, although the showers are shared with guests using the onsite bunkhouse. There's a well-stocked shop at reception, and – best of all – the campsite Barn End Bar (weekends and school holidays only). When the bar's not open you only have to walk up the drive to the onsite Brotherswater Inn. Energetic kids get the use of an entire spare field (except during lambing season), allowing plenty of space for running around and football games.

There are excellent hiking routes starting straight from the site, from easy strolls around Brotherswater – which is a relatively small and unknown lake, yet a favourite of Dorothy Wordsworth, no less – to more challenging ascents up the likes of Fairfield, Helvellyn and High Street. It's also easy to pick up the Fairfield Horseshoe ridge walk, ramble to Priest's Hole cave, or amble all the way to Ambleside. The road outside the site, meanwhile, goes in two directions – three miles up, to the top of Kirkstone Pass (where you can enjoy a pint or a afternoon tea at the agreeable inn there), or three miles down, to the lake at Ullswater. Here, you'll be able to catch a steamer from Glenridding to Howtown or Pooley Bridge, and then stroll back along the lakeshore – secure in the knowledge that, most weekends at least, you can recuperate later with your very own onsite, 100-yard pub crawl, from the Barn End Bar to the Brotherswater Inn.

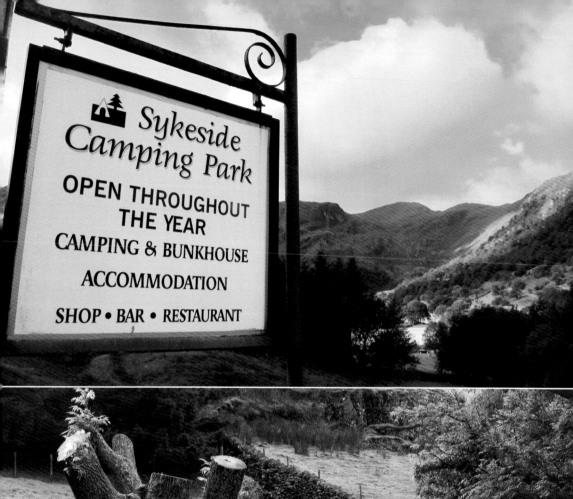

Sykeside
Camping Park
OPEN THROUGHOUT
THE YEAR
CAMPING & BUNKHOUSE

ACCOMMODATION

SHOP • BAR • RESTAURANT

COOL FACTOR Panoramic mountain views and great hiking action right in the middle of the Lakes.

WHO'S IN? Tents, campervans, caravans, motorhomes, dogs – yes. Groups of more than 6 adults (Duke of Edinburgh excepted) – no.

ON SITE Space for 80 tents, 19 motorhomes (with hook-ups), and 5 caravans (on a separate site). Toilet (6W, 4M) and shower (5W, 6M) facilities are clean and heated, but shared with the bunkhouse; shaving sockets and power points available in the shower block. There's also a laundry room (washing machines £3, dryers £1), dishwashing area (with freezer for ice packs), and a shop at reception (daily in summer, on request in winter) selling groceries and camping gear. As well as the Brotherswater Inn (open daily, except Christmas Day), the cosy Barn End Bar is open at weekends (Easter–Oct, plus throughout summer) for meals and drinks in the evening. Play facilities for kids are limited to an empty field. Off-ground BBQs are fine; no campfires.

OFF SITE Boat trips with Ullswater Steamers (01768 482229; www.ullswater-steamers.co.uk) from Glenridding (a 10-minute drive) are available all year round – leave your car at the pier car park for a day cruising and walking round the lake. Staying at Sykeside also gives you the opportunity to explore the lesser-visited eastern side of the Lakes – it's a 16-mile, 30-minute drive, for example, to the magnificent, mainly 19th-century Lowther Castle and Gardens (01931 712192; www.lowthercastle.org), Britain's largest castle and garden restoration project, currently being developed as a major tourist attraction. Lowther is also just south of the enjoyable market town of Penrith (market day is Tuesday), whose own castle lies in picturesque ruins, not far from the town's nice old centre of lanes and alleys.

FOOD AND DRINK The onsite Brotherswater Inn is a quintessential Lake District pub that offers decent grub, draught beer and B&B accommodation for any non-tenters. Otherwise the main local destination for eating and drinking is Ambleside, 7 miles away, up and over Kirkstone Pass, where there's the excellent Zeffirellis (01539 433845; www.zeffirellis.com), an Italian veggie pizza and pasta place with its own cinema and jazz bar. Head the other way, to Penrith, and you can drive to the Gate Inn at Yanwath (01768 862386; www.yanwathgate.com), a renowned gastropub showcasing the best in Cumbrian cuisine and beer. If you really want to push the boat out, the restaurant at the Sharrow Bay hotel (01768 486301; www.sharrowbay.co.uk), also towards Penrith, is Michelin-starred and very much a place for fine dining, despite their claims to have invented sticky toffee pudding! Pop in for afternoon tea if you don't fancy the full gourmet experience.

GETTING THERE From Windermere and the south, take the A592 towards the Kirkstone Pass and Ullswater – head over the pass and down the other side and you'll see the Brotherswater Inn on the left (turn into the pub car park – then drive through for the campsite). Coming from the north and the A66, take the A592 towards Windermere and the Kirkstone Pass – pass Ullswater, drive through Glenridding and Patterdale, and the entrance to the campsite is about 2 miles beyond Patterdale, on the right-hand side of the road, just before the Brotherswater Inn. If you miss this entrance, turn into the pub car park and go on through to the site that way.

PUBLIC TRANSPORT The nearest train station is Windermere (12 miles), from where you can pick up the Kirkstone Rambler (bus 508), which runs at weekends from Easter until October, and every day during the school summer holidays), and handily goes right past the campsite.

OPEN All year except Christmas Day.

THE DAMAGE Tent plus 2 people and a car £13.50–£23.50 (depending on season) per night; campervan (including 2 adults) £17.50–£25 per night; bunkhouse from £14.50 per bed.

hooks house farm

Hooks House Farm, Whitby Road, Robin Hood's Bay, North Yorkshire YO22 4PE   01947 880283   www.hookshousefarm.co.uk

Robin Hood's Bay, near Whitby in North Yorkshire, is an area steeped in romance and intrigue. Its very name is a mystery – there's nothing to link this place with the green-clad hero of Sherwood Forest – but what's certain is that this was once smuggler country: throughout the 18th century illicit gangs unloaded their wares at the water's edge and then used a network of safe houses and secret tunnels to deliver the stash inland. A 10-minute walk from Hooks House Farm and you're right in the heart of this old smugglers' haunt high above the bay, with its unfeasibly narrow streets, although these days you're more likely to stumble across a second-hand bookshop than hidden loot.

Up at the friendly, family-run campsite, the vibe is peaceful, relaxed and low-key – no long list of rules and regulations here. It is next to a road, but you're more likely to be bothered by the cries of seagulls and bleatings of sheep than by traffic. The views, meanwhile, are first-rate – you can watch the tide wash in and out along the whole sweep of shoreline, or gaze across a colourful patchwork of fields, woods, rolling hills and moors. The owners are famously attentive, ensuring that visitors have everything they need, although they can't help with what you mainly need to enjoy Robin Hood's Bay, namely plenty of puff to get up and down the steep hill every day. Although the local coastline is enormously picturesque, the rocky shore is more a rockpool and fossil-hunting kind of place rather than somewhere to sunbathe. Who knows, you might even turn up a forgotten piece of contraband?

COOL FACTOR Panoramic views over sea and moor from a peaceful, low-key site.

WHO'S IN? Tents, campervans, caravans, dogs – yes. Groups – no.

ON SITE Pitches for 75 tents and 25 campervans/caravans across a gently sloping field. A second field is used as a family play area. Facilities include 1 block with 6 showers and 8 toilets and another with 6 private cubicle washrooms; a further block has washing-up sinks, kettle, a microwave, fridge and freezers. Off-ground BBQs fine; no campfires.

OFF SITE The cobbled alleys of Robin Hood's Bay, and the coast, can easily take up most of your time, while Whitby is only 6 miles away. The 21-mile ex-Scarborough-to-Whitby train line runs through the upper village and makes a great hiking/biking route – bike rental from Trailways at nearby Hawsker (01947 820207; www.trailways.info).

FOOD AND DRINK The village has several pubs, including the harbourside Bay Hotel (01947 880278), a pint in which marks the traditional end of the long-distance Coast-to-Coast footpath. Whitby's Magpie Café (01947 602058; www.magpiecafe.co.uk) is considered one of Britain's best chippies. Fish foodies should also try Green's restaurant (01947 600284; www.greensofwhitby.com).

GETTING THERE Heading south from Whitby on the A171 take the B1447, signposted Robin Hood's Bay, and Hooks House Farm is on the right, half a mile before the village. Heading north, ignore the first 2 signs and take the B1447.

PUBLIC TRANSPORT Bus 93 runs between Scarborough and Middlesbrough, via Robin Hood's Bay and Whitby, and stops at the campsite gate.

OPEN 1 March–31 October.

THE DAMAGE Adult £7–£9 (depending on season) per night; child (3–15 yrs) £3; electric hook-up £3–£4 (depending on season).

hadrian's wall

Hadrian's Wall Campsite, Melkridge Tilery, nr Haltwhistle, Northumberland NE49 9PG   01434 320495
www.hadrianswallcampsite.co.uk

The 73 miles of Emperor Hadrian's monumental, Pict-proof stone wall is Northumberland's most famous landmark, and the most visible legacy of the Romans' extended holiday in Britain. You can see it from space with Google Earth if you zoom in close enough, and although its military barracks are long gone, the ruins of this historic structure remain impressively atmospheric. It's easy to imagine how the soldiers must have felt, keeping watch at what was – for them – the furthest outpost of the civilised world. They'd probably dreamed of leaving Dad's vineyard in Tuscany or Mum's riverfront villa in Rome, joining a legion and seeing the world. Instead they ended up here, looking out over mile after mile of Northumberland moor. The wall is now a World Heritage Site, and the good news is that you can still camp just a mile or so from one of the most dramatic sections, at Hadrian's Wall Campsite. The site is terraced on four levels, with top level 'Everest' commanding impressive views and the perfect sunset vantage point. In the summer months, an extra 'wild-camping' field is opened up, with oodles of space for large families. Weary backpackers can also rejoice: there's a strip dedicated entirely to accommodating your aching bones – no need to book, just stagger up on the day. The campsite is well located for walks along Hadrian's Wall Path, an 84-mile National Trail shadowing the line of the wall from coast to coast. The site-owners will even arrange transport to or from your start or finish points, leaving you free to enjoy your linear walk.

COOL FACTOR A stone's throw from Hadrian's Wall – but please don't.

WHO'S IN? Tents, campervans, caravans, dogs – yes.

ON SITE Terraced pitches; 7 hot showers, toilets, laundry and electric hook-ups. Disabled access and facilities. Basic provisions sold on site. Also a bunk barn sleeping 10. No campfires but BBQs with charcoal are available for hire for £5–£10, plus a refundable deposit (the cost depends on the size).

OFF SITE The Housesteads Roman Fort and Museum (01434 344363; see www.english-heritage.org) is just down the road, and the long-distance Hadrian's Wall Path (www.nationaltrail.co.uk/hadrianswall) passes nearby.

FOOD AND DRINK Given the remote location, it's best to come prepared, with lots of supplies. However, there is an onsite shop/café that offers cooked breakfasts and packed lunches, and if your evening's not complete without a pint and a packet of crisps, the Milescastle Inn (01434 321372) is a 15-minute walk back west along the old military road.

GETTING THERE Northeast of Haltwhistle, from the B6318 (Military Road), take the turning to Melkridge. The site is just 300 yards further on the left. From the A69, 1 mile east of Haltwhistle, there's a staggered crossroads at Melkridge village. Take the turning opposite the village and continue for 2 miles.

PUBLIC TRANSPORT The closest public transport goes to Haltwhistle, 3 miles away (either trains or the Arriva 685 bus from Carlisle to Newcastle). Ask nicely and the owners might collect you from there.

OPEN All year.

THE DAMAGE Backpackers £10. Tent and car £10–£15 (depending on size) plus £2.50 per person. Campervan plus 2 adults £15. Caravan plus 2 adults £20. Dogs £2.

demesne farm

Demesne Farm Campsite, Bellingham, Hexham, Northumberland NE48 2BS   01434 220258   www.demesnefarmcampsite.co.uk

Demesne Farm's patch of flat green farmland sits on the outskirts of the sleepy, blink-and-you'll-miss-it village of Bellingham which, just so as you know, is pronounced 'Belling-jum'. Don't ask why. Perhaps it's that, and the location of this rural retreat, right on the doorstep of the Pennine Way, which makes Demesne Farm such a unique place to camp. The site is first and foremost a haven for walkers and cyclists who, after a long day spent tackling the Pennines, may well be in need of a pastoral pillow on which to rest their weary heads, and a nice little village ('Belling-jum', remember) where they can put their feet up. It's only a short wander for a mug of hot cocoa and a sticky bun. The campsite isn't large – just one field given over to campers – but it feels bigger, as it looks out over a glorious expanse of rural England that glows golden as the sun falls: a heavenly view, whether you're a weary walker or not. Over the busy summer months an overflow field is opened to maintain the harmonious balance here, and there's a handy bunkhouse should you need it, or should the local weather turn sour. In nice weather, though, it's a great and authentic farm experience – really rustic with proper farmyard smells and lots of animals in residence. You'll notice that they're used to – and completely unperturbed by – the presence of campers, especially the inquisitive brood of chickens, who will scrabble around your guy ropes and take a peck out of everything in reach. But it's touches like these that make Demesne Farm such a firm favourite with all who visit there.

COOL FACTOR Rural comfort right on the Pennine Way's doorstep.

WHO'S IN? Tents, campervans, caravans, motorhomes, dogs (on leads) – yes. Single-sex groups – no.

ON SITE Approximately 30 pitches; separate male and female facilities with hot showers (50p for 6 minutes). Washing-up facilities and CDP. Campers have use of the drying room in the bunkhouse and there's a secure bike store, too. Quiet time 10.30pm–7.30am. BBQs allowed off the ground if cleared immediately afterwards. No campfires.

OFF SITE The closest and main attraction to the site is Kielder Water & Forest Park (01434 220616; www.visitkielder.com), which just happens to be the largest man-made lake and forest in Northern Europe. You can also wander the historic streets of Bellingham and Hexham, 10 miles south.

FOOD AND DRINK The picks of the pub crop in Bellingham are the Black Bull (01434 220226) and the Rose & Crown (01434 220202). Nearby Hexham's farmers' market has a BBQ-tastic selection of fresh organic meat and veg.

GETTING THERE Take the A6079 to Chollerford and then join the B6320 to Bellingham. In Bellingham, turn right at Lloyds TSB bank and the campsite is 100 metres down here on the right, just past the petrol station and the police station.

PUBLIC TRANSPORT From Hexham train station jump on bus 880 to Bellingham.

OPEN May–October.

THE DAMAGE 2 adults plus car and tent/campervan/caravan £14. Extra adult £6; child (5–15 yrs) £3, under-5s free. Hook-up £4. Bunkhouse £17 for adults/£13 for under-18s.

wales

campsite locator

ISLE OF
ANGLESEY

Liverpool .

. Beaumaris

123

122

Betws-y-Coed .

124

121

125

120

119

118

116

. Welshpool

117

Aberystwyth .

111

110

109

Cardigan .

103

104

102

112

. Hereford

97

David's

98

94 95 99

96

114

113

100

Carmarthen .

Monmouth .

105

101

. Tenby

108

107

115

106

. Cardiff

Bristol .

Bath .

Weston-
super-Mare .

Minehead .

campsites at a glance

For more options, including kid-friendly and cyclist-friendly campsites, please visit www.coolcamping.co.uk

porthclais farm

Porthclais Farm, Porthclais, St David's, Pembrokeshire SA62 6RR   07970 439310   www.porthclais-farm-campsite.co.uk

On arrival at Porthclais Farm, you're greeted by a five-day weather forecast – indicative of the outdoors life that you can lead here, as well as the helpful and informative approach of the owners. They know that people come here to enjoy everything that the Pembrokeshire coast has to offer, from walking the coastal path, to surfing, sailing, fishing, rockpooling and generally pottering around. From the site's lower fields there's only a gorse hedge between you and the coastal path, and the pretty harbour of Porthclais lies just at the bottom of the cliffs. Indeed, with so many enticing outdoor options available, and the cathedral city of St David's only about a 15-minute walk away – either back up the lane, or on a slightly longer route with a view, along the coastal path – you could easily ditch the car for the duration of your stay.

The site, too, has a lovely relaxed attitude, from where to pitch, to what you pitch. In high season it's a lively mix of family frame tents, one-person pop-ups, tipis, bell tents and volley ball/tennis nets. The only real rule is to set up camp 20 foot away from strangers and 10 foot from friends, but that's just a bit of good old common sense. The toilet and washroom facilities are extensive and very good but, if you're camping in one of the lower fields and don't want to get caught short, you may prefer to bring your own toilet tent, which is free of charge. There are no electric hook-ups but you're also welcome to bring your own generator or solar panels. So, all in all, a pretty perfect place to camp.

COOL FACTOR A big but intimate site with 180-degree views of a cracking coastline.

WHO'S IN? Tents, caravans, campervans, groups, dogs – yes.

ON SITE 5 fields covering 24 acres for tents and 1 field for 12 caravans and campervans. Phone charging £1. Freezer pack loan 20p (£1 deposit). 2 shower/toilet blocks with, for ladies 7 toilets, 3 hot showers (50p); for men 3 toilets, 2 urinals, 3 hot showers. 8 outdoor covered washing-up sinks and wetsuit washing tub. Recycling bins galore. No campfires, but BBQ stands can be hired for a one-off fee of £1.

OFF SITE Beaches, the sea, the Pembrokeshire Coastal Path. Visit the Lifeboat station at St Justinian (www.stdavids-rnli.org.uk) or there's the excellent Tyf adventure centre in St David's (01437 721611; www.tyf.com).

FOOD AND DRINK The campsite shop has daily fresh essentials, including milk, bacon and Welsh cakes. St David's has everything else you need, including a WI market on Thursday mornings, and pubs and cafés to suit all tastes and budgets, from the friendly Farmer's Arms (01437 721666; www.farmersstdavids.co.uk) to the more upmarket Cwtch Restaurant (01437 720491; www.cwtchrestaurant.co.uk).

GETTING THERE In St David's, go past the chemist (on your left), then down Goat Street and stay on this road for about 2 miles; look out for the Porthclais campsite entrance on your left, before the harbour.

PUBLIC TRANSPORT Train to Haverfordwest or Fishguard then a Richards Brothers bus (01239 613756) to St David's. 'Celtic Coaster' buses also run via St David's between June and September and will stop on request at Porthclais.

OPEN Easter–October.

THE DAMAGE Tents – adults £7, 5–13 years £3, under-5s free, dogs £2. Caravans/campervans – £18–£21 for 2 people.

caerfai bay

Caerfai Bay Caravan and Tent Park, St David's, Pembrokeshire SA62 6QT   01437 720274   www.caerfaibay.co.uk

Just before you reach the city of St David's, there's a small turning by the visitor centre, which morphs into a single-track lane and finishes at a small car park where the ground suddenly stops, quickly dropping down in a bundle of rocks and heather, a crash of sea spray and a shriek of circling gulls. It's a good spot for your first lingering look at the beautiful Pembrokeshire Coast, a designated National Park covering 240 square miles around the south-western shore of Wales. From here you can see both sides of the coast's character, from the gentle semicircle of Caerfai Bay – a small sandy beach that invites exploration of its rockpools and caves – while off to the right are the cliffs, intimidating and inspiring both in size and in structure. Handily enough, it's also an access point for the Pembrokeshire Coastal Path; and even more usefully, it's the site of the Caerfai Bay campsite.

Not to be confused with the Caerfai Farm campsite on the left side of the lane, Caerfai Bay is a more structured, organised sort of place, where they've made quite an investment into some spotless facilities. There are two tent fields, with nicely spaced grass pitches and a few hard-standing electric hook-ups, but you have to negotiate tarmac drives with speed bumps and pass through a field of caravans to get there. Not everyone's cuppa, and neither are the rules that come with the facilities, though it does make for a well-organised, serene camping experience. And once you're tucked up in your own tent, surveying the stunning views of the coastline, with the knowledge that you can have a free hot shower whenever you want, you'll be glad you pitched up.

COOL FACTOR Cliff-top camping with views to die for.

WHO'S IN? Tents, campervans, caravans, dogs (sometimes) – yes. Parties, groups, dogs in tent-field – no.

ON SITE 3 fields, 2 of which are given over to tents and campervans. Spotless toilet blocks, with free hot showers, baby changing, wetsuit and dishwashing area, recycling. There's also an amenities block with launderette, internet area, phone charging, tourist info, young children's play corner. Office sells camping gaz. No campfires.

OFF SITE As well as the beautiful beaches, you can do a jet boat trip to explore nearby Ramsey Island and the local wildlife (01437 721721; www.thousandislands.co.uk). For a day's cycling, sailing, fishing, and a kids' adventure playground, drive 15 miles to Llys-y-Fran Country Park (01437 532273). Also, about an hour's drive south is Pembrokeshire's zoo, run by TV's Anna Ryder Richardson (01646 651201; www.manorhousewildlifepark.co.uk).

FOOD AND DRINK The organic farm shop at Caerfai Farm, next door, is a great place for essentials and freshly cooked croissants for breakfast. St David's has lots of places to buy food including CK's supermarket, Peter's greengrocer and a butcher. The Grove Hotel (01437 720341; www. grovestdavids.co.uk) does good pub grub. For the best fish and chips head to The Shed at Porthgain.

GETTING THERE From Haverfordwest, take the A487 to St David's. Look out for the visitor centre on the left on the edge of St David's, and take the left just before it. After about ¾ mile, just before the cliff-top car park, make a right.

PUBLIC TRANSPORT Train to Haverfordwest or Fishguard and then a Richards Brothers bus (01239 613756) to St David's (about a 30-minute journey).

OPEN March–mid-November.

THE DAMAGE 2 people plus tent £12–£16.50, campervans up to £18.50.

caerfai farm

Caerfai Farm, St David's, Pembrokeshire SA62 6QT   01437 720548   www.caerfaifarm.co.uk

Caerfai Farm is one of the original pioneers of low-carbon camping. Indeed, this organic, family-run dairy farm has won awards aplenty for its eco-initiatives, for example the landmark wind turbine you pass on your way down the lane. However, you don't have to join the sandals and sackcloth brigade to camp here – it's a welcome-all, traditional campsite, with the usual scattering of tents, the odd campervan, buckets and spades, wetsuits and surfboards.

There are four fields, three of which look out to sea, with the best views had by those in the cliff field next to the coastal path. Yes, you are camping virtually on top of the Pembrokeshire coast, with the pretty little Caerfai Beach just a five-minute stroll down the cliff path. There are adequate washroom facilities here with solar heating, and a fantastic little farm shop that sells some outstanding local produce, including matured Caerfai Cheddar and Caerphilly cheese, all produced on the farm, so no unnecessary food miles. The morning croissant queues are legendary, with kids and adults alike racing back across the grass clutching brown paper bags to enjoy the warm contents with their morning cuppa.

It's an easy hop into St David's, and you're brilliantly placed to explore all the beautiful beaches that North Pembrokeshire has to offer. Do remember, though, that this is the edge of Wales, and glorious sunshine and pancake-flat seas can often be engulfed by howling wind and lashing rain. Regulars (of which there are many) tend to opt for sturdy tents and double-check their pegs and guy-ropes.

COOL FACTOR Low-carbon, cliff-top camping with magnificent views.

WHO'S IN? Tents, small campervans, dogs – yes. Caravans, groups – no.

ON SITE 4 fields, 1 with storm shelter. Water standpipes within 100m of each pitch. Mens and ladies toilet blocks with 1 shower each. 3 additional single showers, plus 2 family showers. Dishwashing room. Laundry room at the farm (across the lane). No campfires.

OFF SITE If you want an adrenalin rush or a soaking try TYF Adventure (01437 721611; www.tyf.com). Surfers should head to Whitesands Beach and wannabes can take lessons with the Ma Simes crew (01437 720433; www.masimes. co.uk). Oriel y Parc (www.orielyparc.org.uk) is a national treasure, especially on damp days, with an art collection, kids' craft days and a cool café.

FOOD AND DRINK The farm shop is packed to the brim with delicious organic produce, including the farm's own cheese, as well as the usual camping essentials. St David's has everything else you might want or need: the Sound Café (01437 721717) is popular with the surfy crowd and renowned for its great breakfasts and tapas evenings. For ice-cream lovers, it doesn't get much better than the gelato at The Bench (01437 721778), made from organic Caerfai milk.

GETTING THERE From Haverfordwest, take the A487 to St David's. Look out for the visitor centre on the left when approaching St David's and take the left just before it. Caerfai Farm is about half a mile down on the left.

PUBLIC TRANSPORT Train to Haverfordwest or Fishguard and Richards Brothers (01239 613756) run buses (about a 30-minute journey) to St David's to tie in with train arrivals.

OPEN May–end September.

THE DAMAGE £7 per adult, children 3–15 years £3.50, car-less adults £4.50, dogs £3. Electric hook-ups £3.

trellyn woodland

Trellyn Woodland Camping, Abercastle, Haverfordwest, Pembrokeshire SA62 5HJ   01348 837762   www.trellyn.co.uk

There's a spot at Trellyn – standing on the rickety wooden bridge, looking upstream as water fizzles and licks at the flow-smoothed stones below – where the woodland canopy overhead is so thick with branches and leaves that, even on the brightest days, the sunlight struggles to find a way in. The dappled yellow that does trick its way through the trees lights the woodland with a mystical hue, sprinkling special magic about the place. You might expect fairies or elves to peek out from behind a tree, do a little dance and disappear again. And, although on our last visit we didn't actually see any, it's impossible to rule it out completely. Trellyn is a magical place. It's calm and remote; a hidden woodland playground. And it's all down to two things – space and trees.

Trellyn stretches across 16 acres of beautiful Pembrokeshire woodland but boasts just five camping pitches, a tipi, a couple of yurts and two new geodomes. That's it. So per pitch that's, er, a lot of space, and a lot of trees. Even calling these 'pitches' is a gross misrepresentation. They're clearings, pockets of solitude carved out of the woodland and furnished with a picnic table, campfire area and full field kitchen. A field kitchen, for those of you that don't know, is a canvas lean-to equipped with gas stove, cooking apparatus, drinking water and all the other paraphernalia required to cook. It's also a stroke of genius, allowing you to cook outside in all weathers and to be creative with your camping meals instead of huddling over a tin of baked beans on a gas burner in the rain. As if that's not enough, there's also the fact that, when you arrive, you'll have a basket of pre-cut wood and kindling all ready and waiting for you, and – even better – when that runs out, you're free to grab the axe and raid the woodshed, chopping down the big old logs and pretending you're Ray Mears. For those camping in the tipi, yurts and domes, raised wooden floors have been built, providing a more comfortable experience, with beds and futons. Rugs, cushions and sheepskins add to the homely ambience, but unlike other more authentic (and smoky) tipi experiences, there is no internal log fire. A wood-burning stove is provided in the yurts and domes for warmth and general cosiness, while tipi-dwellers have the outside campfire and field-kitchen options. Two sociable additions to Trellyn are an outdoor pizza oven – lit when the campers all feel like a get-together, and a wood-fired sauna, for a really relaxing end to the day.

The almost-coastal location of Trellyn means it's a perfect base to explore the attractions of Pembrokeshire. Numerous beaches are just a short drive away, and Abercastle Beach, with its low-tide sand and rockpools, is 100 metres from the campsite. And while there is plenty to do in the area, the best evenings are to be had around the campfire. When *Cool Camping* first discovered this place in 2006, we wrote about how refreshing it was to find such a steadfastly uncommercial campsite and how rare such beautiful, chilled-out woodland sites are. Since then, we've visited hundreds of other campsites and covered just about every inch of Wales hoping to find an equal to the Trellyn experience. We've failed. Trellyn wins. And very good luck to them.

COOL FACTOR Woodland, fires, space, trees and owners who care.

WHO'S IN? Tents, glampers, groups, caravans, campervans – yes. Dogs – no.

ON SITE Campfires allowed. There are 5 tent pitches, each nestled in a shady glade with a campfire, table and grill, plus shared toilets. For more home comforts book 1 of the 2 painted yurts, 1 dragon-painted tipi and 2 geo domes. The paintings are by Pembrokeshire's Jackie Morris – well known author and illustrator – and add to the magical atmosphere at Trellyn. The domes are a new addition – and made from recycled bottles and the timber from a kitchen manufacturer. But rustic they are not: think something from a *Dr Who* set on the outside, with a greenhouse sort of warmth within. Shared facilities for the whole site are immaculately clean, with solar-heated showers, washing-up facilities, toilets, power supply for charging torches and so on. 2 communal freezers and a fridge with ice packs. There's also a huge supply of beach equipment, including fishing nets, surfboards and wetsuits, lent out on a fair usage basis. Electric hook-ups available. Bedding supplied in the yurts and domes, but not the tipi.

OFF SITE Abercastle Bay is only 100 metres from Meadow pitch and then you have the whole of the North Pembrokeshire coast to explore, with its stunning beaches, coves and cliff walks. For trips around Ramsey Island (for seal, dolphin and bird spotting) take a large speedboat with Voyages of Discovery (01437 721911; www.ramseyisland.co.uk). Surf lessons can be booked and equipment hired at Ma Simes in St David's (01437 720433; www.masimes.co.uk). Adrenalin addicts should seek their thrills with Preseli Venture (01348 837709; www.preseliventure.co.uk) or TYF (01437 721611; www.tyf.com), who offer coasteering experiences – where you leap off cliffs into the sea. And for those who are keen on iconic Welsh design, why not visit Melin Tregwynt, a traditional mill, shop and café (01348 891288; www.melintregwynt.co.uk)

FOOD AND DRINK Kev and Claire often put out home-grown veg (yours for a small donation) and their son Matt can provide fresh, locally caught crab and lobster – and he'll even teach you how to cook it, if you want. The Farmer's Arms, up the hill at Mathry (01348 831284; www.farmersarmsmathry.co.uk), and in the opposite direction the Ship Inn at Trevine (01348 831445; www.shipinntrefin.co.uk), are good local pubs, both serving decent pub food. Popular Porthgain Harbour has the evocative Sloop Inn (01348 831449; thesloop.co.uk), which does food, as well as an award-winning seafood restaurant, The Shed (01348 831518; www.theshedporthgain.co.uk). It's a tad expensive and in summer you'll need to book, but the food is great. There's a convenience store at the petrol station at Square and Compass, and St David's and Fishguard have all the food shops that you'll need – from butchers, greengrocers, delis and booze shops to small supermarkets.

GETTING THERE At Mathry (on the road between St David's and Fishguard), turn right just after The Farmers Arms pub and follow the signs for Abercastle. After exactly 1.8 miles you will see the campsite sign and entrance on the left-hand side. If you get as far as the Abercastle village sign, you have gone roughly 100 yards too far.

PUBLIC TRANSPORT Get the train to Fishguard, then the Strumble Shuttle bus, a reliable service that passes the end of the driveway.

OPEN End May–early September (yurts, tipi and domes stay open until the end of September).

THE DAMAGE Weekly bookings only. Camping from £230; tipi from £450; dome from £510; yurt from £565, all per week. Campers must also be members of the Camping and Caravanning Club; non-members can join on site for £40.

ty parke farm

Ty Parke Farm Camping, Parke, Llanreithan, St David's, Pembrokeshire SA62 5LG   01348 837384   www.typarke.co.uk

After deciding they liked the idea of opening a campsite on their farm in the western wilds of Pembrokeshire, Gary and Annie Loch thought long and hard about what kind of site they would wish to stay on, and then they executed it perfectly. Firstly, they were determined to create space for campers to breathe, both spiritually and physically; and the experience had to reflect the original essence of camping – allowing you to be more directly involved with the natural world, with everyone gathered around the fire at night gazing into the flames to a soundtrack of wild creatures. Plus the site reflects their deep commitment to sustainability, with energy provided by wind turbines and solar panels, and much else besides.

The effort to create this natural camping experience has resulted in Ty Parke having just 10 pitches in a space where a hundred might take up residence on other sites, and those nighttime sounds come from their adjacent five-acre Nature Trail, where badgers and foxes warily wander. Ty Parke also offers three yurts for campers who either want something even more authentic, or just don't want to be bothered with tent pegs. Each comes with a wood-burning stove and their own camp kitchen, plus a double bed and two single futons, so they're perfect for young families. Whatever you choose, you're sure to enjoy the experience of this wonderful site: the Pembrokeshire Coastal Path is a short drive away, there are some great cycle rides nearby and the location is perfect. Ty Parke is camping as it should be, with the wilds pushing in around the edges, though without the hardships.

COOL FACTOR Peaceful rural location with acres of space.

WHO'S IN? Yurts, tents, small groups, boats, surfboards – yes. Caravans, campervans, big groups, dogs – no.

ON SITE Campfires allowed. 10 pitches, including 5 'Hideaway' pitches spread out over 30 acres. Each has own firepit and picnic table (there's also a covered cooking/eating area). Drinking water taps in all fields. 2 immaculate family-type washrooms with toilets and free showers, laundry, 2 fridges, a chest freezer, and an electric kettle. The 2 'hideaway' yurts also have their own compost loo. A nature trail snakes around a 5-acre site – part of a 52-acre smallholding. Look out for buzzards, foxes, owls and sheep.

OFF SITE Hire a bike from Pembrokeshire Cycle Hire (www.pembrokeshirecycletours.co.uk) or fulfill an adrenalin rush (coasteering, surfing, kayaking) with Preseli Venture (01348 837709; www.preseliventure.co.uk).

FOOD AND DRINK Eggs and mackerel (in season) are available at the farmhouse. St David's has a small supermarket, CK's, a butcher, greengrocer and deli, as well as many eateries, including the popular new Sound Café (01437 721717). The Farmer's Arms at Mathry (01348 831284; www.farmersarmsmathry.co.uk) is a village local and serves good food. Perhaps best for a pint with a view is the Sloop Inn at Porthgain (01348 831449; thesloop.co.uk).

GETTING THERE The campsite doesn't accept drop-in bookings, so please call for directions. There are signs in the bank and on the gate that say 'PARKE' not 'TY PARKE'. Proceed up the long, bumpy track and follow the signs.

OPEN May–mid-September.

THE DAMAGE Tent pitch £24 per night for a tent and 2 adults; additional adults (over 14 years) £12; children (5–14 years) £6; under-5s free. Camp firewood £3 per very generous tub-load. Yurts from £225 for a weekend break.

Please call at house before pitching your tent

newgale

Newgale Camping Site, Newgale, Haverfordwest, Pembrokeshire SA62 6AR   01437 710253   www.newgalecampingsite.co.uk

About halfway along the stretch of road from Haverfordwest to St David's the road takes a steep dive down to the coast, to the stunning beach that is Newgale. Surfers, kayakers, windsurfers and kite-surfers dot the bright water, families spread out on the sand, and a large field 30 seconds across the road is home to the campsite where many of these people are staying. The campsite is pretty basic – a largely flat, virtually treeless field, with just a low bank separating it from the adjoining A487, from where there's a pretty constant hum of traffic noise. But the location this close to Newgale and the delights of the Pembrokeshire coast is otherwise pure heaven on a hot sunny day (although it can get waterlogged in extreme wet weather), and there's a great surfer vibe in the evenings when everyone's waxed their boards and hung up their wetsuits. If you don't have any of the kit and fancy a go, you can hire everything you need from the Newsurf Beach Shop next to the site. When the weather's fine and you can see the sea shimmering from your pitch, there's no place like it. No surprise, then, that people come back for more, year after year.

COOL FACTOR Camping next to one of Pembrokeshire's best surfing beaches.

WHO'S IN? Tents, campervans, groups – yes. Caravans, young groups, dogs – no.

ON SITE BBQs allowed, but not campfires. Facilities block has 10 toilets and 8 hot showers, with showers for wetsuits behind. Newsurf Beach Shop next door sells essentials.

OFF SITE The harbour village of Solva is 4 miles north-west, and St David's a further 4 miles on, with its cathedral and other attractions. Go horse riding on the beach with Nolton Stables (01437 710360; www.noltonstables.com).

FOOD AND DRINK The Duke of Edinburgh pub right next door is nothing special but has a nice outside terrace. The quirky Druidstone Hotel (01437 781221; www.druidstone. co.uk) is worth the drive; a friendly bar with views and good home-cooked food.

GETTING THERE From Haverfordwest, take the A487 west for 8 miles towards St David's; watch out for the beach (you can't miss it) and the campsite is on the right.

PUBLIC TRANSPORT Trains run to Haverfordwest, from where the regular St David's bus stops at Newgale.

OPEN March–September.

THE DAMAGE £7 for adults and children over 12, children (4–11) £3 per night; no advance bookings accepted.

bower farm

Bower Farm, Little Haven, Pembrokeshire SA62 3TY   01437 781554   www.bowerfarm.co.uk

The Bower Farm campsite is a simple field with simple facilities and the most stunning view. If you want to wake up to the call of farm animals and the distant sound of the sea, this is the perfect spot. The sea you're overlooking is St Bride's Bay and the beach Broad Haven which, when the tide is out, offers a beautiful expanse of golden sand, flanked by low cliffs with rockpools to explore. In the distance you'll also be able to see the unspoilt wildlife reserve islands of Skomer, Ramsay and Grassholm.

The site is a family-run place, an offshoot of the farm's popular B&B, and the field they've given over to it is fantastic – very large, with electric hook-up pitches along the top of the ridge and a few tent pitches mown into the grass, sheltered by a hedge at the bottom. As well as being one of the best, Broad Haven is also one of the more accessible beaches in Pembrokeshire, but if you want somewhere quieter you're well placed to take advantage of all of the North (up towards St David's) and South Pembrokeshire coastline, and the variety that it has to offer – from coastal walks, cycling routes, beaches, outdoor adventures and indoor castles.

COOL FACTOR A simple farm field with a stunning view.

WHO'S IN? Tents, campervans, caravans, dogs, horses – yes.

ON SITE 5 pitches, 3 with electric hook-ups. Basic, but perfectly good facilities include a water pipe in the field and 2 toilets and a shower just outside. Enjoy the small working farm with its many animals. If you have your own horse or dog, they're welcome to stay too.

OFF SITE Apart from the beaches there are lots of opportunities for activities, including horse riding on the beach from Nolton Stables (01437 710360; www. noltonstables.com), river and sea trips from Dale Sailing (01646 603110; www.dalesailing.com) and windsurfing from Haven Sports (01437 781354; www.havensports.com).

FOOD AND DRINK Little Haven, 5 minutes' drive away, has the Swan Inn (01437 781880; www.theswanlittlehaven. co.uk), where you can enjoy delicious food and drink on the harbour wall, or by the fire when it's colder.

GETTING THERE From Haverfordwest take the B4341 towards Broad Haven. After passing through Broadway (about 5 miles) take the single-track road on the corner (signed Little Haven). Bower Farm is first on the right.

OPEN March–October.

THE DAMAGE £25 per pitch per night.

new shipping farm

New Shipping Farm, West Williamston, Kilgetty, Pembrokeshire SA68 0TN 01646 405011 www.campingpembrokeshire.net

New Shipping campsite is a great little spot, situated in a fab location. Initially, its pitches may look like one serried rank, but each of the 12 nicely spaced areas has been created that way for a reason – so that no one can spoil any one else's view. And when you see this you'll very much appreciate this attention to detail, feasting your eyes on the beautiful Cleddau River, with Carew Castle to the south, all surrounded by beautiful countryside.

If you've got a boat, or love walking or cycling, you could easily enjoy a holiday here without going near your car. There's a path from the campsite to Carew Castle and Mill and on to the Pembrokeshire National Park Coastal Path, part of which is stile-free, allowing easy access for everyone. The cycle route starts around the corner, too. As well as being flanked by the river, the site is surrounded by fields of grazing sheep and horses, and is a terrific twitchers' hangout, with regular sightings of kites. Since it's in Pembrokeshire, you're never far away from a beautiful beach, the closest of which include Freshwater West for watersports, Bosherston for swimming and sand dunes, and Tenby for miles of space, complemented by a buzzing seaside town.

COOL FACTOR A small, discreet site with unspoilt views over the Cleddau River.

WHO'S IN? Tents, campervans, caravans, dogs – yes.

ON SITE 12 pitches, some with electric hook-ups. 1 shower, basin and toilet for ladies and the same for gents. Plus an extra ladies toilet at the farmhouse. Fridge, book-swap and internet access in the office. No campfires.

OFF SITE Take a boat trip to Caldey Island from Tenby (www.caldey-island.co.uk) to see the famous monastery. Carew Castle (01646 651782) and Pembroke Castle (01646 684585) are both worth a visit.

FOOD AND DRINK The Carew Inn (01646 651267; www.carewinn.co.uk), is a good pub for food and drink, a 10-minute walk from the site. For shopping, head to the foodie haven of Narbeth and try the delicious Ultracomida deli (01834 861491; www.ultracomida.co.uk).

GETTING THERE At Carew, turn on to the A4075 towards Haverfordwest. After ½ mile cross Carew bridge and turn left towards West Williamston. The campsite is on the left.

OPEN All year.

THE DAMAGE £11.50 per pitch, £13.50 for an electric hook-up for up to 4 people. Extra children £1.50, extra adults £3.50. Dogs and awnings free. Non-members of Caravan and Camping Club can join on site for £40 per year.

north lodge eco camp

North Lodge Eco Camping, Blaenffos, Boncath, Pembrokeshire SA37 0JE   01239 841401   www.eco-camping.co.uk

You are likely to be greeted by sheepdogs Beau and Luke and/or a clutch of rescue chickens as you drive into North Lodge, an unassuming little campsite in the grounds of the former Pant-y-Deri Estate and in the shadow of the Preseli Hills. It consists of a selection of unmarked but secluded pitches set between rhododendron bushes and high hedges, overseen by site owners Jane and Martin Callaby, who make sustainability and recycling a central tenet of the North Lodge experience. That said, the welcome is warm and friendly and above all there's a genuine laidback feeling to the site.

What is especially nice about this part of Pembrokeshire is that the guidebooks and tourist brochures generally overlook it in favour of the more high-profile coastline. Yet you're within easy reach of both Cardigan Bay and the Pembrokeshire coast (one of the most spectacular sections of which is a short drive away), tucked among woods, fields and hedgerows that make up a classic rural Welsh landscape. We think you will find it hard to resist the temptation to walk in the blue-shadowed Preseli Hills in the near distance, from the summits of which you can see most of West Wales on a clear day.

COOL FACTOR Unassuming small site tucked away in one of the least-visited corners of Pembrokeshire.

WHO'S IN? Tents, campervans, small tourers, dogs, families, groups – yes.

ON SITE Communal campfire; pitch campfires allowed at owners' discretion. 10 pitches, 1 hook-up; 'eco-cabin' for up to 5 people with woodburner. Basic but clean washrooms and a shower, 3 loos (2 compost) and communal cooking area. There are pre-erected tents for lazy campers; B&B also available.

OFF SITE Nearby Cenarth has lovely waterfalls and a good selection of pubs/tea rooms as well as the National Coracle Centre (01239 710980; www.coraclemuseum.co.uk). Wales' biggest and best-preserved Neolithic dolmen, Pentre Ifan, is a few minutes' drive away.

FOOD AND DRINK Best option is the Boncath Inn (01239 841241), less than a 5-minute drive away, a traditional pub offering decent pub grub and ales. Just down the coast at Newport, the Cnapan Restaurant (01239 820575; www.cnapan.co.uk) is one of the best eateries in Pembrokeshire.

GETTING THERE The site is on the south side of the B4332, midway between Eglwyswrw and Boncath.

OPEN All year.

THE DAMAGE From £15 per tent for 2 people; set-up tents from £30 per night; eco-cabin from £40; B&B from £55.

ty gwyn farm

Ty Gwyn Camping and Caravan Park, Mwnt, Cardigan, Ceredigion SA43 1QH   01239 614518   www.campingatmwnt.co.uk

Did you ever wonder how *Cool Camping* selects the sites that our team of camping sleuths visit? How one gets the nod and another doesn't? Well we put our heads together and shake out all the years of accumulated camping knowledge first. Then we check out all the hundreds of recommendations sent in by our keenest Cool Campers. Finally we assemble a list of 'possibles'. Then one of our number (the youngest one) trawls the Internet day and night searching for new or previously unknown sites and adds them to the list.

Usually this covers all the possibles, probables and maybes, but in the case of Ty Gwyn, it was nothing to do with any of this. Instead, our oldest and grumpiest correspondent took a dip in the sea at Mwnt, near Cardigan, one day and, after a relaxing swim, went for a walk on top of the airy headland, which provides a spectacular view of the coast north around Cardigan Bay. He was thinking that this may very well be one of the most gorgeous places on the planet. As he scanned the scene he noticed a few static caravans gathered around the nearest farm and, perched on the cliffs just a few hundred metres from the most beautiful beach in Wales, a tiny, single green tent. He felt like he had struck gold, for what he was looking at was Ty Gwyn, a beautiful site close to a stunning beach that none of us had heard or read about. 'There must be a catch' he thought, and so dashed off to interrogate the owner, Martyn Evans, who let him stay and sample the delights of Ty Gwyn first-hand.

Ty Gwyn campsite is part of a farm that occupies a remarkable tract of land that plunges suddenly into the blue dolphin-filled waters of Cardigan Bay, far below. Martyn is the latest member of the family to farm here, and allows campers to share this remarkable place with him. Mwnt's combination of blue-green seas, golden sands, imposing cliffs and even a small, perfectly proportioned whitewashed chapel sitting high above the bay is perfect – even more so when the sun sets spectacularly over the ocean. There isn't a lot to do nearby, but that's the point, and indeed the most obvious activity, other than lazing on the beach or just gazing out to sea, is to follow the Ceredigion Coastal Path, which runs right through the farm's land, either south to Cardigan or – even better – north up to Aberporth, edging the top of the cliffs.

There has never been any attempt to cash in on the location by advertising, nor any other sort of promotional push. So Ty Gwyn, and its simple pleasures of living in the great outdoors in the most sublime of settings, remains relatively unknown. However, even if half of humanity did arrive one day, the way the Evans' have set things up ensures that the uncrowded feel of the site prevails, with just the edges of many, many acres of working meadow mown for camping. Not everyone will love the lack of traditional campsite facilities, but Martyn doesn't necessarily want to become too popular and will limit numbers, if need be, to preserve the idyllic nature of the place. Hallelujah!

COOL FACTOR Almost the antidote to organised campsites, close to the most beautiful beach in Wales, where dolphins may sometimes be seen up close. Absolute tranquillity.

WHO'S IN? Tents, campervans, dogs, caravans – yes. Big groups – no.

ON SITE Campfires allowed, preferably off the ground. 30 pitches, 6 hook-ups, tidy toilet block with 4 ladies and 2 gents toilets and 2 male and 2 female showers (free) plus disabled shower facilities and baby-changing facilities. Dishwashing lean-to, which is pretty basic. Ice packs frozen (50p). Some campers may not like the unconventional land management, which places the facilities quite a long way from certain pitches, and the prows of statics in the top field.

OFF SITE Really the main thing is the location. There is direct access to the Ceredigion Coastal Path (www. ceredigioncoastpath.org.uk), which runs from Cardigan in the south to Ynys-Las, just beyond Aberystwyth, in the north – a length of around 60 miles in all. Then there's Mwnt beach, which is lovely, but not the only great beach in the area, whose number includes the sandy cove at Tresaith, the National Trust beach at Penbryn and the more developed stretch of sand at pretty New Quay. Beaches aside, a car will have to be utilised to find wet-weather entertainment. Nearest is the Rainforest Centre at Felinwynt (01239 810250; www.butterflycentre.co.uk), where the grandiose title translates into a very large greenhouse full of butterflies and moths. Cardigan is only a few miles away, while the reconstructed Iron-Age settlement at Castell Henllys (01239 891319; www.castellhenllys.com) is a few miles beyond Cardigan. There's also the Welsh Wildlife Centre (www.welshwildlife.org) just outside Cardigan, which organises trips to Ramsey Island (01437 721423; www. ramseyislandcruises.co.uk). The Solva Woollen Mill (01437 721112; www.solvawoollenmill.co.uk) and the Palace cinema in Haverfordwest (01437 767675; www.palacehaverfordwest.co.uk) are also options if you don't mind the drive.

FOOD AND DRINK First thing to say is bring copious supplies, as there are no shops nearby. The closest place to eat is the Flat Rock Bistro at Gwbert Hotel (01239 612638; www.gwberthotel.net), 4 miles away, which offers posh nosh with a fantastic view. Or take a drive to dinky little Porthgain Harbour for lunch at the Sloop Inn (01348 831449; sloop.co.uk).

GETTING THERE From Cardigan take the B4548 towards Gwbert, and after 1 mile turn right into a lane, then after 2 miles turn right then immediately left on to a narrow lane to Mwnt. Continue past the beach car park to Ty Gwyn.

PUBLIC TRANSPORT There is a year-round Cardi Bach bus which stops in Mwnt; otherwise buses service Cardigan and Aberporth, from where you can get a taxi.

OPEN Early April–late October.

THE DAMAGE £12 for up to 2 people, extra person £2. Hook-ups £2. Dogs free.

cwrt hen

Cwrt Hen Farm, Beulah, Newcastle Emlyn, Ceredigion SA38 9QS   01239 811393/07811 239768   www.cwrthen.co.uk

Cwrt Hen is no-frills camping at its best; a relaxed, friendly site with a great atmosphere engendered by the affable hosts Gill Baldwin and Chris Cordy, who will be delighted to book you in, show you to your pitch and then talk the pants off you (in the nicest of ways) every time you bump into them. The pride they have in their simple site is obvious – they describe it quite accurately as a 'rustic dog-friendly hideaway' – yet despite Cwrt Hen being tucked away in the heart of the Ceredigion countryside, you're within easy reach of plenty of the county's gems, especially Cardigan Bay.

Nature is allowed to run riot at Cwrt Hen, except in the onsite market garden, whose produce you can buy for campfire meals. The various ponds that fringe the site are left to their own devices, and are home to frogs, toads and newts, and you can also fish for trout. The meadows and woodlands that surround the site are home to badgers, otters, bats and owls, and there's a resident population of ducks and two farm dogs. Indeed, animals are so much a part of the scene here that while well-behaved dogs are allowed to roam around off the lead, children must be booked in in advance.

COOL FACTOR Dog – and animal – heaven.

WHO'S IN? Tents, campervans, dogs (horses and children by arrangement), touring caravans – yes. Groups – no.

ON SITE Campfires allowed. 10 tent pitches, 5 hook-ups. 1 clean and tidy shower block, with 2 toilets and 2 showers (free). Ice packs frozen, phones charged (free). Free-range eggs, fruit and veg available on site. Only downside is that it's a little difficult to find, but maybe that's a plus too?

OFF SITE Cenarth Falls and its salmon leap, and the National Coracle Centre (01239 710980; www.coraclemuseum.co.uk), are just a couple of miles away. Aberporth beach is 15 minutes' drive west and is a great place for kids to play safely in the sea. It's also dog friendly.

FOOD AND DRINK The Ship Inn in Aberporth (01239 810822) does good food, and is next door to the Caffi Sgadan restaurant (01239 811003), which does great fish and chips. In Cenarth the White Hart does decent food (01239 710305).

GETTING THERE Head for Beulah on the B4333 north of Newcastle Emlyn. The site is signposted, but if you get lost just call the site and Gill or Chris will come out and find you.

OPEN All year.

THE DAMAGE Flat rates of £12 per pitch for up to 6 people, £15 with hooks-ups. £15/£18 in August and on bank holidays.

faerie-thyme

Faerie-Thyme, Crwbin, Kidwelly, Carmarthenshire SA17 5DR   01269 871774   www.faerie-thyme.co.uk

Irene and Wish moved over five years ago to this three-acre smallholding in Crwbin, with one aim in mind: to create a campsite that they would like to go back to themselves. They have since made a place where imagination rules and although children aren't allowed everyone is encouraged to nurture their inner child. Have you walked the plank aboard the *Jolly Roger* recently? No, we didn't think so. Well, here you can.

Fun and games aside, Faerie-Thyme is like the best part of a festival's green field, whether you're chilling out by giant dream-catchers or around one of the site's many firepits. And, like Glastonbury, ley lines snake back to a wizard heritage – nearby Myndd LLangyndeyrn is rumoured to be the birthplace of Merlin. If this all feels a bit far-out then bear in mind that Faerie-Thyme was made 'members' recommended best site' by the UK Camping and Caravanning Association – proof that that this place is accessible and well-run as well as being unique and idiosyncratic. It's not for everyone, and you have to buy into Irene and Wish's vibe – but they're so open and friendly that it's impossible for you not to slip under their spell.

COOL FACTOR A truly magical place that will spirit you away from your troubles.

WHO'S IN? Tents, campervans, caravans – yes. Dogs, children, big groups, young groups (under-25s) – no.

ON SITE Campfires allowed in firepits, 6 electric hook-ups and Katie the Caravan for those who want a more comfortable stay. There is a wet room with free showers and the toilets are compost loos. Onsite honesty shop to buy logs, kindling and Irene's handcrafted mementoes.

OFF SITE You'd be daft not to visit the standing stones, and there's a SSSI at Myndd LLangyndeyrn, with an abundance of rare birds. There's also the superb Botanic Gardens in Aberglasney (01558 668768; www.gardenofwales.org.uk).

FOOD AND DRINK Eggs, bacon and sausages are all available on site. Carmarthen's indoor market sells local cheese and Carmarthen ham – a serious rival to Parma ham. Pontyberem's New Inn (01269 871152) has good food and a range of ales, the Smiths Arms (01269 842 213; www.thesmitharms.co.uk) has better food, while the Farmers Arms (01269 871 022) in Llangyndeyrn is recommended for foodies.

GETTING THERE Follow the B4306 to the top of Crwbin village and look for the sign on a gate by a yellow bungalow.

OPEN All year.

THE DAMAGE Tent and 2 people £18–£21.

carreglwyd

Carreglwyd, The Seafront, Port Eynon, Gower, Swansea SA3 1NN   01792 390795   www.carreglwyd.com

The sleepy village of Port Eynon on the Gower Peninsula is dominated by campsites, and static caravan parks occupy various hillside fields above the town. But help is at hand at Carreglwyd, which has five camping fields, of which only the two nearest reception are favoured by caravans, with tents having the run of the place beyond. Pitches nearest the beach tuck in under the shelter of thick hedges, affording views of Port Eynon bay from the higher ground.

All in all, it's a well-organised and well-equipped site, with modern showers that are both clean and free, plus a very good onsite launderette and a small shop at reception for the basics. But above all its direct access to the beach means that it's a perfect place for young families, with a half-mile crescent of calm family-friendly waters and plenty of water sports opportunities that makes it kid-friendly heaven during summer.

Besides the beach Port Eynon is a relatively soulless spot, but there's a more untamed world on the right, towards the tip of the peninsula. This part of the coast is owned and managed by the National Trust, but it feels wilder. Mewslade is a birdwatchers' paradise while Fall Bay is the best unspoilt beach in the area – only accessible at low tide, but that doesn't stop many campers wading there or scrambling over the rocks to this idyllic bolthole. The coastal path to Worm's Head and Rhossili is a spectacular five-mile walk, showcasing the most dramatic stretch of Gower coastline and possibly the best sunset in the UK – proof alone, if it were needed, of why Gower was selected as Britain's first official Area of Outstanding Natural Beauty.

COOL FACTOR Static caravan excess gives way to unspoilt National Trust coastline.

WHO'S IN? Tents, campervans, caravans, dogs (on a lead at all times), families – yes. Big groups, young groups – no.

ON SITE 2 modern amenities blocks have toilets, hot showers, basins, laundry and washing-up facilities. Outdoor showers are available for wetsuits. An onsite shop sells groceries and camping accessories. Electric hook-ups and chemical disposal points also available. No campfires.

OFF SITE Gower Coast Adventures do boat trips from Port Eynon to Worm's Head (07866 250440; www.gowercoastadventures.co.uk), perfect for spotting gannets, guillemots and even puffins. For those after a water-based adrenalin kick, surfboards can be rented and lessons taken from Sam's Surf Shack in Rhossili (01792 350519; www.samssurfshack.com). It's also the perfect place to paraglide off the headland in Rhossili (01239 614140; www.pembrokeshireparagliding.com).

FOOD AND DRINK Among places to eat in Port Eynon, the Smugglers Haunt (01792 391257; www.smugglershaunt.com) does pizzas and pub grub; the Seafarer (01792 380879) does decent fish and chips. A 5-mile walk or bus away in Rhossili village, the Worm's Head Hotel (01792 390512; www.thewormshead.co.uk) serves good food that's very nice washed down with a pint of Worm's Head Ale. It's a stunning spot at sunset, and chef Kate Probert does day cookery courses at her home in Three Cliffs (07976 639352; www.lamusechezkate.com).

GETTING THERE From Swansea follow A4118 to Port Eynon, and the campsite is on the seafront on the right.

PUBLIC TRANSPORT Several buses run roughly every hour during the day from Swansea or Reynoldston and Rhossili to Port Eynon.

OPEN All year.

THE DAMAGE £20 for 2 people, a car and tent, plus £8 per extra person. Children 4–12 years £1, 13–17years £2.

eastern slade farm

Eastern Slade Farm, Lundy View, Oxwich, Swansea SA3 1NA   01792 391374   tynrheol@hotmail.com

Many campsites in the Gower aim big, and as a result they cater for the masses, with lots of facilities but not much soul, and not always the greatest of locations. For a Cool Camper there's no real escape. East Slade Bay has just two facilities: a tap and a portable chemical toilet in a half-acre field. Offsite facilities are also pleasantly sparse. It's a 10-minute scramble over rocks with no formal footpath down to Slade Bay, but once you're down there it's virtually your own private beach – a world away from the chips and postcards of the nearby resorts. If the sun doesn't shine on this south-facing beach there are also plenty of walks to do, best of which are those in the opposite direction to Rhossili. Or there's an excellent multi-terrain route, which takes in Three Cliffs Bay, Nicholaston Woods, Penrice Castle estate, the King Arthur pub in Reynoldston and the Gower ridge walk. If you're hankering for a touch of civilisation, the breakfasts at Oxwich Bay Hotel come highly recommended. And there's also The Mumbles, which is a more refined choice of seaside town – when you hanker for tea-shops or places to eat.

COOL FACTOR Get back to basics and discover the real essence of camping.

WHO'S IN? Tents, campervans, caravans, dogs – yes. Big groups, young groups – no.

ON SITE Campfires allowed. Tap, portable toilet, CDP.

OFF SITE Camping here is really about avoiding the main beach strip of Port Eynon or Llangeneth. For those hankering after civilisation, hop in the car to The Mumbles. It's a pretty little seaside town with decent shops.

FOOD AND DRINK The Oxwich Bay Hotel (01792 390329; www.oxwichbayhotel.co.uk) is just about walkable – otherwise just buy your own drinks and enjoy the often excellent sunsets from the campsite. There are plenty of good tea rooms in The Mumbles, best of which is the Chai Delicatessen & Tea Room (01792 366333), which sells over 30 blends of teas and has an excellent deli counter.

GETTING THERE Follow the signs to Oxwich from the A4118, past the Oxwich Bay Hotel on your left and uphill toward Slade.

OPEN Officially Easter–October, although it's worth calling out of season.

THE DAMAGE Small tent (2–3 people) £10; large tent (4–6 people) £12; dome tent (8 person+) £15; prices include 1 car parking space; extra cars £1.50.

nicholaston farm

Nicholaston Farm, Penmaen, Gower, Swansea SA3 2HL   01792 371209   www.nicholastonfarm.co.uk

If you've been to the Gower before but not to this campsite, the chances are you've already had a taste of the farm. Some of the area's most upmarket restaurants and gastropubs buy Nicholaston Farm produce and Beynon fruit. In summer months you can also pick your own strawberries, raspberries, blackcurrants, redcurrants or gooseberries and scoff them by your tent, or get them whisked into a Berry Boost smoothie as you take in the view of the startling Three Cliffs.

The cliff-top field also has 10 good camping pitches, though you may decide to sacrifice the view and pitch against the hedge for shelter. There's also space for 35 other tents (many with electrical hook-ups) in the back field. The Beynon family are friendly and easy-going and it's a big enough space to accept large groups… if you pass muster on the phone. Both Three Cliffs and Oxwich Bay are largely unspoilt and the walk down to the beaches is either over soft sand dunes, scattered with evening primroses or through forests filled with abundant wildlife. You'd be pushed to see such a varied coastline in such a small space anywhere else in the UK.

COOL FACTOR The fruits of family labour, fresh smoothies and you can pick your own in June and July.

WHO'S IN? Tents, campervans, caravans, big groups, young groups, dogs (by arrangement) – yes.

ON SITE No campfires in any of the 3 fields that take campers; there's a well-stocked farm shop and café, coin-operated showers, and the toilet block has disabled access.

OFF SITE Although there isn't a playground, this site is very child-friendly, a 10-minute walk from Oxwich Bay. Nearby Perriswood (01792 371661; www.perriswood.com) runs archery and falconry activities; Gower Heritage Centre (01792 371206; www.gowerheritagecentre.co.uk) has pet-able farm animals and plenty of history-based activities.

FOOD AND DRINK The best pub is The King Arthur in Reynoldston (01792 390775; www.kingarthurhotel.co.uk/pub) which does hearty food with regional twists such as laverbread with cockles and bacon.

GETTING THERE Head along the B446: Nicholaston Farm is signposted on the left just as you leave Penmaen.

PUBLIC TRANSPORT Gower buses run to Swansea and Rhossili daily between 9am and 4pm. Otherwise a taxi from Swansea will cost you around £30.

OPEN End March–end October.

THE DAMAGE Tent and 2 people £13–£15.

teifi meadows

Teifi Meadows, Fach Ddu, Llanfair Clydogau, Lampeter, Ceredigion SA48 8LE   01570 493220/07967 866371   www.teifimeadows.com

Set in the bucolic heart of Wales, Teifi Meadows is the kind of campsite where you go to sleep to the sound of owls hooting in the trees and wake up to the chirrup of songbirds. The site is made up of one large meadow surrounded by woodland and hedgerows and a small stream, with the resident chickens wandering around – when they're not providing your breakfast eggs.

It's a relaxed and welcoming place, the kind of site where families get to know the owners – Julian and Jane Bransden – as personal friends, and meet fellow campers around the site's firepits while their kids tear around the meadow from dawn until dusk. Not surprisingly, it gets a lot of return visitors.

It's great for dogs and their owners – they have their own dog walking area, and not only are mutts welcome, Julian and Jane are happy to dogsit while owners head out for the day or evening. There are also plenty of nearby attractions if you don't mind jumping in your car, including the village of Llandewi Brefi of *Little Britain* fame (although there's not actually that much there). But for lots of campers the attraction is in simply letting time drift by as they sit outside their tent and do nothing in particular.

COOL FACTOR Ideal for idlers.

WHO'S IN? Tents, campervans, caravans, dogs, kids – yes. Party animals – no.

ON SITE Campfires allowed in firepits. 10 unmarked pitches, 5 hook-ups. Impeccably clean washrooms and 2 free showers, tyre swing for kids, ice packs frozen, farm bacon, sausage, eggs for sale. There's also The Bothy, a converted shepherd's hut with double bed and woodburner.

OFF SITE The lovely coastal village of Aberaeron is 20 minutes' drive away, and the fascinating Dolaucothi Gold Mines a short drive to the south (01558 650177; www.nationaltrust.org.uk/dolaucothi-gold-mines). There's great walking, pony trekking and also mountain biking in the Cambrian Mountains to the east, and good local fishing on the River Teifi.

FOOD AND DRINK The Fishers Arms (01570 422895) in Cellan is a welcoming local with a decent range of real ales and pub grub or, if you don't mind a drive there's the atmospheric Y Talbot in Tregaron (01974 298208; www.ytalbot.com), a classic old coaching inn and gastropub.

GETTING THERE About 5 miles north along the B4343 between Lampeter and Tregaron.

OPEN Easter–October.

THE DAMAGE £10 per pitch, £1.50 per person (under-10s free), £2 for hook-ups.

outer bounds

Outer Bounds, Bwlch Gwynt, Llanrhystud, Ceredigion SY23 5EH   01974 272444   www.campouterbounds.com

Outer Bounds describes itself as a 'small, traditional down-home rural retreat'. It's a tiny site of six-plus plots among wild land peppered with indigenous willows, oaks, hawthorns and redcurrant bushes. Sheep roam the nearby fields and only one or two passing cars might slip along the road each day. Life really doesn't get much more rural than this.

A boutique campsite this is not. There are sizeable pitches and a recently built shower block, but so far that's your rugged lot, although there is now hot water all day during summer, and even electrical hook-ups on some pitches. There are campsite basics like a barbecue and communal table as well as less conventional features like (our favourite) a mini stone circle. Bring a guitar and some incense sticks and, on a starry night, you'll be in hippy heaven.

There are people for whom this campsite won't be right. Dog-owners are out of luck – pets aren't allowed – and older children could get bored. Softies who can't camp without hook-ups will find the amenities a little basic. But anyone looking for countryside calm, broken by nothing more than fish-and-chip suppers, trips to the beach and birdsong, won't be disappointed.

COOL FACTOR Isolated seclusion with easy access to coastal and hill walks.

WHO'S IN? Tents and experienced, no-frills campers, small campervans – yes. Anyone else – no.

ON SITE Campfires allowed. 6-plus pitches offering plenty of privacy. 4 hook-ups. 2 showers, washing-up sink and washing machine. Logs and kindling. It's a trek to the shops, so bring as many provisions as you can carry.

OFF SITE Llanrhystud, 4 miles away, is a pebbly, facility-free beach that's great for sunsets. The Fantasy Farm Park is minutes away by car (01974 272285; www.fantasyfarmpark. co.uk) and among other things features animals, go-karts and pedalos. Nearby Cardigan Bay is famed for its dolphins, porpoises and seals, all of which may be seen along the coast – although you can up the odds of spotting them by taking a boat trip from New Quay.

FOOD AND DRINK The friendly welcome at the Cross Inn is matched by excellent food and a lovely beer garden. There's also the Y Talbot in Tregaron (01974 298208; www. ytalbot.com), which has occasional live music.

GETTING THERE Finding the site is tricky after dark. Call the owners to be directed in.

OPEN End March–end October.

THE DAMAGE From £7.50 per night; kids from £2 per night (3–10 years).

tyllwyd

Tyllwyd, Cwmystwyth, Aberystwyth, Ceredigion SY23 4AG   01974 282216   www.welshaccommodation.co.uk

If you need to get lost for some reason, then Tyllwyd is a good place to end up. It's hard to beat for remoteness, squeezed in between the burbling waters of the River Ystwyth and an unclassified road, high in the hills at the top of Cwmystwyth, about 20 miles inland from Aberystwyth. On the map it looks like the back of beyond, and it is isolated, no question, but happily it doesn't always feel so. Indeed, as a base for both hilly activities and coastal jaunts, Tyllwyd is hard to beat – the hills are literally outside your tent porch, while Cardigan Bay is a short and scenic drive away. Or, of course, you could just sit back and enjoy the peace and quiet of one of the more remote corners of Wales.

Wherever you may be coming from, the journey to Tyllwyd is a long and winding one. Midweek, and out of season, you could set your deckchair up in the middle of the road next door to the site and not have to move it all day, though come a summer Sunday it can seem as though every motorcycle and classic car in the world is parading up and down this lonely strip of tarmac. This isn't actually the nuisance it might seem, happening as it does just one day a week in summer. For the rest of the time those lucky folk camping at this award-winning, carbon-neutral campsite have this lovely road at their disposal, not to mention the joyful sparkling stream of the River Ystwyth to splash about in, and an all-round gorgeous view of the green empty hills of Mid-Wales, all laid out in a soothing, lush, green valley.

Site facilities are good, too, though you have to cross the road to find them at the farmhouse, which once upon a time was an inn catering for travellers on what used to be an important route across Wales. The present occupiers, the Raw family, are as welcoming as their valley, though it should be noted that the midges offer a less friendly reception at times. Nearby are the fascinating remains of what is considered to be the most important non-ferrous metal mining site in Wales, where humans have scratched away at the rock to extract lead, silver and zinc since the Bronze Age. James Raw, the current owner, is in fact descended from captain James Raw who came here from the lead-mining region of the Yorkshire Dales to run the Cwmystwyth mines in Victorian times. (Spare a thought for the miners – most of them were dead of lead poisoning after a few years working here.) The spoil heaps and tumbledown buildings don't detract from the glorious landscapes of high, rolling hills and moors and tumbling, clear rivers, and are worth a wee exploration.

The drive to Rhayader from the site, through the wilds of the Cambrian Mountains, may be famously stunning, but the scenery in the other direction, downstream, is more rewarding, being more complex and intimate. There are first-class mountain-biking routes at nearby Nant-yr-Arian to the north and, about six miles from Tyllwyd, is Devil's Bridge, where you can climb aboard the train to Aberystwyth.

COOL FACTOR Location, location, location.

WHO'S IN? Tents, campervans, tourers, hikers, mountain bikers, dogs (1 per family) – yes. Big groups, party animals – no.

ON SITE 25–30 pitches, 16 hook-ups. Simple but immaculate separate male and female washrooms with hot and cold water, flushing loos, 1 hot shower (free). Small children's play area and sandpit plus paddling in the river. Ice packs frozen. There are some onsite farm walks with printed maps available to borrow from reception, providing a range of routes that varies from a short stroll before supper to a whole day spent wandering or pedalling over the farm's 3000 acres and mountains. Open fires not allowed but BBQ facilities are available alongside picnic tables. Watch out for the midges!

OFF SITE Go to Devil's Bridge, examine the magnificent Mynach Falls and the Punch Bowl and its 3 spectacular bridges, or take a trip on the narrow-gauge Vale of Rheidol railway to Aberystwyth; it runs 2–4 trains most days between April and October (01970 625819; www.rheidolrailway.co.uk). The trip takes an hour and if the weather is kind you can enjoy the ride in its open-topped 'summer car'. Aberystwyth itself is a good choice for a day out if you're craving civilisation; a lively student town in a great location, with all the trappings of a Victorian seaside resort, including a wonderful old cliff railway (01970 617642; www.aberystwythcliffrailway.co.uk) – Britain's longest. It's home also to the prestigious National Library of Wales (01970 632800; www.llgc.org.uk), which is naturally a mine of information on all aspects of Wales and hosts regular exhibitions. Back inland, the Vale of Ystwyth is home to lots of waymarked walks through the old Hafod estate, and Cwmystwyth itself is also worth a stroll, if only for the strangeness of its location, and the abandoned lead mine shafts and equipment all around. To find out more about the mining history of the area, visit Llywernog Mine Museum and Caverns near Bwlch Nant yr Arian (01970 890620; www.silverminetours.co.uk), which has displays on the industry and takes you underground to see a real mine. Finally the Nant yr Arian forest centre to the north (www.forestry.gov.uk), is the place to go mountain biking, with lots of marked trails (and you can see its resident red kites being fed every day).

FOOD AND DRINK Bring everything you need in terms of supplies, because there are no shops or pubs within easy walking distance. The closest place to eat is the Hafod Hotel (01970 890232; www.thehafodhotel.co.uk) at Devil's Bridge, 6 miles away, a lively and attractive pub, with owners who have transformed it into the village hub with a tea room and restaurant. It serves excellent Sunday lunches and also opens every evening for dinner between 7pm and 9pm – booking advised. Otherwise take the Vale of Rheidol railway and make the most of being in Aberystwyth: there's a great Spanish deli there, the sister business of a Narberth original, Ultracomida (01970 630686; www.ultracomida.co.uk), which is perfect for stocking up on camping supplies; and there are also lots of good pubs and places to eat. Try the veggie lunches at the Treehouse (01970 615791; www.treehousewales.co.uk) – or again pick up picnic and campfire supplies and make the most of the site.

GETTING THERE Take the B4575 to the south of Devil's Bridge and turn off for Cwmystwyth on to an unclassified road signposted 'Rhayader' – you'll go straight past Tyllwyd. From Rhayader follow the mountain road to Aberystwyth and you'll pass the site.

OPEN 1 March–31 October. Booking advisable. All other times by prior arrangement only.

THE DAMAGE Tent and car/campervan plus 2 people £12. Children (5–15 yrs) £3. Extra adult £5. Tourer £13. Hook-ups £3. Dogs free but must be on a lead at all times.

fforest fields

Fforest Fields, Hundred House, Builth Wells, Powys LD1 5RT   01982 570406   www.fforestfields.co.uk

It's doubtful whether Ralph Waldo Emerson, or any of the other great American Transcendentalist thinkers of the 19th century, took themselves off camping. After all, equipment wasn't quite so advanced back then. Pop-up tents hadn't even been invented, let alone essential Cath Kidston floral patterns. But if they had ventured out (with giant tent in tow) some of their musings about the human spirit might just have waxed even more lyrical about the euphoric communion between Man and Nature.

It sounds a little on the wishy-washy side, but when you're by the long lake at Fforest Fields, looking up at the twinkling night sky, it's easy to see their point. The lake may be man-made, as is the campsite, its pathways, streams and flower beds, but it has been done with such care and taste that even Mother Nature herself would surely give it her blessing. And if you stand in the middle of this campsite and spin around, the natural scenery that greets the eye full circle is just breathtaking – rolling hills in every direction, forests thick with pine trees, grass, ferns, heather and crystal-clear streams… all the finest organic ingredients that make up a melting pot of countryside idyll. The best bit is that you're free to wander off in any one of these directions, because the land (all 550 acres of it) belongs to Fforest Fields.

There is so much walking to be done; over the hills, through the forests and across the moorland. Maps are available at reception to guide you and there's a six-mile waymarked walk to Aberedw village that's well worth doing, not least because it winds up at a terrific pub. Two fishing lakes allow for more sedate activity and the long lake's cool waters make for refreshing swimming or canoeing in one of the site's kayaks. So the chance to commune with Nature is at an all-time high here. In fact, not far away, at Gigrin Farm in Rhayader, there's a red kite feeding centre, where you can get up close to these majestic birds of prey.

The Transcendentalists would be even more thrilled by the opportunities given to the human spirit to shine here, not just from the tree-hugging and skipping barefoot across the grass there is to be done, but through trust. Campers are welcome to help themselves to locally produced food, wood and charcoal sold in reception and use the laundry facilities by paying into an honesty box. Such are the natures of the owners and campers that trust and honesty abide at this 100-pitch campsite – hopefully to continue for years to come. Campers can also borrow homemade barbecue/campfire structures to cook on in the evenings, plus games and books to keep the entertainment flowing if it happens to rain.

A haven in the Mid-Wales countryside, it's not surprising that Fforest Fields entices people to return year after year. One gentleman loved it here so much that after his first visit he came back every year, always to the same pitch, until he reached the grand old age of 85 – a Cool Camper indeed! Once you've visited, though, it's easy to see the appeal. The natural charms of this place work wonders on the soul and, as Emerson put it, 'In the presence of nature, a wild delight runs through… man, in spite of real sorrows.' He would've just loved it here.

COOL FACTOR The surroundings are stunning and the lake is a magical touch.

WHO'S IN? Tents, caravans and dogs (on leads) – yes.

ON SITE Firepits are available for hire; wood and locally-made charcoal are available to buy. A new timber-framed facilities block has been built and houses loos, showers with underfloor heating and disabled facilities, and a laundry, family room and drying room. The reception sells lots of lovely locally-sourced produce including sausages and organic milk. There are also 2 freezers and fridges, a microwave and phone recharging boxes.

OFF SITE Head into Builth Wells for a look around the town; if you fancy seeing a film (or perhaps a play if one's on) there's the Wyeside Arts Centre (01982 552555; www.wyeside.co.uk), which also has lectures on a variety of topics. For something a bit different there's the National Cycle Collection (01597 825531; www.cyclemuseum.org.uk) at Llandrindod Wells, 8 miles to the north of Builth Wells – a bicycle museum with hundreds of different cycles, the oldest of which dates back to 1819. Those wanting to do a bit of biking themselves should head for Coed Trallwm mountain-biking centre at Aberwesyn, north-west of Builth Wells (01591 610546; www.coedtrallwm.co.uk), which has 3 graded trails of between 4km and 5km in length and a small café – though you'll need to bring your own bike. To see red kites close up visit Gigrin Farm in Rhayader (01597 810243). Finally, if you're lucky enough to be here during August, you may catch the excellent and renowned World Bog-Snorkelling Championships, which takes place over the bank holiday every year at a peat bog just outside Lanwrytd Wells – a truly Welsh institution if ever there was one.

FOOD AND DRINK The Hundred House Inn (01982 570231), ¾ mile away, has a nice atmosphere and does decent food. The Seven Stars Inn (01982 560494) at Aberedw serves fantastic food and lies at the end of the 6-mile waymarked walk from the campsite, so you can build up an appetite and a half. In Builth Wells, the Strand Café (01982 552652) does good breakfasts, lunches and teas, while the Fountain Inn (01982 553920) is a decent boozer with a good choice of ales and an adjoining café. For higher-end food, travel a bit further afield to Lanwrytd Wells, where the Lasswade Hotel (01591 610515; www.lasswadehotel.co.uk) has a fine restaurant serving innovative food at moderate prices.

GETTING THERE From the M5, take the A44 then A481 towards Builth Wells. Fforest Fields is signposted and is on the left, just under a mile from the village of Hundred House. From the M4, take the A40 then A470 to Builth Wells, pass through the town, then at the roundabout take the third exit on to the A481. Fforest Fields is a few miles on.

OPEN Easter–end October.

THE DAMAGE Pitches £4.50, adults £3.50, children (under 16) £2.50, babies free; hook-ups £2.50. Dogs are free, but must be kept on leads and a maximum of 2 per tent/campervan.

pencelli castle

Pencelli Castle Caravan and Camping Park, Pencelli, Brecon, Powys LD3 7LX   01874 665451   www.pencelli-castle.com

There used to be a castle on the site of this marvellously situated campsite; and although it may have been dismantled in the 1550s, the chances are its battlements would be crammed full of flowers if it were still around. Not for nothing have the campsite's owners, the Rees family, won the Wales in Bloom campsite category for over five years now. Paying quiet consideration to a camper's every need is what this dedicated family does so very well, and the main reason why staying here is such a special experience.

You can almost picture the castle as you pitch your tent in one of the three fields. The Meadow is the largest field and is reserved exclusively for tent campers. All the pitches have a backdrop of stupendous views of heather-clad mountains and sheep-strewn, rolling hills, although the drawback is the five-minute walk from here to the facilities. The Oaks and Meadow lie in a horseshoe around the old moat, now part of the Monmouthshire Canal, which runs alongside the site today. You can even launch your boat or canoe directly into the water from the camping field.

The fields are ancient and spacious, with lots of shady, sheltered spots under some of the biggest and oldest oak trees in the parish. Wooden picnic tables are scattered around – perfect if you feel like having a peaceful meal admiring the view – and there are plenty of water points in all the fields. All in all, it's a well-organised and well-planned site, especially good for first-timers, with flat, sheltered pitches, spotless facilities and even a castle themed play area for the kids.

COOL FACTOR Flower-empowered pristine site with good facilities.

WHO'S IN? Tents, campervans, children, caravans – yes. Big groups, young groups, dogs – no.

ON SITE No campfires but BBQs welcome. With 80 pitches and 29 hook-ups over 3 fields, space is rarely an issue, and the facilities are spotless, with 10 showers and 2 family washrooms, a small laundry with fridge-freezer and washing-up facilities. A small shop stocks basics, and there's also a place to store and wash bikes and boots. Some pitches have disabled access and wi-fi. There's a good play area, and children can also follow a nature trail around the site.

OFF SITE The Mon and Brec (Monmouthshire) Canal (01873 830328) runs along the edge of the site, and has boat trips and boats for hire. There is pony trekking at Cantref (01874 665223; www.cantref.com), and a play farm. A network of cycle paths, the Taff Trail (01639 893661; www.tafftrail.org.uk), criss-crosses the area, and you can hire bikes from Talybont Stores (01874 610071; www.talybontstores.co.uk). A combination of driving and walking will get you to the highest peak in the Beacons, Pen y Fan, worth it for the magnificent views.

FOOD AND DRINK Of 4 pubs within a couple of miles of the site, the Royal Oak (01874 665396), literally a few yards away, offers good food and a chance to chat with the locals. For exceptional food, the White Swan (01874 665276), 2 miles away in Llanfrynach, is hard to beat.

GETTING THERE Head towards Pencelli from the A40. Follow the brown signs to the campsite from the village.

PUBLIC TRANSPORT Bus service to Abergavenny or Brecon; Merthyr Tydvill and Abergavenny also have rail stations.

OPEN 3 February–28 November.

THE DAMAGE £8–£10 per person, depending on season; £4.50–£6 for 5–15-yr-olds, under-5s are free.

llanthony priory

Llanthony Priory, Court Farm, Llanthony, Abergavenny, Monmouthshire, NP7 7NN   01873 890 359   www.llanthonycampsite.co.uk

Llanthony Priory resembles a mini Tintern Abbey but, being totally buried in a little-known spot in Wales, amid the enormously gorgeous Black Mountains, in the heart of the Brecon Beacon National Park, it's far less of a tourist trap. And unlike the great ruins of Tintern, it has its very own pub attached. Once you've persevered through the winding country lanes of the Ewyas valley and arrived at these antiquated ruins, it's hard to imagine how a small band of Augustinian monks managed to build such a majestic structure way back in the early years of the 12th century. As you take in the glorious scenery it is, however, easy to see why they bothered.

As well as a public bar in the crypts of the abbey and a hotel occupying the Llanthony Priory's former lodgings, Court Farm – next door to the church opposite and the priory – has riding stables and a field reserved for camping. The facilities are simple and thankfully the Passmore family who own the place are firm believers that Less is often in fact More. For example, rather than having a toilet block obscuring your view of the dramatic mountainside, the two-acre field has a cold-water tap with access to the public toilets in the nearby Priory car park. With no showers near this field, only hardcore campers are going to stay clean.

Bugle (pronounced Bew-glie) bridge is a well-known place to jump into the river on hot summer days, both to cool off – and clean up. The bad news is that even on colder summer days the campsite doesn't allow fires. Never mind: if the chickens, who amble freely around the site, get round to laying, there are eggs available from the farm as well as homemade beefburgers and sausages to sizzle over barbecues on request. And the location, with the dramatic landscape framed by the arches of the abbey's remaining window frames, can't be beaten.

The campsite is rarely full, but because of its proximity to the abbey it remains popular all through the summer and much of the winter. Its other big draw is the omnipresent wall of the Black Mountains either side of the valley. Don't let the hardy climbers who often frequent the campsite put you off: once that initial climb is made, the ridge runs for miles without losing

or gaining much height. All is not lost if you're not a hillwalker either: this valley holds a line of secretive paths and tracks along its entire length, which lead from one heavenly scene to another. The stroll to Cwmyoy, to view its mostly 13th-century parish church of St Michael, which leans improbably all over the place due to subsidence (honestly, it is unbelievable), will be one of life's little highlights. And leaving the confines of this Shangri-La to the north (10 miles as the crow flies or about 35 minutes of winding road) brings you to the bookish town of Hay-on-Wye (Y Gelli) right on the England/Wales border – a nice town in itself, but above all great for loading up on reading matter from its 30-odd secondhand-bookshops before heading back to the site to read in perfect tranquillity.

COOL FACTOR A campsite framed by a ruined abbey and dramatic mountains – what more could you want?

WHO'S IN? Tents, dogs, small campervans, big groups (if booked in advance) – yes. Large campervans, caravans, young groups – no.

ON SITE No campfires, but BBQs allowed off the ground. Cold-water tap and access to public loos. No other facilities.

OFF SITE The countryside at Llanthony is stunning so you may not want to do much or move far once you're settled, indeed there's a spiritual feel to the place that is addictive. A track leads up to join the Offa's Dyke long-distance footpath (www.nationaltrail.co.uk/offasdyke), there's horse riding available (01873 890359; www.llanthonyriding.co.uk), while to the south, in the village of Cwmyoy, the Downey Barn Gallery (01873 890993; www.properdragontales.co.uk), displays and sells the work of children's author Caroline Downey. In Abergavenny, the market is worth a look, with general retail (Tuesday, Friday and Saturday), flea market (Wednesday) and a monthly farmers' market.

FOOD AND DRINK The Llanthony Priory Hotel bar (01873 890487; www.llanthonyprioryhotel.co.uk) – known locally as The Abbey – in the crypt under the Priory ruins, cooks up imaginative bar meals, served in unforgettable surroundings. Treats (01873 890867), in the village, does breakfasts and lunches. The Half Moon Inn (01873 890611; www.halfmoon-llanthony.co.uk) is a short stroll away and serves simple meals between 7pm and 9pm. The best place to eat, though, is the Foxhunter Inn in Nantyderry (01873 881101; www.thefoxhunter.com), whose modern British cuisine is well worth the trip.

GETTING THERE Llanthony Priory is clearly signposted from the A465; keep going down the country roads until you can't drive any further.

OPEN All year.

THE DAMAGE Court Farm charges £3 per person with a discount for families; age 5 and under free.

beeches farm

Beeches Farm Campsite, Tidenham Chase, Chepstow, Gwent NP16 7JR   07791 540016   www.beechesfarmcampsite.co.uk

Beeches Farm has been in the Cracknell Family for several generations, a sheep farm that diversified in the 1940s when Mary Cracknell decided to share the staggering Wye valley views (or God's Window, as they call it) with lucky campers. In time it passed to her son John, who ran it up until 2004, and it's now in the capable hands of his wife Dawn, who looks after the place with the help of her family. She is careful to keep the relaxed and natural ethos of the site intact while maintaining its excellent-if-basic facilities. Arriving here, you wouldn't change a thing...

It's a big site, with many different areas to pitch tents of all sizes. You can take your pick from a spot under an old oak tree to the wind-sheltering hawthorn hedge, and from the edge of the valley to the old path that monks used to traipse along to Tintern Abbey. Each pitch is marked by an off-the-ground tractor wheel – an efficient piece of recycling that doubles as an excellent firepit, and although there isn't a play area as such, old tyres suspended from trees serve just as well.

Above all the site enjoys a beautiful location. There are amazing panoramas of the Wye Valley wherever you pitch and, surrounded by the enchanting Forest of Dean, there is loads to do in the area, from walking and canoeing to hiking the Offa's Dyke footpath that runs alongside. If you are a fan of ruined castles and of walking, then you should try the Three Castles Walk, which takes in the Norman fortresses at Skenfrith, Grosmont and White Castle – a 19-mile circuit that will set you up perfectly for a lazy evening back at the site, sipping a glass of wine and gazing at that view.

COOL FACTOR A big site, with decent facilities and a cracking view.

WHO'S IN? Big groups, young groups, campervans, motorhomes, caravans, families, dogs – yes.

ON SITE Campfires allowed in firepits in every pitch area, with wood available from the site shop. 5 electrical hook-ups, 1 static caravan, coin-operated showers (£1 for 4 minutes), loos use recycled rainwater, extensive washroom and washer-dryer laundry. Fresh eggs are usually available and the farmhouse kitchen can provide bacon and egg sandwiches, hot drinks and cakes by arrangement.

OFF SITE The farm is a stone's throw from Offa's Dyke, the old Welsh border reinforcement that is now a long-distance footpath; you can sample it by way of the more manageable 19-mile Three Castle Walk. There's also an easy walk from Tintern Abbey – itself just a 10-minute drive or 40-minute walk away – to the limestone ledge of Devil's Pulpit. Kayaking and canoeing along the Wye River is highly recommended with Monmouth Canoe (01600 716083; www.monmouthcanoe.co.uk).

FOOD AND DRINK The Brockweir Country Inn (01291 689548) is a 15-minute walk down the valley. Tintern has plenty of good pubs, best of which is the Anchor (01291 689582; www.theanchortintern.com) for its enviable view of the abbey. For a more upmarket offering, drive over Offa's Dyke to the Miners Country Inn in Sling, Gloucestershire (01594 836632; www.minercountryinn.com).

GETTING THERE Turn into Miss Grace's Lane from the B4288 and drive straight for about a mile.

PUBLIC TRANSPORT Buses run to Tintern, from where it's a 45-minute walk to the campsite.

OPEN Easter holidays to November.

THE DAMAGE £6 per adult, £4 for children; children age 3 and under free.

sychpwll

Sychpwll Centre, Llandrinio, Powys SY22 6SH   07980 184842   www.sychpwll.com

Set close to the Welsh border and the confluence of the rivers Severn and Vyrnwy, and tucked beneath the imposing granite outcrop of Criggian Hill, the Sychpwll Centre is both a campsite and a 'rural retreat for the arts, education, nature and human development' according to enthusiastic owner Peter Hendry.

You'll pitch your tent in one of two wildflower meadows surrounded by 'nature corridors' and newt and frog ponds. There is a multi-purpose studio and conference area, a straw-bale kitchen and dining room and new shower/toilet facilities. It's brilliantly done, and there's always a lot going on, but really Sychpwll can be as busy or as peaceful as you like. The two camping fields are big enough to give plenty of space, and they also offer a cabin and ready-pitched bell tents. You can get away from things by taking a hike along the Shropshire Way, Severn Way or Offa's Dyke, or going pony trekking with a local stable. But perhaps the most appealing thing about Sychpwll is that it offers a different side to camping in Wales, in a gentle and pastoral landscape that leaves you no option but to relax.

COOL FACTOR A vibrant yet relaxed rural retreat.

WHO'S IN? Tents, campervans, dogs, artists, sensitive souls – yes. Large rowdy groups, caravans – no.

ON SITE Campfires allowed above ground (firewood £10 for large basket). 15 pitches, no hook-ups. 2 washrooms – one with 3 toilets, 3 handbasins, 1 shower, the other 2 toilets, 2 handbasins, 2 showers. Ice packs frozen, phones charged. Nearest shop is 2 miles away in Llandrinio.

OFF SITE Apart from walking and kayaking there's some great mountain biking in the local Berwyn Hills, and horse trekking from Penycoed Riding Stables (01691 830608; www.penycoedholidays.co.uk).

FOOD AND DRINK The Punchbowl in Llandrinio (01691 830247) is a good option for pub grub; Derwen Farm Shop (01938 551586) at nearby Guilsfield has seasonal fruit and veg and offers basket deliveries of all sorts of local produce.

GETTING THERE Llandrinio is on the B4393, off the A483 Welshpool–Oswestry road – detailed directions from Llandrinio are available on the website.

PUBLIC TRANSPORT The nearest train station is Welshpool, from where there's a regular bus service to Llandrinio, then it's a 1-mile walk.

OPEN All year.

THE DAMAGE £16 a night for a tent and 2 adults.

beudy banc

Beudy Banc, Cwmllywi Uchaf, Abercegir, Machynlleth, Powys SY20 8NP   01650 511495   beudybanc.co.uk

Beudy Banc is located in the heart of some of the world's finest mountain-biking country, but for owner Dafydd Tomos that wasn't enough – so he went and commissioned his own personal single-track downhill trail, the 'Gader Goch Descent'. This twisting descent plummets some 200 vertical metres down a verdant Welsh hillside, where you're far more likely to see red kites than other bikers (assuming you have time to look up).

The Gader Goch Descent can be yours, too, if you stay at Beudy Banc, along with six different loops in the surrounding countryside and some equally appealing road routes and walking trails. You can start all of them from one of the site's three fully equipped bell tents, or pitch your own tent. Alternatively, if you like a solid roof over your head there are the options of a cabin and converted barn, too.

Camping is best, though, in a lovely open meadow, with inspiring views down the Dyfi Valley; once you've settled in you can clamber up for even better views west towards the Irish Sea, north to Cadair Idris and south and east across the glorious heart of Wales. Mountain biker or not, it's a truly blissful location.

COOL FACTOR Your own personal mountain-bike trail.

WHO'S IN? Tents, campervans, dogs, groups – yes. Caravans – no.

ON SITE Campfires allowed. No specific number of pitches for personal tents. 3 bell tents all include camping kitchen and foldaway beds, but bed linen and towels not provided. 1 bright, clean washing-up area, 2 spotless solar showers, 2 compost loos.

OFF SITE Mountain biking is obviously the thing, whether on Beudy Banc's own trails or the various trails around Machynlleth. There's also great hill walking (Glyndwr's Way passes through the farm) and surfing and kite-surfing on the coast at Aberdyfi. The Centre for Alternative Technology (01654 705950; www.visit.cat.org.uk) is a short drive away.

FOOD AND DRINK For eating out, the Wynnstay Hotel (01654 702941; www.wynnstay-hotel.com) in Machynlleth is the best bet.

GETTING THERE East off the A489 towards Abercegir then look out for signs.

PUBLIC TRANSPORT Pick up from Machynlleth station by arrangement, including bikes.

OPEN They're brand new – call for details.

THE DAMAGE Bell tents £40; tents £20. Cabin and bunkhouse rates vary according to season and length of stay.

graig wen

Graig Wen, Arthog, nr Dolgellau, Gwynedd LL39 1BQ   01341 250482   www.graigwen.co.uk

Only mad dogs and Englishmen go out in the rain, right? Well, where does that leave the Welsh? As anyone who's done their research will know, even in high summer the weather can be unpredictable in Wales. Indeed one look at the lush, green valleys (lush, meaning attractive, is a word the Welsh adore) all around and you know that it's thanks to the beauty regime of a wet climate. Of course, the sun does come out in Wales, often within an hour of rain, and there are days and days of dry spells. It's simply potluck as to when to expect sunshine. However, whatever the weather this campsite is an unmissable experience.

The pitches here are positioned to suit most tastes. There is space for 12 tourers or tents at the top of the site, next door to the boutique-style B&B; a parallel track leads from here to two yurts, sleeping two and five, and a so-called 'caban' – a new locally developed timber and glazed structure, which has a rather Scandinavian feel, and will sleep two. Isolated and sheltered among dense woodland, both the yurts and the 'caban' offer total peace and privacy. Back down the track you pass through a top gate and walk down a steep decline. From here you can career off through the hedgerow, heather and bracken to 'wilder' camping spots with firepits on the lower fields, which are open during peak times for tents only. This more low-impact approach to camping has been underlined by recent work to plant native trees, add a compost loo and recycling facilities, all of which helped Graig Wen win the 2009 Green Snowdonia Award for Most Sustainable Campsite.

There are well-maintained new washing facilities with hot showers that are kept spick and span. Viewing benches overlooking Mawddach Estuary offer the best seat in the house at sunset, and there are various annual events: you can sleep under the stars in hammocks, enrol in a fire-making workshop or enlist in a bushcraft course with Heath Dawson. Intrepid explorers could tackle Cadair Idris, the spectacular mountain right at the back of Graig Wen: it's a 10-minute drive to a cheap car park in a farmer's field, avoiding the crowds you get on the summit of Snowdon. And there's the added challenge that, according to legend, if you spend the night on the top of Cadair, you'll come down a poet or, yes, a madman... Or test your animal-spotting skills – owls, nightjars, glow-worms, badgers and kingfishers are all in residence here. There are a couple of rope swings, plenty of trees to climb, occasional wildlife walks and bikes to hire.

You can cycle all the way to the coastal resort of Barmouth (a journey that involves crossing the mouth of the estuary on a stunning bridge) without even seeing a road, and virtually the entire route to Dolgellau in the other direction is road-free, too. In addition to the cycle track along the estuary, there's another family cycling path, plus a stack of more challenging mountain-bike trails at nearby Coed-y-Brenin, around five miles north of Dolgellau.

Back at camp, after a hard day's cycling, it's time to light a campfire, and toasting a few marshmallows on sticks seems like an extremely well-earned treat.

COOL FACTOR Easy access to great walking and cycling in Snowdonia National Park.

WHO'S IN? Tents, campervans, caravans, glampers, dogs, cyclists/mountain bikers, walkers – in fact it's hard to think of anyone who wouldn't enjoy Graig Wen.

ON SITE Campfires allowed on lower fields and communal campfire for touring site; bag of logs £5. 12 pitches at the top; 20–25 in the lower camping fields – though for now these are only licensed to open for just 4 weeks from the last week of July (check the website for dates). 2 yurts, one sleeping 5 and one sleeping 2. 1 caban sleeping 2. Bell tent for hire in August. 2 unisex showers (free), electric hook-ups £3.50 per night. Owners sell eggs, ice cream, marshmallows, and breakfast hampers in high season (local bacon, sausages, bread, juice) for £30. You can hire cruiser bicycles on site (£20) or regular bikes and mountain bikes at Dolgellau Cycles (01341 423332); call for prices. The field nearest the estuary is car-free; wheelbarrows are available for luggage. There are steep hill climbs to facilities, but it'll only make you fitter.

OFF SITE In Dolgellau, the interactive National Centre for Welsh Folk Music, better known as Ty Siamas (01341 421800), has an array of traditional Welsh instruments, which the kids can have a go at playing. There are also occasional live music nights. For something more theme park-like, King Arthur's Labyrinth (01654 761584; www.kingarthurslabyrinth.co.uk), on the A487 between Dolgellau and Machynlleth, is an attraction themed around ancient myths and legends. Check out the handcrafted furniture at the Corris Craft Centre at Corris on the A487. There's also a selection of arts and crafts, including tables, glass works, quilts and jewellery (01654 761584; www.corriscraftcentre.co.uk). Finally, the nearby mountain-bike centre at Coed-y-Brenin (01341 440747; wwww.forestry.gov.uk/coedybrenin) is one of the best in the country, with brilliant forest trails (and bikes to rent), but also plenty of other activities, too, including walking trails, rope swings and walkways, orienteering and geocaching.

FOOD AND DRINK The George III Hotel (01341 422525; www.georgethethird.co.uk) is a 1-hour walk away or 30 minutes by bike. Locally produced lamb, beef and fish can be enjoyed outside in view of the estuary. Stock up on local produce and tasty treats at Dolgellau's Country Market on Thursday mornings, or its farmers' market on the third Sunday of every month. Down at Fairbourne, the unassuming Café Indiana (01341 250891; www.indianacuisine.co.uk) is a pleasant surprise, serving South Indian specialities with a flourish from fresh ingredients and traditional home recipes, and with plenty of non-spicy options available. In Dolgellau, there are a number of good places to eat, most notably the Dylanwad (01341 422870; www.dylanwad.co.uk), which is very homely and does great steaks and local lamb.

GETTING THERE Located on the right-hand side of the A493 just before entering Arthog from the Dolgellau side. Beware – sat nav takes you 2 miles too far!

OPEN Top field 1 March–3 January; lower camping fields currently open end July–August. Check website for dates. The touring site at the top is open for small tents, vans and caravans pretty much all year, but call ahead to check.

PUBLIC TRANSPORT Closest train station is Morfa–Mawddach, 1 mile away; pick up and drop off can be arranged with the campsite.

THE DAMAGE Touring site: £5–£8 per adult and £4–£5 for children under 16; under-5s free; well-behaved dogs on leads £1. Hook-ups £3.50 per night. Tent camping fields: adults £8 per night Sunday–Thursday, £10 per night Friday and Saturday. Under-16s £4 per night Sunday–Thursday and £5 per night Friday and Saturday; under-5s free. £10 one off vehicle charge. Showers free. Bell tent, yurts and 'caban' from £65 per night. To maintain the appeal of this quiet and natural campsite, numbers are limited, so pre-booking is essential.

nantcol waterfalls

Nantcol Waterfalls, Cefn Uchaf, Llanbedr, Gwynedd LL45 2PL   01341 241209   www.nantcolwaterfalls.co.uk

There's a mighty big clue in the name as to what you'll find here – a series of foaming cataracts tumbling into clear shallow waters beside the campsite where kids of any age can splash around or whizz above the River Nantcol on a rope swing; it's little wonder people have been pitching tents here since at least the 1920s.

Nantcol Waterfalls is essentially Snowdonia in miniature – follow the walk from the campsite along the river and you'll pass from open meadows through riverside woodlands, past the lower and upper falls and on to heather moorland, above which rise the craggy Rhinogs, one of the region's least explored mountain ranges. The views here are sensational, taking in not just the mountains but all of Tremadog Bay and out to the Llyn Peninsula – and all within an easy five-minute stroll of your tent.

The site has seen much upgrading in the last few years and has won a whole lot of awards, so it's always popular, which means booking ahead is usually advisable. The narrow woodland road that brings you here is a bit of a mission in a campervan, but it's worth the effort for what is a buzzing, cheerful campsite set among glorious, unspoiled scenery. On a sunny summer's day it couldn't be easier to stroll all of 30 or 40 metres from your tent to the banks of the river and set up shop there for the day as the kids cavort in the waters – in between begging for ice creams from the small campsite shop, which acts as a bit of a gathering point for all and sundry. Camping heaven, then…

COOL FACTOR Waterfalls, woodlands, rope swings and mountains – what's not to like?

WHO'S IN? Tents, campervans, dogs, touring caravans, kids, hikers – yes.

ON SITE Campfires are allowed, but only with manufactured logs (£4 per bag) as this is a woodland preservation area. 62 tent pitches, 23 campervan/tourer pitches, 32 hook-ups. 9 toilets including disabled facilities, plus a dishwashing area and CDP. Separate men's and women's showers and washrooms including 1 disabled shower, which are all built to a high standard with local stone cladding and a slate roof. Baby-changing facilities, launderette. Natural children's play area by the river including rope swing. Wi-fi (£5/day; £10/week). Small shop, ice packs frozen and phone charging (free).

OFF SITE There are several short circular walks from the campsite and the Rhinogs are easily accessible for day walks. The coast is 10 minutes' drive away and Harlech Castle (01443 336000; www.harlech.com) and the Italianate village of Portmerion (01766 770000; www.portmeirion-village. com) are within easy reach.

FOOD AND DRINK The Ty Mawr Hotel (01341 241440; www.tymawrhotel.com) and the Victoria (01341 241213; www.victoriainnllanbedr.com) in Llanbedr are a good bet for an evening out, with Ty Mawr in particular specialising in a range of real ales (they have an annual beer festival) and good pub meals.

GETTING THERE Follow the minor road east from the centre of Llanbedr – the site is signposted.

OPEN March–November.

THE DAMAGE £8 per adult, £4 kids (4–16 yrs), £1 dogs, £4 hook-up, inclusive of pitches. 3 self-catering cottages and static caravan also available – see website for prices.

cae gwyn farm

Cae Gwyn Farm, Bronaber, Trawsfynydd, Gwynedd LL41 4YE   01766 540245/07776 019336   www.caegwynfarm.co.uk

Cae Gwyn has in the past been voted 'Most Beautiful Farm in Wales', and it's hard to disagree when you sit outside your tent watching the sun set. The land over which you gaze has both Nature Reserve and SSSI status, and should the urge take you it's possible to follow footpaths through the meadows and moorlands and up on to the mighty Rhinogs, from where the views over Snowdonia and the coast are sensational.

However, most campers at Cae Gwyn come not to walk but to ride their mountain bike at the next door Coed-y-Brenin Mountain Bike Centre – Britain's oldest, biggest and maybe best trail centre. Cae Gwyn is a working sheep farm (so dogs are not allowed during lambing), with three fields set aside for campers. The fields are big and spacious, while there's a 10-person camping barn and B&B rooms in a 200-year-old converted barn for those who don't appreciate life under canvas. There's a nice vibe to the place, with bikers and hikers swapping tips on the best trails, while loquacious owners Dave and Sue Hill impart useful advice on how to avoid the summer midges and where to enjoy the best pint.

COOL FACTOR Next door to some of the world's best mountain-bike trails.

WHO'S IN? Tents, small campervans, mountain bikers – yes (book in advance). Caravans – no. Dogs by arrangement.

ON SITE Campfires allowed as long as off the ground. 40-plus pitches (plus camping barn and B&B). Washroom with 5 showers and 4 toilets – clean but a tad 'rustic'; washing-up room with fridge-freezer, microwave, kettle. Wi-fi, bike lock-up.

OFF SITE Mountain biking at Coed-y-Brenin (01341 440747; www.forestry.gov.uk/coedybrenin), which also has a 'Go Ape' centre. There's also a downhill trail at Antur Stiniog, a few miles north (01766 832214; www.anturstiniog.com).

FOOD AND DRINK The Rhiw Goch Inn (01766 540374) is a lovely old pub that serves real ale and great food. You can get a lift there for a small charge from site owner Dave, and there's 10 per cent discount for campers and a free lift back afterwards.

GETTING THERE The site is on the left side of the A470, just north of Coed-y-Brenin.

PUBLIC TRANSPORT The T2 coach (Lloyd's Coaches) from Aberytswyth/Bangor passes the site, and pick-ups from Barmouth and Blaenau Ffestiniog stations can be arranged.

OPEN All year.

THE DAMAGE £8 per person inclusive of pitch, bikes and hot showers.

lechrwd riverside campsite

Llechrwd Farm, Maentwrog, Gwynedd LL41 4HF   01766 590240   www.llechrwd.co.uk

Like it says on the tin, Llechrwd is set beside a river – in this case the gently flowing River Dwyryd, which on a sunny day becomes the focal point of activity. Kids and dogs splash around in the shallows, more adventurous types swim in the deeper waters, picnickers relax in the shade of overhanging trees, creating a general impression that all is well with the world, which indeed is exactly what camping should be about.

With a choice of pitches in either a top or bottom field, the site itself, plus Llechrwd's easy riverside and wildflower meadow walks, should be enough to keep many campers happy. But there's a whole stack of additional fun to be had around here, from walking the surrounding hills to heading to the nearby coast at Tremadog Bay or visiting nearby tourist attractions like Harlech Castle, Portmeirion and Llechwedd Slate caverns, the last of which will keep the whole family occupied. Or you can just enjoy a tootle on the nearby Ffestiniog Mountain Railway, through the glorious Vale of Ffestiniog. And when the action is over the riverbank offers the perfect location at which to finish the day with a cold beer beside a warm campfire.

COOL FACTOR Easily accessible riverside camping in the heart of Snowdonia.

WHO'S IN? Tents, campervans, caravans, dogs, families, disabled – yes. Party animals – no.

ON SITE Campfires allowed in firepits. 30 tent pitches, 8 caravan pitches, 22 hook-ups. Neat, clean toilet blocks, with 7 toilets and 3 (free) showers, washing machine and tumble-dryer. Basics such as bread and milk available on site.

OFF SITE Llechwedd Slate Caverns (01766 830306/01766 832214; www.llechwedd-slate-caverns.co.uk) with its underground mine tours, zip wires, mountain bike trails and Victorian miners' pub, is 5 miles away.

FOOD AND DRINK There are 2 excellent pubs with food within a mile: the Grapes in Maentwrog (01766 590365; www.grapeshotelsnowdonia.co.uk), one of the most famous coaching inns in North Wales, and the Oakley Arms in Tan-y-Bwlch (01766 590277; www.oakleyarms.co.uk).

GETTING THERE The site can be found off the A496 between Maentwrog and Ffestiniog.

PUBLIC TRANSPORT Buses from Harlech, Portmadog and Blaenau Ffestiniog stop right outside.

OPEN April–October.

THE DAMAGE Tent plus 2 people and a car from £11, caravan/campervan with hook-up from £15. Dogs 50p.

rynys farm

Rynys Farm Camping Site, nr Betws-y-Coed, Gwynedd LL26 0RU   01690 710218   www.rynys-camping.co.uk

Decisions, decisions. Everywhere you turn there are choices to be made: three dozen digital TV channels; thousands of mobile phone tariffs; bargain bucket or supersize with fizzy and fries? But Rynys Farm is a no-nonsense campsite run by Carol Williams, a no-nonsense sort of woman, who gives you only two choices. Do you want to pitch in the upper field (spectacular but windy) or the lower field (spacious and secluded)? Simple, done, enjoy your stay.

Based on a working farm nestled in a cleft of soft, green hill above the town of Betws-y-Coed to the east of mighty Snowdon, the views here are gorgeous: gentle, soft and comforting, with the odd tractor and bleating sheep to provide a dose of reality. Nearby Betws-y-Coed is great if you like craft shops, outdoor wear and ice cream and was probably a real gem before the invention of the internal combustion engine. Now it suffers from having the A5 and its 18-wheelers rumbling through the middle of town. But who cares? Rynys Farm is plenty big enough to spread out and relax in. Both fields catch the morning rays, bask in the warmth during the day and, as evening sets in, are raked by the sun setting slowly somewhere by Snowdon. The site rolls and dips, as you would expect in this most mountainous corner of Wales, with the occasional rocky outcrop here and there, so you may have to search a little for a perfectly flat pitch, and there is some road noise from the A5 down in the valley. But it's all pretty simple, really, and the last decision of the day is only whether you'll want to stay here another day.

COOL FACTOR Views to die for.

WHO'S IN? Tents, campervans, dogs (on leads), caravans – yes. Big groups, young groups – no.

ON SITE Campfires allowed as long as off the ground. 40 pitches, 26 hook-ups. An old stone building has WCs and showers (2 of each) and a kitchen and washing room plus a pool room, and there's another, separate male and female WC. Shepherd's hut available all year and sleeps 2 people, includes a fridge, stove and all cooking utensils. Ice packs frozen and phones charged for free. Free-range eggs available from the farm. 1 static caravan between the 2 fields.

OFF SITE Old Bishop William Morgan's house at Ty Mawr Wybrnant, is a bit of a treasure trove of rural Welsh life, and even if you don't fancy going in, there's an adventure to be had just getting there. The rutted track carries on to Conwy Falls, a hairy journey by car but great on foot or by bike. Otherwise there's the famous Snowdon Mountain Railway (0871 720 0033) and a kiddies' train running out of Betws-y-Coed railway station.

FOOD AND DRINK 10 minutes' walk from the site, the Silver Fountain (01690 710456) does decent pub grub and real ales. In Betws-y-Coed try the Bistro Betws Y Coed (01690 710328; www.bistrobetws-y-coed.co.uk), although the Conwy Falls Café (01690 710696; www.conwyfalls.com) is equally good.

GETTING THERE To the south of Betws-y-Coed, the site is on the left-hand side of the A5 up a steep minor road.

PUBLIC TRANSPORT Regular buses from Betws-y-Coed stop at Conwy Falls café, 5 minutes' walk from the site.

OPEN The site is open for tents all year, but caravans and campervans are only allowed Easter–October.

THE DAMAGE Adults £7.50 per night, children £2.50 per night, £2 for a caravan, dogs 50p. Hook-ups £3. Shepherd's hut £45 per night.

gwern gôf isaf farm

Gwern Gôf Isaf Farm, Capel Curig, Betws-y-Coed, Snowdonia LL24 0EU   01690 720276   www.gwerngofisaf.co.uk

Gwern Gôf Isaf Farm is all about mountains – breathtaking, wild mountains, that tower above this traditional farm site nestled between the Tryfan and Capel Curig mountains in Snowdonia's Ogwen valley. It was on this dramatic hillside that Sir John Hunt trained before leading the 1953 Everest expedition and, now owned by the 7th generation of the Williams family, Henry and Kirsty, it still welcomes experienced climbers looking to scramble to Tryfan's 3,000-foot peak.

Behind Tryfan, the amazing Glyder Ridge and Carneddau mountain range offer more stunning scenic climbs; and on longer stays you might take the short drive to Pen-y-Pass, to tackle the biggest pile of them all, Snowdon (or, to be precise, Yr Wyddfa). Less ambitious campers can always make do with the moderate nine-mile walk along the old road between Capel Curig and Bethesda, or just a trip on the Snowdon Mountain Railway.

The campsite may have seen mountaineer legends pass by its door, but its awesome location allows everybody to get a taste. It's as wild as you would expect – stray sheep, chickens and ducks share the garden; the facilities are basic; midges can be relentless and the ground can be hard. If planning to travel during wetter months, you might consider the bunkhouse, a compact and cosy bunker behind the farmhouse made of stone. Otherwise don your hardiest boots, grab your toughest mullet, and get among the mountains. Anyway, toughing it out is what this site is all about – if those famous rock-jocks before you could stand it, then why can't you?

COOL FACTOR Amazing vertical, rocky scenery and a whole gamut of challenging walks.

WHO'S IN? Tents, hikers, groups, young groups, campervans – yes. Dogs – no.

ON SITE 50 pitches, washroom equipped with 5 WCs, 3 showers and washing-up sinks. 2 bunkhouses sleep 6 and 16, mattresses and pillows are provided – BYO sleeping bag and cooking utensils.

OFF SITE The Snowdon Mountain Railway (0844 493 8120; www.snowdonrailway.co.uk) at Llanberis will take visitors to the summit in no time. Bodnant Garden, near Conwy, is one of the most beautiful gardens in Wales. If you're a two-wheeler fan, get cycling: the campsite lies on the Sustrans mountain-bike route between Tryfan and Bangor. A couple of miles from the site, the National Mountain Centre, Plas y Brenin (01690 720214), runs short courses in canoeing, orienteering and climbing.

FOOD AND DRINK The café on Snowdon's peak sells Welsh pies and Welsh Oggie pasties. Local specialities like mussels, black beef and salt marsh lamb are among many goodies on the menu at nearby Bistro Betws Y Coed (01690 710328; www.bistrobetws-y-coed.co.uk). The Riverside Chocolate House, Pentrefoelas (01690 770296; www.riversidechocolatehouse.com), is home to a tea room and shop.

GETTING THERE Follow the A5 from the M54, all the way to the site. From the north take the A55, then the A5 through Bethesda.

PUBLIC TRANSPORT Train to Bangor, then infrequent bus to Capel Curig, directly past the site.

OPEN All year.

THE DAMAGE Tents £5 per person per night, campervans and caravans £12–£15 per night (kids 2–8 years half price, under-2s free). Bunkhouse £12 per person per night.

aberafon

Aberafon, Gyrn Goch, Caernarfon, Gwynedd LL54 5PN   01286 660295   www.aberafon.co.uk

Let us not beat about the bush – this campsite scores on the old 'location, location, location' chestnut, in a beautiful spot sandwiched between the beach and the mountains on the Llyn Peninsula, 10 miles south of Caernarfon. Negotiating a steep, narrow lane to the site, past the bumbling stream by the amenities block, feels like you are descending into a secret valley within the mountains. Drive past a covered games room and the owners' lovely house, past rows of white tourers and down to a joyous coastal Beach Field, a grassy patch so close to the sea as to be virtually in it. It can only be accessed by small vehicles and features 16 pitches with seven electric hook-ups.

Both grassy tiers of the campsite sharply meet the rugged coastline and there is a tiny, partly sandy, wild beach full of rockpools to explore. Braver swimmers might attempt a quick dip – a little wild swimming is all part of Aberafon's package – but there are sandier swimming beaches along the peninsula. There is even a slipway to launch your boat from, should you happen to carry one with you.

Co-owner Hugh is an extreme-sports fan, so he'll approve of anyone that wishes to canoe downstream, hike through Snowdonia, or try wakeboarding at the local sporting venue, Glas Fryn Park, near Pwllheli. Hugh has regularly jumped off Gyrn Goch mountain, which overlooks the campsite, strapped to a paraglider. If you're feeling equally adventurous, sign up with the local paragliding school. Otherwise, just let the kids safely run riot: happy kids make happy parents, after all.

COOL FACTOR As good as camping on the beach.
WHO'S IN? Families, tents, campervans, caravans, dogs – yes. Groups – no.
ON SITE Campfires permitted on the beach, wood available to buy. 65 pitches, for tents and tourers, 40 hook-ups. Clean but basic facilities – 1 shower/WC block, with 13 WCs, 6 showers (3 M/F), 4 urinals. Laundry facilities, dishwasher, ice-pack freezing, hook-ups at some pitches, TV and pool room. Onsite shop for daily essentials, open summer holiday only. BBQs permitted off the ground.
OFF SITE Cycle and walking tracks lead from the site to Clynnogfawr and Trefor, and bikes can be delivered (01753 798902; www.velovert.co.uk). The soft play and ten-pin bowling at Glas Fryn Park near Pwllheli is a wet-weather option, and they have go-karting, archery and wakeboarding activities too (01766 810202; www.glasfryn.co.uk). Caernarfon's Castle is a delight (01286 677617), and you can pick up the Welsh Highland Railway to Porthmadog there (01286 677018; www.whr.co.uk).
FOOD AND DRINK The nearest supermarket is a mile away in Clynnog Fawr. After a strenuous hike, treat yourself to a Hillwalker's Platter at the Y Bueno hotel, Clynnog Fawr (01286 660785; www.y-beuno.wales.info).
GETTING THERE Aberafon is just off the A499, 2 miles north of the small village of Trefor. Taking the A449, after Clynnog Fawr proceed to Gyrn Goch and look for the brown Aberafon tourist sign on the left.
PUBLIC TRANSPORT The nearest train stations are at Bangor and Pwllheli. Buses run regularly from Bangor and drop you near the campsite entrance.
OPEN Easter–end October.
THE DAMAGE Adults £7.50, children £3.50, dogs £1.75; hook-ups £3.

penrallt

Penrallt Coastal Campsite, Tudweiliog, Gwynedd LL53 8P   01758 770654   www.penrallt.co.uk

Don't spoil it, will you? laughed the elderly solo traveller as he zipped up his two-man tent. He was, he said, here to explore the Llyn Peninsula on foot, and to bask in Penrallt's peaceful embrace at night. A neglected football lay near his tent, a reminder of the scores of kids that had played here in the school holidays. In the corner, the first arrivals of the owners' annual conservation weekend were settling. Penrallt attracts all sorts, united through a love of wild, rugged coastline and of the wildlife that thrives nearby.

The owner, Sue, proudly pointed out many wildflowers on our walk to the cliffs via her small homemade labyrinth, a lovely spot overlooking the sea. There were so many blooms, it was hard to keep up. 'Striving for Sustainability' is her and her partner Pete's motto, and for their efforts they have received a Green Dragon Award. The facilities aren't luxurious but they are adequate and in keeping with the site's environmentally-friendly, wild and rugged vibe.

Tents pitch up around the edges of the 'Sea View' field leaving space to play in the middle. There's a family field, too, with eight pitches that can be booked out as a group. An old boat, swings and climbing tree and the generous space for ball games and riding bikes, tend to appease youngsters more than any day-trip off the site. The stretch of coast alongside Penrallt has a well-marked scenic path. One direction leads to the small harbour at Porth Ysgaden and a lovely beach at Porth Towyn, where you can spot seals. In the opposite direction, there's a mile of empty golden sands at Traeth Penllech – perfect bucket-and-spade territory.

COOL FACTOR This place is all about the Llyn Peninsula, its environment and wildlife.

WHO'S IN? Everyone, from 4 wheels to 4-legged friends.

ON SITE Campfires are permitted at the discretion of the owners. 35 pitches, 20 hook-ups. South Field has space for 15 caravans. 2 pilgrim pods (similar to tipis) each sleeping 4 should be in place for 2013 season. A fully-equipped static, 'The Dorchester', sleeps 6. BBQs allowed off the ground, bricks provided. The 2 washrooms are basic, stone outbuildings, with 4 shower cubicles and WCs, plus a family shower room. Fridges for hire, a freezer for ice packs, a washing machine and washing-up sinks, book swap, recycling bins.

OFF SITE If you only do one thing, walk to the famous Ty Coch Inn (www.tycoch.co.uk) in Porthdinllaen, but enquire about tides before you set off. The pub can only be reached on foot; it takes 30 minutes each way, or you can drive a little nearer and park in the National Trust car park at the golf club. You'll never forget the views or location.

FOOD AND DRINK There are 3 local breweries, no less. Try the tasty Purple Moose Bitter from Porthmadog or a traditional bitter, Brenin Enlli, from Cwrw Llyn brewery in Nefyn. There's also Orchard Cider in Morfa Nefyn, which organises cider-tasting weekends (www.welshcider.co.uk). Selective Seafoods on the other side of the peninsula, inland from Tudweiliog, sells prepared crabs and lobsters (01758 770397; www.selectiveseafoods.com).

GETTING THERE Follow the A487 south from Caernarfon, then the A499 south, and the B4417 south-west; half a mile beyond Tudweiliog turn right and you're there.

PUBLIC TRANSPORT Regular buses run to and from Pwllheli.

OPEN Easter–end September.

THE DAMAGE Tent, campervan, caravan and 2 adults £10–£12, additional adults £4, children £2, hook-ups £3. Pods £15 per person; 6-berth static £275–£350 per week.

All are welcome to walk this
LABYRINTH
as a place of meditation

You may leave a stone to
build the lines
The centre is kept clear

scotland

campsite locator

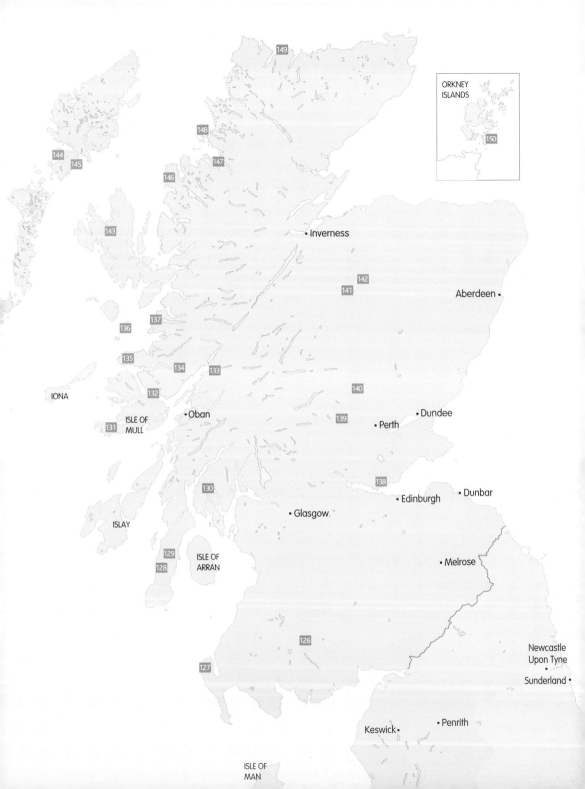

ORKNEY
ISLANDS

149

148

144
145

147

146

143

137

136

135

134   133

132

IONA

131   ISLE OF
       MULL

130

ISLAY

129
128   ISLE OF
       ARRAN

• Inverness

142
141

• Aberdeen

140

139   • Dundee
       • Perth

138

• Edinburgh   • Dunbar

• Glasgow

• Melrose

126

127

Newcastle
Upon Tyne

• Sunderland

Keswick •   • Penrith

ISLE OF
MAN

campsites at a glance

For more options, including campsites with views and romantic retreats, please visit **www.coolcamping.co.uk**

marthrown of mabie

Marthrown of Mabie, Mabie Forest, Dumfries, Dumfries and Galloway DG2 8HB   01387 247900   www.marthrownofmabie.com

Huddled around a life-preserving fire that illuminated the gloom of their Iron-Age roundhouse, our ancestors eked out a living in places like Mabie Forest. Today you can follow in their footsteps in what has to be one of Europe's only reconstructed Iron-Age roundhouses that you can actually stay the night in. Get down and dirty while cooking your own food over the fire, enjoying the pleasures of an alfresco toilet and a dense and moody forest where little has changed over the last few millennia.

Marthrown is a special place in so many ways. The forest itself is awash with native Caledonian trees, with characterful old Scots pines each managing the wilful Scottish trick of being a different shape to the rest of their brood, as well as birch, rowan and juniper. Edging over the grassy mound that separates the heart of the 'multi-activity centre' from the roundhouse, you half expect to find a gaggle of Iron-Age hunters crowded around a clearing where Celtic songs and stories were once celebrated in wild ceilidhs.

Today, the roundhouse – an impressive construction that manages to stand up to the full might of the Atlantic weather systems sweeping in off the coast – is similarly full of life. Perfect for groups as it sleeps up to 16, it inevitably plays host to the occasional stag and hen party, and is also popular with groups of friends looking for something a bit different. And different it is: you camp around the central woodburner (in place of the old open fire), perfect for cooking up something tasty and keeping the place cosy. Just

nearby is a canvas tipi that sleeps an additional four people and a Mongolian yurt with room for four, but the roundhouse is the real star. Tents are also welcome and it is possible to hire the whole site for exclusive use.

Rather than just sticking up the roundhouse and leaving it at that, the family team behind Marthrown has made an effort to recreate other earthy features, which fit neatly into today's vogue for all things clean and green. Rather than clog the local sewage system there is a simple, highly effective odour-free straw urinal as well as a compost toilet and an 'outdoor' shower. Luxurious extras include a sauna and hot pool that are free of charge for guests.

The surrounding forest, which is alive with red squirrels and woodpeckers, is one of the best locations in Scotland for mountain biking. All skill levels are catered for, with everything from easy and gently undulating forest trails that are perfect for beginners to some seriously testing 'black runs' that fling you and your wheels at high speed through tough terrain.

Back at camp, the atmosphere is one of relaxation and all-round bonhomie. However you spend your day at Marthrown, the highlight is getting back around the stove,. whether you are in one big group or sharing space with complete strangers. Taking a star-lit stroll and then walking back to the welcoming and gently smoking arms of the simple dwelling is a strangely comforting experience that people have been enjoying for thousands of years.

COOL FACTOR Enjoy the simple life and cosy nights by the fire like your ancestors.

WHO'S IN? Tents, glampers, groups, parties (stag, hens and weddings) and dogs – yes. Caravans and motorhomes – no.

ON SITE Wooden facilities building houses a kitchen, hot showers, composting loo and urinal. Large woodburner/campfire in the Roundhouse and firepit outside. The Marthrown Challenge course is a low ropes climbing circuit that has sorted the men from the boys on many a stag weekend (needs to be booked in advance; no need for helmets or instructor; under-16s must be accompanied by an adult). There's also a Finnish sauna and spacious wood-fired hot tub in the grounds. BBQs are allowed under the covered all-weather area. Campfires are not permitted in the woodland camping area.

OFF SITE You can hire a bike from dedicated cycle centre 'the shed' (01387 270275; www.cycle-centre. com) just a mile away and explore the forest, which has been opened up as part of the excellent Seven Stanes programme (01387 702164; www.7stanes.gov. uk). Forrest Estate Experiences (01644 430015; www. forrestestateexperiences.com) offer the chance to try your hand at clay pigeon shooting, fishing and all sorts of outdoor activities. Not far away is the tiny village of New Abbey, which is home to the expansive ruins of the oddly named Sweetheart Abbey (01387 850397; www.historic-scotland.gov.uk), a 13th-century complex whose widowed founder carried the heart of her dead husband with her for life. Nearby Dumfries, to the north, is south-west Scotland's largest town and was the home of Scottish national poet Robert Burns, who spent the last 5 years of his short life here and was buried at St Michael's church in the town. There's an impressive mausoleum, and you can also visit the poet's house, which remains much as it was in the 18th century and has been turned into a small museum devoted to Burns (01387 255297; www. dumfriesmuseum.demon.co.uk/brnsho.html). Burns wrote 'Auld Lang Syne' just to the north of Dumfries, at Ellisland Farm (01387 740426; www.ellislandfarm. co.uk), now a museum.

FOOD AND DRINK On the site you can get breakfast for £5.50 or a light brekkie for £4 and 3-course dinners for £13.50, but you have to book all meals in advance. For groups of 40 or over, Marthrown offer a hog roast (price on application). In terms of eating out, you're spoilt for choice in Dumfries, 5 miles away. The Globe Inn (01387 252335; www.globeinndumfries.co.uk) was Robbie Burns' favourite watering-hole and as such is worth a visit for its Burns memorabilia and an interior barely changed since the poet drank here. A couple of the best places to eat in are the riverside Coach and Horses (01387 279754), which serves hearty pub grub, and the Hole in the Wall (01387 252770), although both only serve lunch. For evening meals, try the excellent Linen Room (01387 255689) whose modern Scottish menu won't disappoint.

GETTING THERE Leave Dumfries on the A710 towards New Abbey. 1.6 miles after you reach Islesteps, look out for the right turn to Mabie Forest and Mabie House Hotel. When you come to the sign for Mabie House Hotel the road bears left and you will see signs for Marthrown of Mabie. The site is a mile from here along a winding forest track.

PUBLIC TRANSPORT Bus 372 from Whitesands in Dumfries stops at the bottom of the road; from there it's a 1½-mile walk into the forest. If you have a heavy load, it's perhaps best to opt for a taxi from Dumfries.

OPEN All year.

THE DAMAGE From £16 in low season and £17.50 in high season per person in the roundhouse; 1–3-person tents £15; family tents £25. The Mongolian yurt costs from £60 per week night and £125 per weekend night in low season and £70/£150 in high season. Duvets, towels and sleeping bags are available to borrow.

north rhinns camping

North Rhinns Camping, Glengyre Cottage, nr Leswalt, Kirkcolm, Stranraer DG9 0RG   01776 853630   robingooge@btinternet.com

'Our number one rule?' smiles Rob Googe, the co-owner of North Rhinns. 'You must be laid-back.' And, with his wife Kath, he has created a hideaway campsite that makes you want to be just that. This gem of a site harks back to the golden days of camping that your grandfather may have told you about, when he tramped along some sun-dappled byway with no real plan in mind, and needed no more than a few grassy feet of a local farmer's orchard to be completely happy.

When the Googes came here in 2010 they found a small forest run wild with bracken and brambles, and saw the potential to create the campsite they had always wanted to stay at themselves. Inch by inch they hand-cut pitches according to the shape of the land and the feel of the space. So each spot has its own character – one is perfect for watching the sunset, another completely lost amid the trees or favoured by grazing deer at dawn. Find the one that suits you best and settle down.

As you do, you'll begin to discover more special things about this deceptive site. The trees you thought were all pines also include young oaks and odd exotics (is that really a eucalyptus?). That odd 'ack-ack' noise isn't a misfiring tractor but a boisterous buzzard, and that vole isn't actually scurrying away from you, but the barn owl that happens to be sat on the fencepost. This is a site you'll want to tell your friends about – but not too many of them, as it truly is one of the best-kept secrets in UK camping.

COOL FACTOR Rural hideaway that puts the solar-powered spotlight on small camping.

WHO'S IN? Tents, small campervans, dogs (on leads) – yes. Caravans, big campervans – no.

ON SITE Campfires allowed. About 10 pitches and 4 hook-ups (pay-as-you-go card). Immaculate new washblock with disabled loo and walk-in shower room big enough to hose down the muckiest of pups. Socket for a hairdryer. Picnic tables and firepits (you can buy wood, kindling and matches on site).

OFF SITE There is a well-stocked village shop 2 miles away in Leswalt. The local sea fishing is fantastic – Rob will point you towards the best spots. There's a sandy beach 2 miles away, and the holiday town of Portpatrick is 10 miles away. The 200-mile coast-to-coast Southern Upland Way passes just 5 miles away on its way from Portpatrick to Cockburnspath on the east coast (www.southernuplandway.gov.uk).

FOOD AND DRINK The hotel in the lighthouse at Corsewell Point, 9 miles from the site, does fine food and does yummy tea and scones, too (01776 853220; www.lighthousehotel.co.uk).

GETTING THERE From Stranraer head west following signs for Leswalt, Kirkcolm. After the golf course go straight on at the roundabout into Leswalt; pass the shop on the left and continue straight up a steep hill, after which the site is 1 mile further on, signed beside the first cottage on the left.

PUBLIC TRANSPORT Bus 408 runs from Stranraer to Leswalt (www.dumgal.gov.uk), a 2-mile walk from the site.

OPEN March–October (although out-of-season enquiries are welcome).

THE DAMAGE £8 per person, children half price; under-5s free. £1 to use hook-ups plus a charge for electricity used.

'Dolphins, seals (x3), a sparrowhawk, gannets, sea otter (large) and buzzards (daily)' – so read the tally for just a few days on the campers' wildlife spotting board at Muasdale. Given that we visited on a quiet weekend in late September, there were probably more seals on the site than campers!

Certainly, if you want to get away from it all, this is a fine place to do it. Muasdale lies in the middle of the western shore of the long Kintyre peninsula. A few miles further down the coast is the beautiful Machrihanish beach, with its epic three-mile sweep of sand and soaring dunes. This marks the start of the Mull of Kintyre, one of the most remote and rugged corners of the whole British mainland. Paul McCartney bought a farm near here in the 1960s and felt sufficiently moved by the scenery to compose a certain, rather catchy tune about it. If he could escape Beatlemania here, the chances are that you will find your own little sanctuary, too.

Muasdale is one of the most modest campsites you'll find anywhere: a simple grassy strip and a snug campers' bothy with laundry, fridge and a games room. However, it's what's around that makes this site extra special: the grass simply drops away to an elegant crescent of sand. On arrival, you know you ought to put your tent up, but once you clock that beach you'll find it's impossible not to skip down and at least throw one stone into the surf to stake your claim on this exceptional spot.

muasdale

Muasdale, Tarbert, Argyll PA29 6XD   01583 421207   www.muasdaleholidays.com

Later, when all your pegs are sunk into the firm sandy soil, you can return and mooch barefoot at your leisure, watching the waves and hatching grand plans. Tread softly when you reach the rocks at the southern headland; this is where the sea otter likes to frisk about at dawn and dusk.

You might feel like exploring further afield, and Muasdale is beautifully placed for some adventuring. Campbeltown, 15 miles to the south, is known as one of Scotland's best whisky-making areas. At one point, in fact, there were 30 distilleries here, shipping vast amounts of spirit, but local production now consists of just three quality operations, which are well worth nosing out.

The site also makes a good base for a spot of island hopping. Gigha is just up the coast, while the Islay and Jura ferry is a few miles further on. One of the most fun islands to visit is also one of the least well-known – indeed you might notice that Alison and Adrian, the site owners, have posted the tide times of Davaar Island in the common room area. The island lies in the loch just east of Campbeltown; you reach it along a shingle causeway that is flooded at high tide, hence the need for tide tables. After a day's adventuring on Davaar – it's known for its caves – you can return to Muasdale to settle down in your camp chair, dig out your binoculars (or borrow the site's pair) and start counting seals.

COOL FACTOR Marvellous midge-free mini-site on the very edge of the ocean.

WHO'S IN? Tents, campervans, caravans, dogs (must be on lead on site and under control on the beach), family groups – yes. Big groups, young groups – no.

ON SITE 10 pitches (all with hook-ups). The new washroom facilities suit the size of site and are spotlessly clean. Fridge-freezer and laundry with coin-operated washing machines and tumble-dryers, as well as an iron and board. The games room has pool and table-tennis tables, but the site makes a big point of not being overloaded with amusements and activities. You can hire binoculars and BBQs are allowed off the ground. A fish van stops by every Thursday. The site is right beside a road, although you can use the beach to walk to the local shops. No campfires.

OFF SITE There's loads to do in the area. The island of Davaar has plenty to keep you occupied for a day. Time your visit well and you can have 4 or 5 hours there, exploring its lighthouse, viewpoint and excellent caves, one of which has its own famous 18th-century painting on a flat rocky wall. At Ardminish Bay on Gigha you can hire boats, kayaks and wet suits (07876 506520; www.gigha.net/gighaboats/index.htm). There is a popular sub-aqua club in Campbeltown (www.campbeltownsac.co.uk), and the Seabird Observatory at Machrihanish (07919 660292; www.machrihanishbirds.org.uk) offers bird-lovers a dream day out. The classic golf links at Machrihanish (01586 810213; www.machgolf.com) is a wonderfully scenic course, and boasts what is widely reckoned to be golf's best first hole. Or you can go pony trekking at Crosshill, 10 miles away (01586 551791). There is also the recently revived whisky industry at Campbeltown, which is focused on 3 distilleries – Springbank, Glengyle and Glen Scotia. Springbank (1586 552009; www.springbankwhisky.com) runs regular guided tours and has a brilliant shop

if you feel like buying. Finally, there's Campeltown's slightly incongruous Linda McCartney Memorial Garden, complete with a bronze statue of the ex-Beatle's first wife, commissioned by Paul to remember the many happy times the couple enjoyed on their nearby farm.

FOOD AND DRINK There is a shop 5 minutes' walk away for buying camping and food supplies. For sit-down eating, Muneroy in Southend (01586 830221; www.muneroy.co.uk) is a top-notch tea room with some of the best home-baking in Scotland. Gallery 10, also in Campbeltown, (01586 554074) offers stylish snacks and lunches served in an easy-going atmosphere. And for full meals, there's the restaurant at the Ardshiel Hotel (01586 552133; www.ardshiel.co.uk), which serves lovely local lamb and game, along with a good assortment of veggie options, and has a bar that is very well-stocked indeed with different malt whiskies.

GETTING THERE Take the A82 from Glasgow, then the A83 through Inverary, Lochgilphead and Tarbert. Muasdale is 22 miles south of Tarbert, alongside the A83. Alternatively, use the ferry from Gourock to Dunoon, then take the A885 north, and then the B836 to the A886, then the A8003 to Tighnabruaich and ferry from Portavadie to Tarbert; after that it's a further 22 miles south to Muasdale. Alternatively, if you fancy arriving in style, there is a small airport at Campbeltown, served by www.flybe.com, who fly from Glasgow, Orkney, Shetland, Belfast, Birmingham and the Isle of Man.

PUBLIC TRANSPORT There are regular bus services from Glasgow that pass right by the site, but the journey takes 4 hours. See www.westcoastmotors.co.uk and www.citylink.co.uk for more details.

OPEN Easter–end September.

THE DAMAGE Tent pitch £10 per night, caravan/campervan pitches £13.50. All pitches in £15.50 July and August. Adults £2, children (5–15years) £1.25 and dogs £1.25.

point sands holiday park

Point Sands Holiday Park, Tayinloan, Tarbert, Kintyre, Argyll PA29 6XG   01583 441263   www.pointsands.co.uk

Everyone returns to Point Sands. A favourite summer spot for seals and dolphins, it has recently seen little terns, one of the UK's rarest sea birds, come back to nest in the sandbanks after 23 years. At the same time, peace-loving campers who discover this sanctuary never stay away for long.

The campsite feels particularly welcoming after returning to the day-to-day care of a resident family. They are giving the site a deserved dose of love (and investment) – modernising the facilities, adding homely touches and generally being on hand to cheerfully dispense local knowledge and barbecue grub.

Most of the campsite area is no more than a kick of a beach ball from the private beach. This is clean and, thanks to the shelter of the nearby islands, safe. There is also a section known as the 'old camping field', which offers an inland pitch close to a wildlife-stuffed wetland. The site has plenty of room for kids to run free, while adults can find their own corner in which to kick back and watch the sun go down.

The island of Gigha floats tantalisingly close (and is easy to explore thanks to the nearby ferry), while further north are the rounded Paps of Jura and glimpses of the whisky-paradise of Islay. An amber-fringed twilight, with the dunegrass whispering and the waves sighing on the shore, has an energy that is nothing short of magical. Youngsters may find it's the place they look back on in years to come and realise that's where they fell in love with camping. And to which they will then return with their own family one day…

COOL FACTOR A welcoming site with woods, coastal walking and a feeling of closeness to the water that is hard to beat.

WHO'S IN? Tents, campervans, caravans, dogs, boats – yes.

ON SITE Campfires allowed on beach. 50 pitches and 40 hook-up points. Loos (including disabled) and showers are being upgraded. 2 showers for each gender (20p coins). There is a good onsite shop selling fresh bread, groceries and BBQ staples, a kids' playground, and a café that is open daily in high season and on weekends at other times. The site is quite large and can feel busy at peak times. There are several statics, although these are secluded in their own wood.

OFF SITE The Kintyre Way long-distance footpath runs right through the site. Follow it out to Rhuahaorine Point to gaze in peaceful wonder at the hills of Jura. The island of Gigha will tempt you into a visit at some point and the ferry is just a few hundred metres away.

FOOD AND DRINK The onsite Cara Café serves fish and chips; the Seafood Cabin at Skipness (01880 760207; www.skipnessseafoodcabin.co.uk) is a short drive away and will have seafood fans salivating for its fresh fish and shellfish.

GETTING THERE Take the A82 west from Glasgow, then the A83 at Tarbet. Continue through Inverary, on to Lochgilphead and then head south to Tarbert. The site is signposted shortly after Clachan.

PUBLIC TRANSPORT Regular bus services run from Glasgow, but do take 4 hours. See www.westcoastmotors.co.uk and www.citylink.co.uk for more details. You can also fly from Glasgow to Campbeltown, see www.flybe.com.

OPEN April–October.

THE DAMAGE Tent plus 2 people £15; pitch with hook-up £10; family ticket £20.

glendaruel

Glendaruel Caravan Park, Glendaruel, Argyll PA22 3AB   01369 820267   www.glendaruelcaravanpark.com

Trees, trees and yet more glorious life-affirming, oxygen-pumping trees are the main attraction at this remote, 22-acre escape on Argyll's sleepy Cowal Peninsula. Glendaruel sits in a hollow at the foot of its eponymous glen, shrouded by woodland. There are only 10 pitches for tents, most set in a generously sized grassy field away from the caravans and statics, and red squirrels and rabbits often outnumber campers. A recent arrival has been the Little Camping Lodge: a cosy wooden bolthole that can sleep up to four and is a great wet-weather option, with the owners planning to pop up another couple of lodges over the next few years. More conventional campers can use the campers' kitchen-cum-dining-room.

A variety of paths snake their way into the thick web of surrounding forests, with a large grass field also on hand for wee ones to run around in, and a couple of swings and a bijou playground. Cowal itself is not well-known, even among most Scots, so its quiet roads tend to be ideal for cycling and hiking, while the surrounding waters dish up a rich bounty of seafood that can be enjoyed in the local restaurants and pubs.

COOL FACTOR If you love trees this is the place for you, 3 steps beyond the middle of nowhere.

WHO'S IN? Tents, campervans, dogs, caravans, young groups – yes. Big groups – no.

ON SITE 10 pitches. Basic toilet block, shower and laundry. Campers' kitchen. Kid's swing and playground. No campfires.

OFF SITE Walking trails snake off into the towering forests, while a variety of circular cycle routes await around the Cowal Peninsula. The Cowal Way (www.visitcowal.co.uk/the-cowal-way.html) is a glorious 57-mile walking trail that rumbles right through Glendaruel. The impressive Kilmodan Carved Stones (www.kilmodan-colintraive.org.uk) are just a few miles south.

FOOD AND DRINK Creggans Inn (01369 860279; www.creggans-inn.co.uk) is an atmospheric old place on the shores of Loch Fyne – enjoy a traditional ale from the Loch Fyne Brewery to go with your oysters. Inver Cottage (01369 860537; www.invercottage.com) is a friendly restaurant bursting with local produce such as hand-dived scallops.

GETTING THERE Take the Western Ferries (www.western-ferries.co.uk) ferry from Gourock to Hunter's Quay, then follow the A885 north, B836 west and finally the A886 north.

OPEN April–October.

THE DAMAGE Tent and 2 people from £16.

fidden farm

Fidden Farm, Knockvologan Road, nr Fionnphort, Isle of Mull PA66 6BN   01681 700427

If the effort of getting there makes the arrival all the sweeter, Fidden Farm is a sugar overload. Not to mention utterly gorgeous. A three-hour drive from Edinburgh only gets you to Oban, where you'll have to jump on a ferry to Mull, which may just be the most scenic ferry ride you've ever taken. Arriving on Mull, you might be lucky enough to see an otter playing on the rocky shores of Craignure, before negotiating the remaining 40-odd miles across one of Britain's most spectacularly inhospitable landscapes. Some sections are single track, so you'll have to weave around the odd car, bike, Highland cow or red deer, and you may well arrive cursing. But not for long.

Fidden Farm enjoys one of the finest locations of any campsite in the UK. The grass tufts of this deeply informal place to camp give way to a rugged coastline indented with pretty little sandy coves, while the Atlantic stretches off into the distance broken only by the hulk of the Isle of Erraid. There is not much to do here but take in the setting and look out for bottlenose dolphins, whales and sea eagles. You certainly won't want to leave – and that's not just because of that epic journey home.

COOL FACTOR Fidden Farm has one of the most scenic locations of any UK campsite.

WHO'S IN? Tents, campervans, caravans, dogs, big groups, young groups – yes.

ON SITE Campfires allowed. 40 pitches. No hook-ups. Simple toilet portacabin with toilets and showers.

OFF SITE The most popular nearby destination is the Isle of Iona, with its beguiling abbey (01681 700512; www.historic-scotland. gov.uk) and white sand beaches. Another option is the island of Staffa, renowned for its incredible basalt pillars, which inspired Mendelssohn's 'The Hebrides'. For walkers, a thrilling option is being dropped by boat on the Isle of Erraid, where the hero of Stevenson's novel *Kidnapped* is bundled ashore. Suitably equipped walkers can also follow the Stevenson Way (www.stevensonway.org.uk), which battles its way through 50 miles of Mull's toughest terrain.

FOOD AND DRINK In Fionnphort the Keel Row (01681 700458) serves up a hearty menu featuring local seafood. The Ardachy House Hotel (01681 700505; www.ardachy.co.uk) has superb local lamb and hand-dived scallops.

GETTING THERE Take the Cal Mac ferry (www.calmac.co.uk) to Craignure and from there head south on the A849. On arrival in Fionnphort, turn left and follow the signs.

OPEN Easter–October.

THE DAMAGE £6 per person per night.

the shielings

The Shielings, Craignure, Isle of Mull, PA65 6AY   01680 812496   www.shielingholidays.co.uk

Long before the word glamping had ever come into the camping lexicon, Mull-based Shieling Holidays (the brainchild of David and Moira Gracie) were offering nights under canvas for those not keen on pitching their own tents. Their 16 starched white shielings may not be quite as glamorous as some places these days, but they are supremely flexible, and eight en-suite shielings are also available (with their own toilet and hot shower). Designed for a maximum of six inhabitants, they also boast cookers, worktops, electric lighting and gas heaters. You can either bring your own bedding, crockery, cutlery and kitchenware or hire it.

There are camping pitches, too, for those who prefer to pitch their own tent, and the location could not be more dramatic. The waterfront site sits right on the strategic Sound of Mull, guarding the gateway to the Hebrides. Just across the water lies Morvern, while in the distance a flurry of mountain peaks vie for attention, including Ben Nevis. Otters are resident on the rocky foreshore and porpoises and dolphins also regularly make an appearance. Many visitors just recline and watch the wildlife and the ferries travelling between the mainland and the isles. For hikers, Mull's biggest attraction is Ben More, the only island Munro (a mountain with a peak over 3,000ft/914m) outside of Skye. Much more accessible is Dun da Ghaoithe, Mull's second highest peak, which rears up behind the site – a good half-day's walk, but one that offers life-affirming views and the chance to spot red deer and eagles. Back by the Sound your tent awaits and a cosy congratulatory sundowner enjoyed with *that* view.

COOL FACTOR Glamp or camp with the pioneers.

WHO'S IN? Tents, campervans, caravans, big groups, young groups, dogs – yes.

ON SITE Campfires allowed (designated communal area). 16 shielings. 90 tent pitches. Excellent toilet and shower facilities. Swing, sandpit and games for children. Communal TV. Communal firepits and benches with views. Launderette. Astroturf tent pitches handy in poor weather, special tent pegs available if needed. Bike hire available. Wildlife trail on site.

OFF SITE Duart Castle (01680 812309; www.duartcastle. com) lies just a few miles to the east of the site. Across the bay is a lovely community pool and spa at the Isle of Mull Hotel (01680 812544; www.crerarhotels.com). Further afield the island capital of Tobermory is a picturesque treat, and is home to the Tobermory Distillery (01688 302647; www.tobermorymalt.com).

FOOD AND DRINK The Craignure Inn (01680 812305; www.craignure-inn.co.uk) does a decent pint, and this cosy pub also has a restaurant offering wild Mull venison, smoked trout from Tobermory, Mull Cheddar and Mull Brie. Tobermory has a better choice of eating options including the excellent Café Fish (01688 301253; www.thecafefish. com), where the freshest of fish and shellfish is perfectly prepared. Mull's best pub is in Tobermory, the Mishnish (01688 302009; www.mishnish.co.uk).

GETTING THERE From the ferry turn left on the A849. After 400m turn left again and follow the signs.

PUBLIC TRANSPORT Cal Mac ferry (www.calmac.co.uk) from Oban on the mainland to Craignure on the Isle of Mull.

OPEN Camping March–November; shielings April–October.

THE DAMAGE Tent with two adults from £16 per night (£2.50 discount if no car). Shielings £32 for 2 people (minimum 2 nights); en suite shielings from £48.

caolasnacon

Caolasnacon, Kinlochleven, Argyll PH50 4RJ   01855 831279   www.kinlochlevencaravans.com

Some Scottish campsites enjoy an epic setting shrouded by mountains, others sit by an ice-blue loch or huddle by a wee burn that ripples through the heart of the site. Caolasnacon boasts all three, as well as catatonically relaxed owners who let campers pitch where they want and light campfires too. Yes, they take caravans and have some statics, but they also treat campers with respect and nothing really detracts from what is definitely the most appealing campsite in the area.

The pitches by the loch are ideal for kayakers and canoeists, who can just launch out into Loch Leven, while walkers will want to pitch further inland for the easiest access to the mountains – the Mamores across the water to the north, and Glen Coe's epic mountainscapes to the south. More sedentary souls can take a trip on one of the world's great railway journeys, the West Highland Line, from the bustling nearby tourist hub of Fort William. Many new arrivals soon ditch their grand touring plans, though, and just idle by the loch soaking up the epic views and scanning the water, wild hillsides and big skies for seals, otters, red deer and the site's resident pair of golden eagles.

COOL FACTOR The sweeping panorama, with mountains, loch and burn.

WHO'S IN? Tents, campervans, dogs, caravans, big groups, young groups – yes.

ON SITE Campfires allowed. 50 pitches. Clean and efficient washrooms with decent showers. Pitches near loch can be windy, but it does give some protection against the midges.

OFF SITE Canoeing on Loch Leven and world-class walking and climbing in Glen Coe (0844 4932222; www.glencoe-nts.org.uk). Ice Factor (01855 831100; www.ice-factor.co.uk) in Kinlochleven offers ice climbing and winter skills training year-round.

FOOD AND DRINK The legendary Clachaig Inn (01855 811252; www.clachaig.com) may infamously refuse to serve Campbells, but otherwise this is a welcoming Glen Coe pub amid epic mountain scenery. On the opposite shores of the eponymous loch, Lochleven Seafood Café (01855 821048; www.lochlevenseafoodcafe.co.uk) is one of Europe's finest places to savour shellfish.

GETTING THERE Take the A82 down through Glen Coe then turn right along Loch Leven for the final few miles to the site.

OPEN Easter–October.

THE DAMAGE Tent and 2 people from £10.

resipole farm

Resipole Farm, Loch Sunart, Acharacle, Argyll PH36 4HX   01967 431235   www.resipole.co.uk

The fact that Resipole has its own slipway says it all – this is a place where adventures are launched. A family-run site for two generations, it sits on a serene swathe of grass on the edge of the Arnamurchan peninsula, the most westerly, and one of the wildest, parts of the British mainland.

Its position at the fringe of nowhere means you can make discoveries in every direction. The trees behind the site are part of the Sunart Oakwoods, a special conservation area bursting with unusual beasts and birds, including ptarmigan, pine martens and even wildcats. Behind the site stands Ben Resipole, a hill just shy of 'Munro' status, and a less-tramped gem. The ascent from sea level will have you puffing happily and your mind will be well and truly blown by views to Skye, the Outer Hebrides and Ben Nevis. The path starts just beside the laundry room, which is handy if the Scottish weather turns grumpy. Even when you're standing by your tent with a cup of tea, make sure you keep your binoculars close and your camera charged – look over the fence and you might see seals, dolphins, otters or porpoises, not to mention new campers arriving by kayak.

COOL FACTOR The three 'W's – water, wildlife, walking.

WHO'S IN? Tents, campervans, caravans, groups, dogs – yes.

ON SITE 60 pitches with hook-ups, hardstandings and grass available. An energy-saving washblock has hot showers, hairdryers, a dishwashing area, washing machines, dryers and disabled toilets. Shop with food and camping essentials. No campfires on site, but they are permitted on the shore.

OFF SITE This site is all about the great outdoors – explore on foot, by bike or take to the water. There are at least 50 walks in the area, several bike trails and nature reserves.

FOOD AND DRINK The Salen Hotel (01967 431661; www.salenhotel.co.uk), 3 miles west, has a formal dining room and a more laidback sunroom. The Strontian Hotel (8 miles the other way) does cracking lunches and its cosy bar has lots of fine whiskies (01967 402029; www.thestrontianhotel.co.uk).

GETTING THERE Take the A82 north from Glasgow through Glencoe; 4 miles after Ballachulish Bridge, turn left and take the Corran Ferry across to Ardgour. Turn left out of the ferry port; follow the A861 through Strontian for 8 miles.

OPEN March–October.

THE DAMAGE Tent with 2–4 people £8 plus £3 per person; large tent (5+ people) £11.50; pitch with hook-up £13.

ardnamurchan

Ardnamurchan Campsite, Ormsaigbeg, Kilchoan, Acharacle PH36 4LL   01972 510766   www.ardnamurchanstudycentre.co.uk

Ancient Celtic traditions say that over the western sea, beyond the edge of any map, lies the afterlife. Sitting at Ardnamurchan campsite it's certainly easy to believe, as you watch the sun torch the ocean between the scattered Hebrides, that you're as close as you can get to Heaven on Earth.

The site clings to the coast just a few miles from the tip of a rocky finger of land that's as far west as Britain goes. You approach it (slowly) via a ferry and a sinuous single-track road that hems in the crumpled and craggy landscape and makes getting here an escapade in itself. The site is situated to the west of the beautiful village of Kilchoan, on a small south-facing croft that has stunning views down the Sound of Mull to

Morven and Mull. This far-flung location makes it the most westerly campsite on the British mainland.

Remarkably, it has been brought into being by one man, Trevor Potts, who has turned an old croft into this Elsyian camping field. The site may seem rough-and-ready at first glance, a slice of wild hillside only just tamed, but as you settle in you'll appreciate just how much Trevor has done to make the site welcoming. Every pitch has been cut from the slope and levelled by Trevor's own hand, and he has recently vanquished a field of seven-foot high bracken to open up a new camping area. Pitches range from neat nooks with hook-ups near the washblock to wilder spots closer to the shore. If you camp right at the bottom of the slope you will be lulled to sleep by the wash of wave on rock. If the weather is being boisterous, you may even find the spray will splash your tent! The facilities are humble and homely, with surprisingly powerful showers. Flowers add a burst of colour to the whitewashed walls, and there can't be many washblocks that have their own whale skeleton to fascinate campers on the way to the loo.

The foreshore is rough, rocky and just right for a scramble. You can catch creatures in the rockpools, throw stones at the waves or simply watch the ferries weaving their way along the sound to islands that seem off the edge of the world. You'll be amazed how quickly a day can glide by when you have so much of nothing to do, although at some point you may want to explore

the peninsula, and you'll be delighted to discover Ardnamurchan packs a surprise around every corner. Just a few miles away are the glorious sands of Sanna, lapped by turquoise waters. The drive there takes you through a jagged, almost extra-terrestrial landscape of steep cliffs and snaggle-toothed ridges. If you'd visited 55 million years ago you'd have witnessed an epic volcanic spectacle. Fastforward through a few Ice-Age scourings and today you see a rocky ring more than three miles across. Further on around the coast, another age of history was brought back to life at Swordle Bay in 2011, when archaeologists unearthed a rare treasure – a Viking burial boat, virtually intact, although you can't see much more now than the mound of stones that marks the spot. You can, however, watch an occasional summer recreation of the boat's burial – an impressive sight. Back at the site, it's not hard to understand why people have been coming here for thousands of years.

COOL FACTOR Ideally placed to unlock the secrets of one of the least-known parts of Britain.

WHO'S IN? Tents, campervans, groups, dogs – yes. Large motorhomes, caravans – no.

ON SITE 20 pitches and 4 campervan hook-ups, 2 loos and 2 free, powerful showers. You can also hire 1 of 2 caravans and a bothy. Washing-up area with fridge. Internet access. No campfires.

OFF SITE Stroll on the sandy beach at Sanna, reached by passing through an extraordinary volcanic landscape. Visit the lighthouse at Ardnamurchan Point, the most westerly part of the British mainland, and climb the tower (01972 510210; www.ardnamurchanlighthouse.com). Nearby Ben Hiant is a terrific wee mountain with superb views. You can also pop over to Tobermory on Mull by ferry from Kilchoan (www.calmac.co.uk).

FOOD AND DRINK There's a fine and fun coffee shop in an old stable at the Ardnamurchan Lighthouse (01972 510210; www.ardnamurchanlighthouse. com). Bar meals and finer evening dining are on offer at the Kilchoan House Hotel (01972 510200; www. kilchoanhousehotel.co.uk). There's also food available at the Sonachan Hotel (01972 510211; www.sonachan. com), on the way to the lighthouse.

GETTING THERE From the Corran Ferry head all the way out west along the A861 through Strontian. At Salen turn left on to the B8007 and on to Kilchoan. The campsite is half a mile beyond the village shop (Ferry Stores).

PUBLIC TRANSPORT City Link buses (08705 505050) and trains (Scotrail 01397 703791) run to Fort William, from where Shiel Buses run a daily service to Kilchoan Post office (01967 431272), which is less than a mile from the campsite.

OPEN April–September.

THE DAMAGE £7.50 each person over 14 years, £3 for 14 years and under (under-5s free). Hook-up £3.

cleadale campsite

Cleadale Campsite, 13 Cleadale, Isle of Eigg PH42 4RL   01687 482480   www.eiggyurtingandcamping.co.uk

Nothing can prepare you for the view at Cleadale. Admittedly, the journey here does a pretty good job of warming you up – especially if you see dolphins, minke whales or an orca on the ferry over. And the island of Eigg itself gets ever more spectacular as you approach, with its serried banks of sheer cliffs and the insolent snub nose of An Sgurr towering over the harbour. Any geologists on your boat will be in heaven; birdwatchers may well be spontaneously combusting. But it's only when the local minibus rattles its way up and over the ludicrous ribbon of tarmac that passes for a road on the island, and drops you down into the cluster of crofts in the northern corner, that you really get it.

First you look seawards. Ah, you think, look at that – a sweep of green land, a white sand beach, a shining Hebridean sound and the jagged crown of the cuillin of Rum. JRR Tolkien holidayed here, and you can bet he had Rum in mind when he imagined the Misty Mountain. It's amazing. Then you heft your bag and turn to look at the campsite – and realise you will be staying at the bottom of a vast and curving cliff, an amphitheatre tiered infinitely steeply as if for the sole purpose of giving the eagles an epic perch from which to observe the sunset.

The campsite itself is as wild and wonderful as its setting. The pitches aren't the flattest and the dishwashing sink is outdoors. But if you're the kind of person who likes watching buzzards coast from the cliffs as you wash the pasta from your plate, you'll love the view at Cleadale.

COOL FACTOR The view... and, er, that's it. No other reason is needed.

WHO'S IN? Tents, dogs – yes. Campervans, caravans, big groups, young groups – no.

ON SITE 10 pitches, no hook-ups. This is as close to wild camping as a campsite gets. There are 2 composting loos (1 of which would win a national 'Loo With a View' competition by a mile). A newly built campers' shower and loo will be operational by 2013. There is also a yurt and a self-catering bothy. Eigg's only shop is on the other side of the island, so make sure you bring supplies. The site sells free-range eggs and seasonal organic vegetables grown on the croft when available. No campfires.

OFF SITE There are 2 excellent beaches within 15 minutes' walk, one of which, the Singing Sands, has natural arches, caves and waterfalls. The crofting museum, a couple of houses along, is fascinating. Take the path just past the Lageorna restaurant up on to the cliffs for an airy and unforgettable circular walk.

FOOD AND DRINK If you fancy a special treat, the restaurant Lageorna (01687 482405; www.lageorna.com), is just 2 minutes' walk from the campsite and offers fine food in a friendly atmosphere, with lovely views.

GETTING THERE Only islanders' vehicles are allowed on Eigg. A minibus service travels between the pier and Cleadale twice a day. You can hire bikes (call Jamie on 01687 482405) and residents are happy to give lifts if you stick your thumb out. There's usually plenty of traffic the hour before/after boats come in. Or you can walk to the croft from the pier in about an hour.

OPEN April–September. Bothy year-round.

THE DAMAGE £5 per tent per night. Showers are available on request from the house for £2. Yurt £35–£40 per night. Bothy £30–£35 per night.

invercaimbe

Invercaimbe, Arisaig, Inverness-shire PH39 4NT   01687 450375/07919 872309   www.invercaimbecaravansite.co.uk

Invercaimbe might be the only campsite in the country that is linked to the beach by a children's slide. Well, that's just one way on to the sand that seems to surround the site. Actually you can also jump, step or flop down from your pitch straight on to the bright white strand.

This working croft has been in the same family for 270 years, and as soon as you arrive you'll see why they've been so keen to hang on to it. The perfect little beaches curve like scallop shells round two sides of the headland and open on to a rocky foreshore. Here, as the tide goes out, you'll discover a mysterious playground of sands, lagoons and rockpools. You can't help but feel 10 years old here; the urge to dig canals and take crabs hostage is all but irresistible. Even if you only dangle your toes in the cool turquoise waters you'll instantly feel your cares washing away.

The sea is so much a part of this site that everyone becomes a little amphibious. Couples don wetsuits and splash through the rising shallows like dolphins. Children run from and taunt the incoming waves like oystercatchers. Kayakers awkwardly launch themselves into the foam where they become as fleet and sleek as seals. Then, as the sun begins to drop drowsily into the west, most people grab a cup of something wet and warming and perch on the rocks to watch one of the most spectacular sunsets in the land. It's hard to take your eyes off the kaleidoscope of colour in the sky, but you must be careful that you don't let this waterside wonderland capture your spirit completely. After all, where do you think mermaids come from?

COOL FACTOR Bordered by white sands and shallow lagoons on 2 sides, this site boasts knockout views over the sea to Skye.

WHO'S IN? Tents, campervans, caravans, groups, dogs – yes.

ON SITE Campfires allowed. 18 pitches, 16 hook-ups. There are 4 toilets, 2 showers, a laundry and dishwashing room. The best way to book a pitch is to text Joyce, who also keeps a freezer stocked with essentials: burgers, buns, veg, ice cream, and beef reared on the croft – about as organic as you can get.

OFF SITE Ferries from Arisaig and Mallaig visit the beautiful nearby small isles and also Skye (Arisaig Marine 01687 450224; www.arisaig.co.uk; Cal Mac 0800 066 5000; www.calmac.co.uk). Arisaig Marine also has sealife-watching trips. There are walks along the side of Loch Morar and the Jacobite Steam train runs from Mallaig (www.westcoastrailways.co.uk/jacobite/Jacobite_Details.html). It's also worth visiting the working harbour of Mallaig, 9 miles away, to try some fresh fish or just watch the boats come and go.

FOOD AND DRINK Treat yourself to lunch or supper just 10 minutes' walk up the hill at the stunningly situated Cnoc na Faire (01687 450249; www.cnoc-na-faire.co.uk). The Rhu café in Arisaig, 2 miles away, is fab for both quick bites and more leisurely meals (01687 450707; www.caferhu.com).

GETTING THERE Take the A830 from Fort William through Glenfinnan towards Mallaig. After you pass through Arisaig look out for the signposts to Invercaimbe.

PUBLIC TRANSPORT Trains run direct to Arisaig from Glasgow, and Scottish City Link buses run from Edinburgh, Glasgow and Inverness via Fort William (www.citylink.co.uk).

OPEN March–October.

THE DAMAGE £12 for a 2-person tent.

gimme shelter

Gimme Shelter, 2 Dales Farm Cottage, Duloch, nr Dunfermline, Fife KY11 7HR   01383 417681
www.camping-fife-near-edinburgh.blogspot.co.uk

Many campsites talk a good environmentally friendly game, but few put it into practice quite as well as Gimme Shelter, situated amid the meadows and hills just a few miles from the Forth Bridge. Recycling is practised religiously, there are no showers or hot water, and toilets are of the sawdust-composting variety – not trendy off-the-peg numbers but, like most things here, self-built and brilliantly improvised. Rainwater is collected in various systems, including an old wine barrel, and a woodburner has been made from an old toolbox and a rejuvenated gas bottle. Rat race escapees Chris and Yvonne Barley may have been dubbed hippies a decade ago, but today many Gimme Shelter devotees proclaim them visionaries.

Gimme Shelter's DIY style is undeniably impressive, from the handcarved wooden furniture that adorns every pitch to the funky but solid 'camping shack' made of oak and fir beams salvaged from the nearby dockyard, which boasts a large living space and two balconies that are ideal for sundowners. The camping fields, like the site itself, give away the Barleys' tastes in music – choose between 'Strawberry Fields' and 'Rising Sun'. All have their own campfires and are set amid rich woodland. Gimme Shelter's other stab at glamping is a brilliantly reinvented caravan: it does give shelter, but very much in the Gimme Shelter style, where less is definitely more. As for things to do nearby, there are plenty, with Dunfermline and its historic abbey on your doorstep and Edinburgh just a half-hour train ride away aross the famous Forth Bridge.

COOL FACTOR Eco-friendly site that doesn't just talk the ecotalk but very much walks the eco walk.

WHO'S IN? Tents, groups – yes. Caravans, campervans, big groups, dogs, young groups – no.

ON SITE Campfires allowed. 24 pitches, though the number varies as some can be knocked out by the weather. No hook-ups. Cold water but no showers (though there are some available at a nearby leisure centre). Fire-starting essentials are available to buy, and there's communal fridge space and use of a microwave and kettle. It can get muddy in wet weather though Chris and Yvonne have laid strips of an old tennis court down as paths to make life easier.

OFF SITE Wee ones love Deep Sea World (01383 411880; www.deepseaworld.com) just down the road, and a string of beaches to the east. Alternatively, head by train into Edinburgh or hop off before at Dalmen, (or drive over the Forth Bridge), to explore historic South Queensferry. Hopetoun House (0131 331 2451; www.hopetoun.co.uk) on the suburb's outskirts is renowned as 'Scotland's Versailles'.

FOOD AND DRINK Inverkeithing is within walking distance for basic supplies, but is not great for eating out. The Wee Restaurant (01383 616263; www.theweerestaurant.co.uk) in North Queensferry is superb, with creative cooking and fresh local produce. The Albert Hotel (01383 413562) in the same village does decent food and has a bar said to be a favourite of local writer Iain Banks.

GETTING THERE Follow the signs from the Forth Road Bridge for Inverkeithing, drive through the main street north to join the B981. The site is signposted on the left.

OPEN All year.

THE DAMAGE £6 per person per night; £6 per car for first night only, subsequent nights half price for children, under-2s free).

comrie croft

Comrie Croft, Braincroft, Crieff, Perthshire PH7 4JZ   01764 670140   www.comriecroft.com

Before the Act of Union and the birth of the modern British state many Scots lived on crofts – smallholdings of land where communal living was the norm. In the heart of deepest Highland Perthshire this communal, everyone-in-it-together ethic has been recreated at Comrie Croft. Run by a cooperative of like-minded, environmentally aware individuals, this is no mere campsite. Yes they take tents, but they've also got Swedish katas (a sort of Scandinavian tipi), an onsite Tea Garden and a superb bike shop, the latter handy for exploring the network of trails that snake off up the Croft's wooded hillside.

First-timers might feel most secure down in the main camping field by all the facilities, but more adventurous souls will want to push on up into the forest where secluded pitches await, each with its own campfire. Four of the site's five katas are up here too, complete with woodburning stoves and sleeping areas strewn with animal skins. Not exactly super-chic glamping, but supremely cosy nonetheless.

There is little need to leave the Croft. Down by the car park is a superb camp store, stocking everything from fluorescent tent pegs to free-range eggs and fresh local meat. Up the hill are those trails. You can walk them, but biking provides a much better way of exploring the hillside, though the tough red route is not for the fainthearted – you can brush up on your technique first at their skills park. On a busy day – and most weekends are busy – Comrie Croft buzzes with life, just as the traditional crofts once did in this charmingly scenic corner of Highland Perthshire.

COOL FACTOR Communal eco-aware living under canvas in charming Highland Perthshire.

WHO'S IN? Tents, dogs (main camping field only), groups, young groups – yes. Caravans, campervans – no.

ON SITE Campfires allowed. 32 pitches. 5 katas. Solar- and wind-powered amenities block with toilets and good free showers (including disabled access seat). Note the more secluded pitches up on the hillside and upper meadow are a bit of a trek from the toilets – not great at night. Excellent camping store. Blue and red mountain trails, with bike hire and helmets available, plus a network of marked walking trails as well as picnic areas.

OFF SITE The high land beyond the Croft is tough going, but opens up sweeping views of Strathearn for adventurous, well-equipped hikers. The Auchingarrich Wildlife Park (01764 679469; www.auchingarrich.co.uk) is a handy family attraction just south of Comrie.

FOOD AND DRINK The onsite Tea Garden is a welcome addition, serving breakfast, lunch and huge homemade cakes. Nearby Comrie has a reasonable chippie (07514 678833) and the Royal Hotel (01764 679200; www.royalhotel.co.uk), with a characterful bar in the main hotel and a more pub-style affair just outside. Their restaurant, under the smooth hand of chef patron David Milsom, serves delicious Perthshire lamb and salmon.

GETTING THERE 2 miles out of Comrie on the Crieff road heading east, signposted on the left.

PUBLIC TRANSPORT A seasonal bus service, Breadalbane Explorer (01877 384768), stops at the Croft.

OPEN All year.

THE DAMAGE Tents from £7 per adult, £3.50 under-16s. Katas from £50 per night. £1 off for those arriving without a vehicle.

inver mill

Inver Mill Farm Caravan Park, Dunkeld, Perthshire PH8 0JR   01350 727477   www.invermillfarm.com

Birnam Wood boded ill for Macbeth, but it makes for a wonderfully tranquil weekend's camping. Deep in the heart of the gnarled, twisted glen where the River Braan joins the Tay, are the picturesque villages of Dunkeld and Birnam. They are surrounded entirely by magical woods, so if you like idling in a leafy bower, Inver Mill is the site for you.

Most of Inver Mill is geared towards caravans, but there's a sweet little tent section that snuggles on a curve of the River Braan. The only hubbub in this corner results from the minor battles between herons and fishermen for the best bankside spots. You might think there isn't much to do in this simplest of sites, but it's beautifully placed at the edge of a wanderer's paradise. A spider's web of paths crisscrosses the local woods, taking you deep into the hills or right into Dunkeld itself, where the cathedral is a must-see. You should also explore the Hermitage, a secretive wooded valley that is home to the tallest trees in Britain, and Ossian's Hall, a temple above a crashing cascade where salmon leap in late summer. It's such a seductive place you may put down roots of your own.

COOL FACTOR Unwind under the greenwood tree.

WHO'S IN? Tents, campervans, caravans, dogs – yes. Big groups – no.

ON SITE 65 pitches overall; separate, secluded tent area with 12(ish) pitches and some hook-ups. Good heated shower/toilet block with free hot showers, shaver/hairdryer points and disabled toilet. Laundry/dishwashing area, hairdryer and iron for hire and CDP. No campfires.

OFF SITE Walking and cycling are excellent in the immediate area. Fishing on the Tay is justly famous. Very young children will love the Beatrix Potter garden in Birnam.

FOOD AND DRINK The Taybank in Dunkeld (01350 727340; www.thetaybank.co.uk) does amazing stovies (if you don't know, what they are you HAVE to find out), local ales and is a folk-music mecca. The Scottish Deli ('Menzies' locally) is the place to stock up on picnic grub (01350 728028; www.scottish-deli.com).

GETTING THERE The site is signposted from the A9 at Dunkeld.

PUBLIC TRANSPORT Get a bus or train to Dunkeld and then walk the 1½ miles to the campsite.

OPEN March–October.

THE DAMAGE Solo backpacker £10, 2-person tent £14, hook-ups £2. July/August £2 supplement. No credit cards.

rothiemurchus

Rothiemurchus Estate, Coylumbridge, nr Aviemore, Inverness-shire PH22 1QU   01479 812800   www.campandcaravan.com

If you *seriously* like trees, the Rothiemurchus campsite is the type of spot you might not want to tear yourself away from. It's one of the best places in Scotland to enjoy vast swathes of indigenous Caledonian woodland, with a flurry of Scots pine, birch and juniper forests and wood-shrouded lochs.

The award-winning campsite is set within the Rothiemurchus Estate, right on the edge of the Cairngorms, the UK's largest national park. Campers can choose from the main woodland pitches or burn-side ones beside the flowing Am Beanaidh. Bikes can be hired nearby and there's an easy circular route taking in the lochs of Morlich and Loch an Eilein. The latter is one of the prettiest in the country, with a ruined castle and beaches fringing its edges. Alternatively, visitors can enjoy the views with minimal effort aboard the Cairngorm Mountain Railway.

Rothiemurchus is the sort of site that ticks so many different boxes. It works for those looking to get away from it all, those wanting to explore on a bike or those who fancy a walk off into the challenging Cairngorm Mountains. And did we mention all the beautiful trees?

COOL FACTOR Trees, trees and more trees.

WHO'S IN? Tents, tourers, caravans – yes. Dogs – no (except in caravans).

ON SITE Several woodland and riverside pitches plus 1 on an island. 17 hardstandings for the caravans in a separate area. Heated amenity block with hot showers, toilets, dishwashing area and laundry.

OFF SITE Archery, hiking, canoeing and more at the Rothiemurchus Centre (01479 812345; www.rothiemurchus-activities.co.uk). Near Aviemore, the Macdonald Highland Resort (www.aviemorehighlandresort.com) has swimming pools and restaurants.

FOOD AND DRINK The Old Bridge Inn (01479 811137), 2 miles away, is an atmospheric pub that specialises in local dishes such as peppered leg of venison.

GETTING THERE Heading north on the A9, take the first turning for Aviemore and follow the signs for Rothiemurchus. The site is visible after a couple of miles on the right side.

PUBLIC TRANSPORT Regular bus services run from Aviemore to the Cairngorm Mountain Railway, passing the campsite on the way (08712 002233).

OPEN January–October and December.

THE DAMAGE £8 per adult per night and £2 for kids aged 5–16. In July and August adults are £9 per night, kids still £2.

lazy duck

Lazy Duck Hostel and Camping, Nethy Bridge, Inverness-shire PH25 3ED   01479 821642   www.lazyduck.co.uk

The Lazy Duck campsite is well named. Its resident Aylesbury Ducks are so relaxed that the site owners David and Valery once had to bring in nanny ducks as the Aylesburys were too lazy to bother hatching their own eggs. The site seems to have an equally soporific effect on campers, and new arrivals soon slip into a similarly relaxed state here, as doing very little becomes the main aim of the day.

To call the Lazy Duck a campsite is perhaps a little misleading. It's more a chilled forest clearing, blessed with a sauna and a bush shower, where swings and hammocks dangle from the tall trees and man and duck idle side by side. It just happens to have plenty of room for four very lucky tents and their (maximum of three) inhabitants. With typical unassuming attention to detail, David and Valery ask you to move on every three days to another spot to save the grass. Welcome new comforts include the Campers' Shelter, where you can relax by a chimenea in the evening and meet your fellow lotus-eaters. Another welcome addition is the Woodman's Hut, a seriously romantic log cabin-style getaway for two.

If you want to shun the laidback ways of the Aylesburys, the Speyside Way runs nearby, and is waymarked and open to cyclists, too, though the kissing gates are a bit of a hassle when you're on two wheels. You can also tackle the Spey in a canoe or kayak, or just sample some of its famous produce on a choice of distillery tours – this is serious whisky country. After a few drams, a swing in a hammock is the perfect recreation at a site where relaxation is practically mandatory. Just ask those ducks.

COOL FACTOR If you are lucky enough to snare a pitch you can feel what it is like to be as gloriously idle as the famously lazy ducks.

WHO'S IN? Tents (maximum 3 people) – yes. Caravans, campervans, dogs, big groups, young groups – no.

ON SITE Campfires enouraged (in chimeneas). Wet weather cooking facilities. Sauna available at a nominal charge. Hammocks and swings. Toilet, bush shower and washbasin by the camping area.

OFF SITE Of many distillery tours our favourite is Aberlour (01340 881249; www.aberlour.com), which is open for visits every day between April and October (otherwise Monday–Friday). The site is within the Cairngorms National Park (01479 873535; www.cairngorms.co.uk), which has numerous outdoor activities on offer. Ornithologists will enjoy the nearby Loch Garten (01767 680551; www.rspb.org.uk), with its resident ospreys. The resort town of Aviemore is close by and also has plenty of wet weather options, shops, cafés and a swimming pool.

FOOD AND DRINK A fishmonger visits on Wednesdays, and nearby Nethy Bridge has a post office and store and a superb butcher, Mustards (01479 821245). The Old Bridge Inn (01479 811137; www.oldbridgeinn.co.uk), on the edge of Aviemore, serves local Moray fish and Speyside steaks and has a cosy bar. The Mountain Café in Aviemore (01479 812473; www.mountaincafe-aviemore.co.uk) does spot-on burgers, superb cakes and fantastic coffee.

GETTING THERE From Aviemore take the B970 into Rothiemurchus, which turns left for Nethy Bridge after Coylumbridge. The site lies south of Nethy Bridge on the Tomintoul road. GPS lands you a mile away!

OPEN May–October.

THE DAMAGE £10 for tent sleeping 1 person, £15 for 2, £20 for 3.

GARDEN GROWN
Fresh Rocket + Sorrel

PICK YOUR OWN LETTUCE
A HEAD

skye family camping

Skye Family Camping, Loch Greshornish, Borve, Arnisort, Edinbane, Portree, Isle of Skye IV51 9PS   01470 582230 (no calls after 8pm)

Skye Family Camping is having something of an identity crisis. Officially, it's a Camping and Caravanning Club site with the tendency towards formality that such status entails. But, this being Skye, it can't help but be a little bit wild and wonderful in a *Cool Camping* way.

It's a working croft on the shore of Loch Greshornish, with cattle, sheep, ducks and chickens. Here, croft and campsite go so neatly hand in hand that it seems everyone has their own corner in which to be happy. The chickens willingly produce eggs for the benefit of hungry campers, and the staff's name badges and matching fleeces are neatly cancelled out by the rock-star hairdos of the highland cows.

Yes, there are lots of caravans, but the tent field is completely separate, a campsite within a campsite. Gloriously, it has by far the best views, its smooth grass sweeping almost down to the loch itself. With the weather likely to be on the boisterous side even in summer, you may also be very glad of the site's first-rate facilities. The dog-walking path that runs along the waterline doubles as an otter-spotting trail, and you can't feel rule-bound when there are eagles soaring overhead.

COOL FACTOR A beautifully civilised campsite nestled amid the wilds of Skye.

WHO'S IN? Tents, campervans, caravans, dogs – yes. Big groups, young groups – no.

ON SITE 105 pitches with hook-ups available, 2 camping huts. The loo block is modern, spacious and scrupulously clean. Onsite shop selling most everyday items, and eggs laid on the croft. A fish van visits every Tuesday morning. No campfires.

OFF SITE Take an eagle-spotting boat trip in Portree (07795 385581; www.skyeboat-trips.co.uk). Dunvegan Castle (01470 521206; www.dunvegancastle.com) is the oldest continuously inhabited castle in Scotland, with magnificent gardens.

FOOD AND DRINK The Edinbane Inn (01470 582414; www.edinbaneinn.co.uk), at the head of Loch Greshornish, has local ales and is one of Skye's best bars for traditional music.

GETTING THERE From Portree take the A87, then the A850 for Dunvegan. The site is on the right just after Flashader.

PUBLIC TRANSPORT Citylink buses 915 and 916 run from Glasgow to Kyle of Lochalsh and on to Portree. From here Stagecoach bus 56 (Portree to Glendale service) stops right outside the site and also goes to Edinbane.

OPEN March–October.

THE DAMAGE £7.90–£9.65 per adult. £7.10 per pitch. 1 night's camping hut accommodation £37.

horgabost

Horgabost, Isle Of Harris HS3 3HR   01859 550386

The beaches on the west coast of Harris are a competitive lot: 'Look at the creaminess of my sands' 'marvel at my deliciously turquoise waters' and 'aren't I *enormous*'. But Horgabost sits confidently in the middle of all this one-upmanship, safe in the knowledge that it is probably the best of the lot.

Pitching on the machair dune grass right above the beach, which gives you a grandstand view of the sand, sea and isle of Taransay, makes you feel like you've discovered somewhere truly new; and the site's undulations only add to its mystery – whole Duke of Edinburgh Award groups can be carbonising sausages in a nearby hollow and you wouldn't know they were there. For many years it was purely a wild camping site, and that free-spirited vibe has deliberately been kept by the owners, Richard and Lena Maclennan. They pop by to keep things clean and post information, but generally leave everyone to get on with having a seriously relaxing time. As for the beach, it too, despite its grandeur, is a marvellously relaxing place to be; indeed you know you're at a chilled-out site when you get chatting with a fisherman and end up swapping a bottle of beer for a mackerel.

COOL FACTOR Wild camping by a wildly beautiful beach.

WHO'S IN? Tents, campervans, caravans, groups, dogs – yes.

ON SITE 50 pitches, no hook-ups. The loos and shower blocks are just metal containers, but inside are clean and homely. Dishwashing sinks. No campfires.

OFF SITE Walk out to the 16th-century temple at Northton. Pick up some Harris Tweed in the shop at Tarbert (harristweedandknitwear.co.uk). Visit the eagle observatory on the road to Huisinish. Or just hang out on the beach.

FOOD AND DRINK Croft 36 (01859 520779) in Northton does amazing seafood, plus they will deliver to your tent. The Temple Café in Northton (07876 340416), inside a low stone house overlooking a serene sandy bay, does lunches that are even more spectacular than its setting. Gus's mobile shop pops by every Tuesday and Friday.

GETTING THERE From Leverburgh head north-west on the A859, passing Northton and Borve. From Tarbert turn south on the A859, passing Seilebost. The campsite is opposite the small settlement of Horgabost.

PUBLIC TRANSPORT Bus W10 runs from Stornoway to Leverburgh and passes the site (01859 502441).

OPEN May–October.

THE DAMAGE 1–2 man tent £7, 3+ man tent £10.

lickisto blackhouse

Lickisto Blackhouse Camping and Yurts, 1 Lickisto, Isle of Harris HS3 3EL   01859 530485   www.freewebs.com/vanvon

Ever been to a party where you meet someone and you keep thinking you ought to be talking to your old pals but you're having so much fun that you spend the whole night happily wittering to your new chum? Lickisto is the campsite equivalent of that magnetic personality.

Perched snugly above a sea loch on Harris, it is perfect for exploring the wilds of the east coast or the breathtaking beaches of the west, but many, many campers barely leave the site, so drawn are they to its rock-star charisma. Harvey and John, its owners, have transformed a rough and rocky croft into a relaxing retreat, where the love they have lavished on their labours can be clearly seen and felt. The camping pitches are personally cut

by John, and are separated from each other by wild grasses and heather, giving everyone their own individual space; plus there are a couple of yurts for lazybones, pitched high up on the site to give splendid ocean views. Each comes with woodburning stove, running water, futons (with linen), gas stove, carpets and candles. Harvey even pops a homemade loaf in, so don't forget your butter and jam.

The site has its own restored blackhouse, where you can cook a meal, play Jenga, have a shower or simply slouch on a leather sofa and dream. Pluck a fishing rod from the wall and you can try catching your supper from the loch. And guests are also free to enjoy the fruits (and veg) of the polytunnel – the lemon basil will be perfect should you hook a fish.

Lickisto is proud to be low impact and small-scale, and this is a responsibility that the owners live and breathe. When John was re-roofing the blackhouse he learned traditional thatching techniques and used local heather to do the job. Take a close look at the wooden bridges and walkways that dot the site – they are made from telegraph poles discarded at the roadside by a telecoms company. It's creative recycling that benefits everyone and fills your head with ideas for how you could do the same.

When you arrive, John or Harvey is usually on hand to give you a welcoming tour of the site. It's a seductive introduction and, as you wind down little paths between stands of high rushes, cross tiny bridges and turn unexpected corners to reveal perfect pitches hidden behind

brightly flowering bushes, you may be forgiven for thinking Harvey is actually a white rabbit in disguise, leading you into Wonderland.

The resident wildfowl are only too happy to make your acquaintance, and the ducks, in particular, have an engaging habit of wandering up and eyeing you in a way that clearly says, 'Have you finished with that biscuit?'. You are welcome to have a fire by the shoreline, where John has fashioned a fine seat from an old rowing boat. Stretch your legs out there of an evening, looking out down the slender sea loch and, if you watch closely enough, there's a good chance you'll see the local otter making his evening commute back down the loch with his supper in his mouth. That's what counts as rush hour at Lickisto.

COOL FACTOR The space and beauty to get in touch with your own wild inner self.

WHO'S IN? Tents, campervans, dogs – yes. Caravans, big groups – no.

ON SITE 15 pitches, 4 campervan spaces with hook-ups. There are also 2 gorgeous yurts if you really want to enjoy the atmosphere without putting your tent up. You can wake up to sunrise over the loch and fresh bread courtesy of Harvey. 'Bathroom byres' with 3 loos, 3 showers and loads of character. Blackhouse where campers can cook, chat and chill. The site is better suited to small or medium-sized tents: large 'multipods' could find it difficult to pitch. A polytunnel with home-grown veg and herbs is open for campers. Bring midge repellent. Campfires are allowed on the foreshore.

OFF SITE There are several art galleries on the spellbinding East coast of Harris. You'll see why when you drive along the road. Pick up some genuine Harris Tweed in the shop at Tarbert (harristweedandknitwear.co.uk). Visit the eagle observatory on the road to Huisinish

(www.north-harris.org/north-harris/the-north-harris-eagle-observatory).

FOOD AND DRINK Soak up some inspiration (and stunning home-baking) at the nearby Skoon Art Café (01859 530268; www.skoon.com). The Temple Café in Northton (07876 340416) is also worth a stop if you're exploring the island, making delicious food in as tiny a kitchen as you'll ever see.

GETTING THERE From Tarbert take the A859 south (towards Leverburgh); after 5 miles take the left turn to Lickisto – the campsite is 1½ miles further, on the left.

PUBLIC TRANSPORT Bus W13 meets the ferry and the Stornoway bus, ask for Lickisto. The bus stops at the top of the road to the campsite.

OPEN March–October.

THE DAMAGE Camping £12 per person, kids half-price, 'small uns nothin', Price includes use of Blackhouse, free showers and fresh bread every day (eggs too, when the chooks deliver). Yurts £70 per night (extra person £20, larger kids £10).

sands

Sands Caravan and Camping, Gairloch, Wester Ross, IV21 2DL   01445 712152   www.sandscaravanandcamping.co.uk

The shop at Sands is possibly the most remarkably stocked campsite store in the country. So much so that, as you check in, you might think the owners James and Marie have gone a wee bit over the top. But then you pitch your tent, breathe in the sea air, look out through the dune grass at the islands and mountains and realise that venison steaks, champagne and inflatable canoes are EXACTLY what you need right now.

That's the thing about Sands, it keeps surprising you. The winding road that leads north out of Gairloch seems to be heading nowhere, then a sliver of grassy land gradually unfolds into a wide and welcoming apron bordered by swooping dunes and an epic seascape. Driving in, your first impressions are of a large caravan site, but campers have their own area of rolling duneland with plenty of tent-sized pockets for you to hide away in. This starts just down a winding track from the shop, and it's worth continuing along to check out the whole site before choosing your spot. Pitches range from secluded hollows to breezy eyries, while the spots in the southern corner are ideally placed by the site's own slipway – perfect for launching kayaks and returning out on other watery adventures.

There are also 10 heated wooden wigwams should you fancy taking it a little easier for a few nights. These come with firepits (campfires are not allowed anywhere else) and sublime views of the sunset as standard. Wherever you are, it won't be long before you're winding your way through the dunes and down on to the beach to paddle in the irresistibly turquoise water. And even if this is surprisingly cold, don't worry – the shop sells wetsuits, too.

The beach, of course, is the campsite's glory. In the day its gently sloping sands call one and all for a happy shift of castle-building, swimming and general larking about. Then, when your work is done, you can perch in the grass at the top of the dunes, taking pride in your achievements and watching the blazing sunset over the far tip of Skye. This is a dreamer's place, and as the sun finally slides into the western ocean, the island of Longa drops into shadow, becoming a humpbacked sea monster, settling down to rest for the night. With a beach to dig up, dunes to jump down, rocks to graze knees on and woods to go heffalump-hunting in, it's ironic that the campsite also has an adventure playground – it's not like it needs one. However, it's a beauty, and is set right in the middle of the site, forming the perfect spot for young teens to gather and eye each other sheepishly while their parents read the paper. Arrive when the sun is shining and you might also wonder why there is a games room. Well, it has been known to rain in the north-west of Scotland, and you may find yourself very glad of the owners' foresight. There is also a large indoor cooking and washing-up area, complete with several benches; and James and Marie are building a small café on site, which should be open by summer 2013. They are also planning to lay out a few mountain-bike tracks on some adjacent land. Like there isn't enough to do here already…

COOL FACTOR With a beautiful beachside location, this is a particularly good family site with serene views of Skye and the Hebrides.

WHO'S IN? Tents, campervans, caravans, dogs on leads – yes.

ON SITE The washblocks are rather aged but they're also huge and kept very clean. Hot showers are free. There is a large indoor kitchen and dining space, a dishwashing area, electric hook-ups, a laundry, a games room, plus bike and canoe hire and a children's adventure playground. A new café is being built for summer 2013. The shop is very well stocked and is licensed. No campfires (except for wigwam guests).

OFF SITE The beautiful path to Flowerdale Falls, which are located 1 mile south of Gairloch, offers an energetic family ramble. The Gairloch Heritage Museum (01445 712287; www.gairlochheritagemuseum.org) is a great local museum that will have you stepping back in time to soak up some local history.

FOOD AND DRINK The Mountain Coffee Company in Gairloch (01445 712316) has a terrific selection of outdoor and adventure books, and the cakes are pretty thrilling, too. The food at the Old Inn at Flowerdale (01445 712006; www.theoldinn.net) is worth seeking out, and it tastes particularly delicious if you sit outside and enjoy it under the trees by the river. Tootle around the loch to the Badachro Inn (01445 741255; www. badachroinn.com), which snuggles by the seashore in a sheltered bay, where you can choose from 50 malt whiskies or simply enjoy a pint of the local ale by open fires and watch the boats come and go on the peaceful waters of the loch.

GETTING THERE Take the A832 to Gairloch. From there follow the B8021 coastal road north towards Melvaig. The Sands Holiday Centre is 4 miles along this road on the left.

OPEN April–September.

THE DAMAGE Tent and car plus 2 people £14.50 low season, £16.50 high season. Extra adults £5, kids (5–16) £2.

badrallach

Badrallach, Croft 9, Badrallach, Dundonnell, Ross-shire IV23 2QP   01854 633281   www.badrallach.com

How does it feel to get to the end of a track that's eight miles from the nearest main road, in a lost corner of north-west Scotland? That's a question that Badrallach's owners, Mick and Ali Stott, have put a great deal of thought and effort into answering.

To start with, if you've come this far, there's a pretty good chance you'll be aiming to get away from it all – including other people. So there are individual camping pitches hidden away between bushes and behind rowan thickets. You navigate between these on a web of little paths and bridges that will have younger campers playing hide-and-seek for hours. And now that you are

here, you will probably want to sit quietly, rest, and simply gaze at the amazing scenery. Doing this is so much more fun with a fire crackling at your feet, and so firepits are duly provided. If you should venture out on the hills, you will probably get wet/muddy/sweaty/all three in the course of a day, so you want showers that do more than tickle and tease. The loo block itself may be in an old farm building, but it is still one of the brightest and most welcoming washing facilities we've ever been in.

It's also fun to play table tennis, but it seems a shame to be inside when there are all those lovely mountains to look at – so why not put the table outside? It's bonkers considering the weather, but hey – it works. And finally, since this part of the world is the haunt of the mischievous highland midge, Mick and Ali have installed a 'Midgebuster' – an ingenious device that attracts the insects then literally hoovers them up so they can't bother you any more. Well, that's the theory; it's still advisable to bring some repellent!

Nature has also laid on a smorgasbord of adventures for you to savour. Sit at Badrallach for any length of time and you'll become fascinated by mighty An Teallach, the mountain that sits over the loch, hunching its shoulders and glowering. If you do climb this splendid hill, remember it is one of the most precipitous ridges of any mountain in Britain and you should be fully prepared (in mind as well as body). If you fancy a more casual wander there are paths running directly from the campsite along the foreshore and up to Beinn Ghobhlach, the hill

behind the site. The campsite also looks over Little Loch Broom, which is reached by a short path. If you are a paddle-fanatic you'll find the crinkled coastline fascinating to explore. Just further along is Scoraig, one of the remotest communities in Britain, which is only accessible by boat or a five-mile walk. But that's just the kind of thing you'll have time for. You can bring your own craft or hire kayaks and inflatables on site. There are also sea-fishing rods available, so if you've ever thought you might like to live a more nautical life but haven't been able to learn the ropes, Badrallach is the perfect place to dip your toe in the water.

Once you've been at Badrallach for a few days you will settle into a new rhythm of existing. Time drifts here and pulls you along with it. So when you are finally packing up, you find yourself asking a very different question – how will it feel when you return to the world at the end of the road eight miles away?

COOL FACTOR Where the end of the road is the start of your adventure.

WHO'S IN? Tents, groups, dogs, caravans, campervans, motorhomes – yes. Hardstandings – no.

ON SITE Campfires allowed. 12 pitches, hook-ups available. You can also rent the gas-lit cottage, stay in the bothy or rent a caravan for a more luxurious stay. The site is a long way from any shop, so come prepared.

OFF SITE Outdoor adventuring is the name of the game here, and it's a great place for walking, climbing and kayaking. Kayaks, inflatables and sailing boats are available for hire to residents subject to experience and weather. You can also hire fishing rods. Corrieshalloch Gorge is a spectacular chasm (20 minutes' drive) that you can reach easily from the road.

FOOD AND DRINK The Dundonnell Hotel (01854 633204; www.dundonnellhotel.com) has a restaurant and also does fine bar meals with frequent live music. If you're prepared to head further afield, the Frigate Café in Ullapool is a classy continental bistro that seems to have got lost and turned up in the far north-west of Scotland (01854 612969; www.ullapoolcatering.co.uk). It has a great little kids' area and a backroom where you can hide from the weather with a hot chocolate.

GETTING THERE Take the A9 north from Inverness on to the A835 to Ullapool. Approximately 10 miles from Ullapool, at Braemore Junction, turn left on to the A832 for 10 miles then turn right on to the single-track Badrallach road for approximately 8 miles.

OPEN All year.

THE DAMAGE 1-person tent £9, 2 people £13; campervan/caravan/hook-ups £16. The bothy is £8.50 for 1 person per night, 2 people £14.50. Caravan rental is £45 per night.

port a bhaigh

Port A Bhaigh Campsite, 211 Altandhu, Achiltibuie, Ullapool, Ross-shire IV26 2YR   01854 622339   www.portabhaigh.co.uk

Inverpollaidh is an incredible landscape, even by the standards of the Scottish Highlands: sugar-loaf mountain peaks erupt from the moors, lochs shine like molten stepping-stones across the wilderness, and otters chomp on salmon beside crashing waterfalls. You might think this is beautiful enough, but you then realise it's all adjacent to an equally amazing seascape, complete with islands, cliffs, hidden coves and sandy beaches… and then you pretty much run out of superlatives.

Astonishingly, this corner of the country has been without a proper campsite for several years – until Catriona and David Last decided to turn a section of the family croft into a new site. The location could hardly be better: a decent-sized strip of land stretching from the local pub (which they also own) to the beach, with hills all around and views out to Isle Ristol.

They have gone the extra mile here to ensure that you have a good time, levelling the pitches, installing a few hook-ups and building one of the loveliest toilet and shower blocks you'll find in any campsite in the country, with the result that the site offers the best balance of wilderness and civilisation you could hope for. You can sit in your tent and look out at the seals loafing on the rocks or scramble up the hill for an uninterrupted view of the island-studded western ocean; you can also enjoy a steaming hot shower, do your laundry, and pop your milk in the fridge before sauntering up to the pub for an evening's live music. Something tells us that this is a site that will be around for a long, long time…

COOL FACTOR A civilised site at the edge of an incredible wilderness.

WHO'S IN? Everyone welcome!

ON SITE 50 pitches (a 'wild' section plus an area with hook-ups). Lovely new washblock with 6 showers, 4 loos, laundry, a disabled loo, baby changing, fridge, freezer and beer fridge. Hot food on hand thanks to the pub at the top of the hill – you can even order a breakfast bacon roll the evening before. The beach would benefit from a willing scout group to pick up some of the flotsam. No campfires.

OFF SITE Achiltibuie Garden (01854 622202; thehydroponicum.com) is a unique garden and growing house promoting the benefits of hydroponics. In case you're inspired to grow your own tomatoes, chillies or salad, kits are available to take home. There are often ceilidhs in the local community hall, and sea tours to the Summer Isles are great for seal spotting (07927 920592; www.summerisles-seatours.co.uk). There is a general store and a craft shop at Polbain, 1 mile away.

FOOD AND DRINK The campsite is on the croft opposite the local pub, Am Fuaran (01854 622339; www.amfuaran.co.uk), and shares the same owners. In fact, owner David also fishes for shellfish from his boat at Old Dornie, so bag something fresh for the BBQ or head to the pub to sample langoustine, squat lobster or crab, straight off the boat.

GETTING THERE From Ullapool drive north on the A835; after 8 miles, turn left for Achiltibuie. After approximately 10 miles turn right to Achnahaird and follow the road to Altandhu. The site is opposite the Am Fuaran pub.

OPEN Easter–October.

THE DAMAGE Small tent £9, family tent £11, adult £4, child (5–16 yrs) £2; hook-ups £4.

sango sands

Sango Sands Oasis, Durness, Sutherland IV27 4PZ   01971 511726   www.sangosands.com

Sango Sands' unique north-facing location at the very top of Scotland means that in summer you can watch the sun both rise and set over the ocean. That is if you aren't lying in your sleeping bag, exhausted from all the outdoor adventuring that you can't help yourself doing in this wild and windswept corner of the land.

There are several fields to camp in, and the most picturesque spots are by the steep slopes above the beaches. But there are other thoughtfully prepared areas for tents, which give children ample room to kick a ball away from nearby cars. It was in one of these quieter spots that we were joined for breakfast by a playful stoat.

The place boasts an embarrassment of sandy blessings with not one but two spectacular beaches easily reached by tracks from the site. The land and sea might meet here, but it's clear that they don't really get on. The beach is scattered with black rocks carved from ancient cliffs by centuries of northern storms. The power of the waves makes it a favourite spot of surfers and you can hire boards nearby if you fancy joining in. Or if the waves aren't too pounding it is possible to swim.

That's the thing about Durness: it may be remote but there's a lot to do. A few miles west is the aptly named Cape Wrath, where the Vikings turned for home after a successful marauding session. You can visit it by catching a ferry and then a minibus – there's a lighthouse, the highest sea cliffs in Britain and a thrilling sense of freedom. Then you can return to your tent on its cliff-top eyrie and stay awake for that late, late sunset.

COOL FACTOR Near-mystical cliff-top spot at the far end of Britain.

WHO'S IN? Tents, campervans, caravans, groups, dogs – yes.

ON SITE 120+ pitches, 64 hook-ups. 3 washblocks, 1 solely dedicated to showers (free). Waste disposal, dishwashing and laundry facilities. Fantastically, everyone has the use of a kitchen with free gas. Campers need to book if a hook-up is required. No campfires. Note: although the campsite itself is dog-friendly, the Oasis pub on the campsite is not.

OFF SITE Balnakiel craft village is an old MOD station that now has lots of individual galleries, cafés and workshops (www.durness.org/Balnakeil%20Craft%20 Village.htm). Durness golf course welcomes visitors and has a terrific last hole over the ocean. Smoo Cave is the largest sea cave in Britain and is just a 15-minute walk away. There is a peaceful public garden dedicated to John Lennon in Durness village – he regularly holidayed here as a boy.

FOOD AND DRINK The site has its own bar and restaurant (the Oasis) just along the cliff, which often has live music.

GETTING THERE Take the A9 north beyond Inverness, then the A836 and A838 to Durness. The site is right in the middle of Durness village.

PUBLIC TRANSPORT There's a bus service from Inverness and a post bus from Lairg. See Traveline (www.travelinescotland.com) for times.

OPEN April–October. Camping available at other times but without facilities.

THE DAMAGE Flat rates for adults £6.50, plus first child £4, second child £2.40, additional children free. Hook-ups £3.70.

wheems organic farm

Wheems Organic Farm, Wheems, Eastside, South Ronaldsay, Orkney KW17 2TJ   01856 831556   www.wheemsorganic.co.uk

Not for nothing did the poet and novelist George Mackay Brown say that the Orkney imagination was haunted by time. There's something other-worldly about the Orkney Islands. There's been a human presence here for thousands of years; the living in places like Skara Brae and the dead in the Neolithic burial chamber of Maes Howe, whose entry shaft is perfectly aligned with the setting sun on the winter solstice.

The land's been smoothed over by the prevailing winds, and the resulting views are of rolling hills and water, water everywhere between the 70 islands that make up the archipelago. The dun hills are the colour of the tweed of a geography teacher's jacket, and the sky can do everything from broody to menthol-clear.

Wheems is owned and run by Christina, a former oboist with the Scottish Chamber Orchestra, and Mike, a landscape architect. Their outlook on life, the universe and camping is to keep things small, share in the beauty of the place and pass on the philosophy of eco-living. For those seeking creature comforts, Mike has constructed two solid wooden bothies. These are insulated with sheeps' fleeces and have double-glazed doors that open on to a small deck that overlooks the bay – perfect for those travelling light or requiring more comfort.

On your way back south try, if you can, to stop at the small Italian chapel on Lamb Holm, built by and for the POWs while they were here, and skillfully preserved. Like most things in the Orkneys, it's a simple and unassuming place, but beautifully done.

COOL FACTOR Philosophically spot-on organic eco-camping with a warm welcome.

WHO'S IN? Tents, campervans, dogs (on leads), small caravans, big groups, young groups – yes. Large caravans – no.

ON SITE Campfires allowed. There are 20 pitches, some with hook-ups. 2 showers and 3 WCs in a wooden building and a covered kitchen area with 2 cookers and a fridge-freezer, plus books and games for the kids.

OFF SITE Wander around the labyrinth of stone-paved streets in Kirkwall, which is just a 20-minute drive away.

FOOD AND DRINK Wheems' own organic fruit, veg and eggs are on sale in their shop. Alternatively, Creel (01856 831311; www.thecreel.co.uk) in St Margaret's Hope is widely regarded as one of Scotland's best restaurants, serving set 3-course menus (with just 2 choices for each course) for £40. While you are there, stop off at the Murray Arms (01856 831205; www.murrayarmshotel.com) for one of their delicious local beers.

GETTING THERE The easiest route from the mainland is the passenger ferry from John O'Groats to Burwick or the car ferry from Gills Bay to St Margaret's Hope. Follow the road from the ferry up through the village to the top of the hill and the main road to Kirkwall. Turn right then left (at the soldier's statue). Follow this road for a mile or so until the crossroads (where there's a postbox). Go straight over and the farm is down the hill on the left.

PUBLIC TRANSPORT There's a reasonably frequent bus service in the summer months from Kirkwall to St Margaret's Hope (plus there's the ferry) but then it's a 2-mile walk from the village.

OPEN Early April–end October.

THE DAMAGE Tent pitches £7–£15 per night, bothies £35. Cars £2; dogs free.

index

acknowledgements

Cool Camping: Britain (1st edition)
Series Concept and Series Editor: Jonathan Knight

Researched, written, and photographed by:
Jonathan Knight, Alf Alderson, Jules Brown, Dan Davies, Sophie Dawson, Keith Didcock, Martin Dunford, Richard Happer, Norm Longley, Scott Manson, Paul Marsden, Robin McKelvie, Mirio Mella, Andrea Oates, Sam Pow, Hayley Spurway, Andy Stothert, Paul Sullivan, Alexandra Tilley-Loughrey, Mandy Tomlin, Richard Waters, and Dixe Wills.

Editor: Martin Dunford **Design:** Kenny Grant, Diana Jarvis **Maps:** Nicola Erdpresser **Proofreaders:** Leanne Bryan, Claire Wedderburn-Maxwell **Index:** Diana LeCore **Editorial Assistants:** Shelley Bowdler, David Jones

Published by: Punk Publishing, 3 The Yard, Pegasus Place, London, SE11 5SD

UK Sales: Compass DSA Limited, Swan Centre, Fishers Lane, Chiswick W4 1RX; 0208 996 9500; sales@compass-dsa.co.uk

All photographs included in this book have been licensed from the authors or from the campsite owners except the following: Sea Barn Farm © Clive Dibben, 2nd Pillar Projects and Graig Wen © Visit Wales/Phil Boorman

No photographs may be reproduced without permission. For all picture enquiries, please contact enquiries@coolcamping.co.uk

Front cover photo: Aberafon photographed by Andy Stothert

Chapter header photos (p8, 198, 266) all © Andy Stothert

Maps ©MAPS IN MINUTES™ Reproduced with permission.

The publishers and authors have done their best to ensure the accuracy of all information in *Cool Camping: Britain*, however, they can accept no responsibility for any injury, loss or inconvenience sustained by anyone as a result of information contained in this book.

Punk Publishing takes its environmental responsibilities seriously. This book has been printed on paper made from renewable sources and we continue to work with our printers to reduce our overall environmental impact.

A BIG THANK YOU! Thanks to everyone who has emailed with feedback, comments and suggestions. It's good to see so many people at one with the *Cool Camping* ethos. Go forth and camp, one and all!

HAPPY CAMPERS?

We hope you've enjoyed reading *Cool Camping: Britain* and that it's inspired you to get out there. The campsites featured in this book are a personal selection chosen by the *Cool Camping* team. We have visited hundreds of campsites across Britain to find this selection and we hope you like them as much as we do. However, it hasn't been possible to visit every single campsite. So, if you know of a special place that you think should be included, please visit www.coolcamping.co.uk to tell us all about it. You can also leave reviews of other *Cool Camping* sites you've visited.

www.coolcamping.co.uk